THE HISTORY OF OKLAHOMA

THE HISTORY OF OKLAHOMA

by

Arrell Morgan Gibson

New Edition

UNIVERSITY OF OKLAHOMA PRESS

NORMAN

BY ARRELL MORGAN GIBSON

The Kickapoos: Lords of the Middle Border (Norman, 1963)
The Life and Death of Colonel Albert Jennings Fountain (Norman, 1965)
Fort Smith: Little Gibraltar on the Arkansas (with Edwin C. Bearss) (Norman, 1969)
The Chickasaws (Norman, 1971)
The Canadian: Highway of History (New York, 1971)
Wilderness Bonanza: The Tri-State District of Missouri, Kansas, and Oklahoma (Norman, 1972)
(editor) *Frontier Historian: The Life and Work of Edward Everett Dale* (Norman, 1975)
The West in the Life of the Nation (Lexington, Mass., 1976)
America's Exiles: Indian Colonization in Oklahoma (Oklahoma City, 1976)
Will Rogers: A Centennial Tribute (Oklahoma City, 1979)
The American Indian: Prehistory to the Present (Lexington, Mass., 1980)
Oklahoma: A History of Five Centuries (Norman, 1981)
(editor) *American Notes: Rudyard Kipling's West* (Norman, 1981)
The Santa Fe and Taos Colonies: Age of the Muses, 1900-1942 (Norman, 1983)

Library of Congress Cataloging in Publication Data

Gibson, Arrell Morgan.
    The history of Oklahoma.

Includes index.
    1. Oklahoma—History.   I. Title.
F694.G47   1984   976.6   83-40325
ISBN 0-8061-1883-0

The paper in this book meets the guidelines for permanence and durability of the Committee on Production Guidelines for Book Longevity of the Council on Library Resources, Inc.

To
Derek Morgan Ash,
the
youngest Sooner

CONTENTS

ILLUSTRATIONS

Photographs not otherwise credited are from the Western History Collections, University of Oklahoma Library.

MAPS

PREFACE

THE HERITAGE of Oklahoma is rich and diverse. Known by the conquistadors, Coronado and Oñate, Oklahoma's southwestern rim continued under Spanish influence into the middle of the seventeenth century. The French came to Oklahoma during the eighteenth century. Restless *coureurs de bois* (bush rangers), led by Bernard de La Harpe, traveled the Grand, the Arkansas, the Canadian, and the Red rivers, mingling with the native tribes and establishing a loose confederacy.

Integrated into the United States by the Louisiana Purchase, in 1803, Oklahoma was on the southern flank of a far-flung defense system in which Fort Smith, Fort Gibson, and Fort Towson were strategic links. For nearly a century thereafter, while many areas in the Louisiana Territory were becoming states in the Union, Oklahoma was reserved as Indian Territory. Thus Oklahoma provided a home for more than fifty immigrant tribes, who joined the native Kiowa, Comanche, Wichita,

Caddo, Quapaw, and Osage tribes. These early settlers included black immigrants who came as slaves of the Five Civilized Tribes—the Cherokees, the Choctaws, the Chickasaws, the Creeks, and the Seminoles—who had been driven from their eastern homes over the Trail of Tears. To this complex ethnic community were added the Indian agent, the trader, and the missionary.

Indian Territory had a natural bounty of minerals, especially lead; it had grain, meat, cattle hides, and horses, produced on the territory's ranches and farms; and it was inhabited by Indians whose fighting abilities were well known. Because of those advantages, during the Civil War (the war between the North and the South) in 1861 this borderland was coveted by the Union and the Confederacy alike. Courted by both, the nations of Indian Territory committed themselves to the cause of the Confederacy (the southern states). The Confederacy, well-intentioned but helpless to meet its treaty promises to the Indian nations, abandoned its grand design in the West in 1863. Thereafter, for two painful years, Indian Territory faced Union (the federal government) reconquest and Reconstruction (when the South was being rebuilt and once more governed by the United States).

Hardly had the Indian Territory recovered from the ruin of war when it became subject to railroad construction, rapid economic development, and "Boomer" raids, all aimed at overrunning the Indian nations and opening their territory to settlement. Boomers were illegal homeseekers. Beginning in 1889, with a nucleus of homesteaders in the Unassigned Lands, settlement encroached into the Sac and Fox country and overran both the Cheyenne-Arapahoe Reservation and the vast Cherokee Outlet. By 1900, the Indians had lost tribal ownership of their lands throughout Indian Territory, except in the eastern parts that were the domain of the Five Civilized Tribes. Even this domain fell in 1907, when Oklahoma Territory and Indian Territory became the state of Oklahoma.

Between the end of the Civil War and statehood, the stamp of the West was indelibly imprinted upon Oklahoma. Cattle trails, ranches and stock-raising syndicates, mining boomtowns, railroad construction, military posts, cavalry and Indians, outlaws and lawmen, and the homesteader all became a part of Oklahoma's historical mosaic.

The knowledge of this fascinating heritage is derived from many sources, most of them found in the Oklahoma Historical Society Library and the University of Oklahoma Library. Writings by Oklahoma historians have provided substance and scope for producing this narrative of the Sooner State's past. A special debt is due Professor Robert E. Bell for his research and writing on Oklahoma prehistory. Grant and Carolyn Foreman, pioneer Oklahoma historians, produced books and articles of immense value to those trying to understand the many dimensions of Oklahoma's past. The basic work in Oklahoma history accomplished by Roy Gittinger, Muriel Wright, Joseph B. Thoburn, Victor Harlow, Edward E. Dale, and Edwin C. McReynolds provides a foundation that is indispensable for understanding and writing new versions of the state's past. The writings of the late John W. Morris extend the richness of sources on the natural environment of Oklahoma and its utilization by Oklahomans yesterday and today.

ARRELL MORGAN GIBSON

Norman, Oklahoma

THE HISTORY OF OKLAHOMA

Chapter 1. **THE NATURAL SETTING**

Geographic and Cultural Position

OKLAHOMA properly belongs to the Southwest geographic region of the United States. Geographers and historians, however, have various opinions about where Oklahoma should be placed among the American states. Some argue that Oklahoma is a part of the West. Some say it belongs to the South; others, the Middle West; and still others, the Southwest. Oklahoma has been said to be the most northerly of the southern states, an extension of the Midwest, and, by way of compromise, a border state.

Actually, Oklahoma falls between the East and the West and between the North and the South. It connects states that are easily identified with these regions. Oklahoma is also a mix; its natural and social environments are a blend of North, South, East, and West. The greatest influence, though, comes from the South and the West. Most of the state's early settlers, for example,

including the Five Civilized Tribes, were from the South. Its Indians, cavalry, frontier military posts, outlaws, lawmen, traders and trappers, ranching and trail drives, and homesteaders are definitely a part of the American West. Thus, because Oklahoma has been influenced most by the South and the West, it belongs to the geographic region called the Southwest.

Physical Environment

OKLAHOMA'S physical environment—its landforms, soils, climate, natural resources, trees, plants, and grasses—is a blend of contrasts and extremes. The state's nearly seventy thousand square miles, about 45 million acres, are surrounded by the states of Missouri, Arkansas, Texas, New Mexico, Colorado, and Kansas. Oklahoma's boundaries are rich in history. For instance, the Red River on the south and the 100th meridian on the west were for several years the boundary separating the

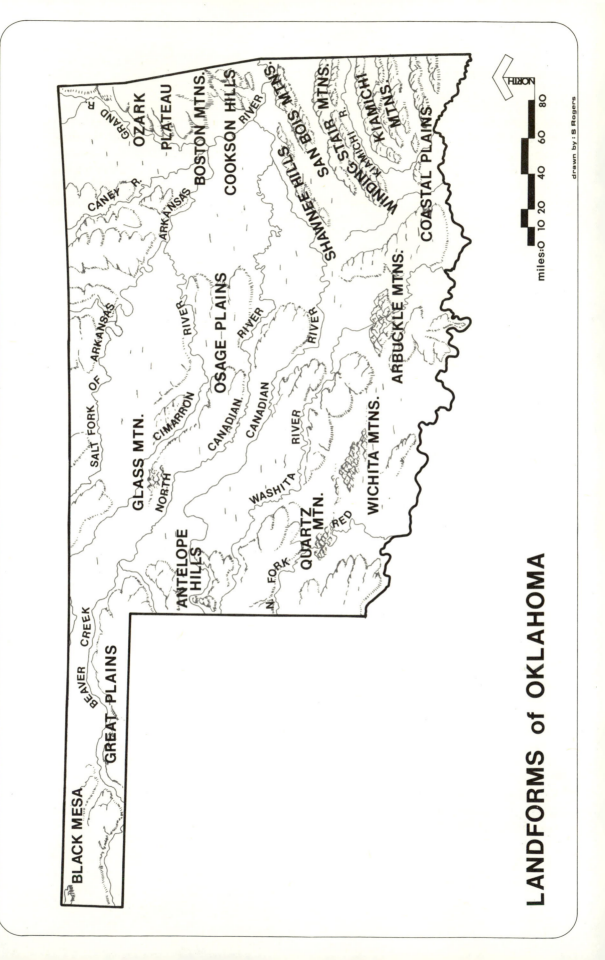

LANDFORMS of OKLAHOMA

drawn by : S Rogers

miles: 0 10 20 40 60 80

United States from foreign nations. At one time or another, Spain, Mexico, and the Republic of Texas all bordered what is now Oklahoma.

Oklahoma's northern boundary is the 37th parallel; its extreme southern point touches 33° 35' (minutes) latitude. Most of the state's western boundary is the 100th meridian, but its far western boundary, at the end of the long, narrow strip of territory called the Panhandle, is 103° longitude. Oklahoma's extreme eastern line is 94° 29' (minutes) longitude.

Among the states of the Union, Oklahoma ranks eighteenth in size. It is larger than the six New England states combined. It is also larger than any single state east of the Mississippi River. The state is divided into seventy-seven counties. The largest of these in size is Osage County in the north, and the smallest is Marshall County in the south.

The surface of Oklahoma is composed of a variety of landscapes. The state drains from northwest to southeast. The elevation ranges from 5,000 feet above sea level at Black Mesa in the far-northwestern corner of the Panhandle to 325 feet above sea level in the southeastern corner on Red River. Oklahoma's mean elevation is 1,300 feet above sea level.

The state's irregular countryside, created by scattered mountains and hills, causes local changes in drainage. For example, some streams flow north or west before they bend to the normal northwest–southeast drainage pattern. The general slope for the entire region is six to eight feet per mile.

Oklahoma is drained by two great drainage systems. One is the Arkansas River drainage, which carries about two-thirds of the state's runoff, and the other is the Red River drainage, which carries the other third. The Arkansas River forms as a snow-fed, fast-running, clear mountain stream in the Colorado Rockies. After entering Oklahoma, this river gathers the Salt Fork, the Chikaskia, the Cimarron (or Red Fork), the Verdigris, the Grand, and the Illinois rivers. All these flow from the northern areas of the state.

The principal southern feeder of the Arkansas River is the Canadian. This stream, which crosses the Texas Panhandle into Oklahoma, is often wrongly called the South Canadian. The North Canadian, formed by the joining of the Beaver River and Wolf Creek in the northwestern corner of the state, enters the Canadian River at North Fork Town near present-day Eufaula. Nearby, a stream flowing from the south across Pittsburg County joins the parent stream. In early times this stream was known as the South Canadian, but it is now called Gaines Creek. Gaines Creek is the true South Canadian.

The other major drainage stream for Oklahoma, the Red River, begins on the high plains of the Texas Panhandle and forms Oklahoma's southern boundary from the 100th meridian eastward. The Red River picks up the North Fork, the Washita, the Boggy, the Blue, and the Kiamichi rivers on its way.

Oklahoma contains four major mountain systems—the Ozark, the Ouachita, the Arbuckle, and the Wichita formations. The Ozarks extend into northeastern Oklahoma from southwestern Missouri and northwestern Arkansas. Clear, surging creeks and rivers, including the Cowskin (Elk) and the Illinois, drain the western slopes of the scenic Ozarks.

South of the Arkansas River in east-

Glass Mountains, Major County.

ern Oklahoma is a series of local mountain systems, including the Kiamichi, the Sans Bois, the Winding Stair, and the Jack Fork, all of which are associated with the parent Ouachita formation in western Arkansas. The Arbuckle Mountains, which cover one thousand square miles in south–central Oklahoma, are of interest to the naturalist and the geologist because the base material of which the mountains are made is exposed at the surface.

On Oklahoma's southwestern boundary are the Wichita Mountains. Mount Scott (2,464 feet), Mount Sheridan, and Saddle Mountain rise quite visibly from the surrounding Great Plains. The Wichita Mountains include the Quartz Mountains, which mark the valley of the North Fork of Red River.

Oklahoma's prairies and plains are marked here and there by ancient mountain systems, now worn down into low-lying hills, buttes (hills with steep sides and flat tops), and mesas (high, broad, flat tablelands with rocky slopes). These include the Osage Hills of north–central Oklahoma, the Glass (pronounced "gloss") Mountains of northwestern Oklahoma, the Antelope Hills in the valley of the Canadian River near Oklahoma's western border, and the majestic Black Mesa, a lava cap in the far-northwestern corner of the state.

Rock material from the mountain systems—limestone, sandstone, granite, gypsum, and shale—has weathered, broken down, and eroded to produce a variety of soils. Black limestone soils, which come from the Ozark and the Arbuckle mountains, are the most fertile in the state. Most eastern Oklahoma soils outside the limestone belts are

6

Oklahoma landmark, chimney rock.

made from a base of clay and shale mixes. In central and western Oklahoma the red-orange soil, formed from shale and clay rock material, is also fertile.

Oklahoma's climate is transitional, linking weather systems of the North and the South and those of the East and the West. The state's climate is generally considered temperate but with variations because of the blending of horizontal and vertical climate zones. A humid belt in the South joins with the more variable, colder, continental climatic belt in the North. The horizontal climatic zones in Oklahoma are the humid belt from the East and the dry from the West. The mixing of these kinds of climate produces weather that is generally pleasant and mild but with wide variations.

Oklahoma's annual average tempera-ture is about 60° F. The state's summers usually have several days above 100° F. Oklahoma winters sometimes produce subzero temperatures, but the bitterly cold periods seldom last very long.

Oklahoma's climate variety includes sudden changes in temperature; there are "northers" carrying destructive blizzards, and violent thunderstorms containing hail, lightning, heavy rainfall, and occasionally a deadly, destructive tornado. No part of Oklahoma is free from winds, but the western half of the state, in the Great Plains, receives a steady air flow most of the year, generally from the south. As a result, the scattered trees in that part of the state are permanently bent toward the north.

Rainfall distribution varies more than temperature. Oklahoma City, near the center of the state, averages 32 inches a year, but in the southeast the average

Buffalo herd grazing on the plains of western Oklahoma.

is 56 inches. In the arid northwest the precipitation average is only 18 inches. In 1949 a record yearly rainfall of 67 inches was recorded in the Kiamichi Mountains of southeastern Oklahoma. The smallest annual precipitation recorded in the state was 8½ inches at Boise City in the Panhandle during 1934.

Oklahoma is rich in a variety of minerals useful for modern civilization. Coal deposits are scattered across eastern Oklahoma. Oil and natural gas have been found in most of Oklahoma's seventy-seven counties. Rich lead and zinc beds occur in Ottawa County in northeastern Oklahoma. Granite, limestone, clay, gypsum, and gravel have provided materials for constructing buildings and roads. Traces of gold and silver, found in the Wichita Mountains at the turn of the century, set off a miners' rush to that region.

Just as Oklahoma is a transition zone in climate, so it is in plant life. More than one hundred thirty different kinds of trees have been identified as native to the state. Mixed hardwood forests, found in the eastern part of the state, contain stands of maple, sweet gum, oak, hickory, pecan, walnut, sycamore, dogwood, and redbud. Pine, cedar, and cypress also grow there. Wild grape and sumac clumps add variety to the larger forest species.

Oklahoma's eastern forests gradually blend into the prairies and plains of the central and western regions, but even on the grasslands forest growths appear now and then, especially along the watercourses. These forests include stands of cottonwood, elm, blackjack, post oak, willow, hackberry, cedar, and wild plum.

One of Oklahoma's most interesting vegetation belts is the Cross Timbers. A thickly packed, stunted forest five to thirty miles wide, it runs almost diagonally from the southwest toward central Oklahoma. The forest consists of blackjack, post oak, and shinnery oak laced together by a tightly woven, tangled undergrowth of wild grapevine and greenbriar. The Cross Timbers serve as a divide between the bluestem-dominated prairies to the east and the short-grass plains of western Oklahoma. Scattered through the eastern forests are grassy parks and glades that gradually blend with the prairies

A drawing of how prehistoric Oklahoma may have looked.

of central Oklahoma, where bluestem and goldentop grasses flourish.

Beyond the Cross Timbers are the Great Plains, an arid zone generally west of 98° longitude. Grasses predominate in this part of the state. Short, curly grama, mesquite, and buffalo grasses form a thick sod that was used by pioneers to construct walls for houses and sheds. Sage and varieties of cactus also grow on the Great Plains. Rivers and creeks in this portion of the state are lined with cottonwood, willow, and hackberry. Shinnery oak, mesquite, and cedar clumps are also found in this area of limited rainfall.

Oklahoma's wildlife is just as varied as its physical landscape. In prehistoric times Oklahoma's forests, prairies, and plains were the habitat of creatures now long extinct—the Columbian mammoth, the mastodon, the giant primordial bison, and the diminutive camel and horse. These also existed during the Ice Age, which produced a climate in Oklahoma that nourished plants now extinct—subtropical trees and shrubs and broad savanna-type grasslands.

About eight thousand years ago, the present environment evolved, and it came to sustain plants and wildlife familiar to us today. Prehistoric Indians and, after 1541, Europeans, found deer, elk, antelope, black bear, raccoon, timber wolf, coyote, fox, beaver, prairie dog, panther, and wildcat in abundance. Alligators were seen in the Red River. Most visible and useful for humans was the American bison or buffalo, which roamed western Oklahoma in great herds.

Oklahoma's wildlife community has included the horned toad and other lizards, such nonpoisonous snakes as the garter, bull, green, ribbon, coachwhip, and black, and poisonous snakes, such as the timber, prairie, and diamondback rattlers, the copperhead, and the vicious cottonmouth.

Oklahoma streams contained many bass, perch, and channel and flathead catfish. The forests and meadows were the home of flocks of wild turkeys, prairie chickens, quail, ducks, geese, and passenger pigeons so numerous their flights darkened the sky. Every kind of bird found in the area from the Mississippi River to the Rocky Mountains flourished in early Oklahoma. These included mockingbirds, sparrows, orioles, thrushes, blackbirds, bluejays, larks, warblers, robins, bluebirds, roadrunners, scissortail flycatchers, and at times the now-extinct Carolina parakeet.

9

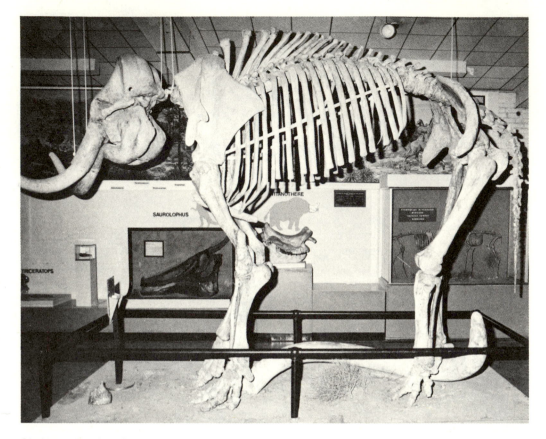

Skeleton of extinct Columbian Mammoth.

Prehistoric People in Oklahoma

OKLAHOMA's natural environment, with its mild climate and abundant wildlife, served as a home for humans at least fifteen thousand years ago. This makes the state one of the oldest areas in the United States in terms of human occupation. We know of Oklahoma's historic past from the written records left by European visitors to the area, beginning in 1541. Oklahoma's past before 1541 is told through the investigations and writings of archaeologists (scientists who study the past by examining the remains of early cultures) and anthropologists (scientists who study the beliefs and customs of people). These scientists' studies show that human life existed in Oklahoma even in that period called the Pleistocene Age, down to about eight thousand years ago.

Then, as now, Oklahoma was in a good condition to support human life. The environment, however, was not what it is today. There were, for example, savannas, swamps, and waterholes throughout central and western Oklahoma. These attracted the Columbian mammoth and other creatures

Prehistoric drawings, Cimarron Canyon, Oklahoma Panhandle.

that Oklahoma's earliest people—wandering families of big-game hunters—sought out for food and hides. The moderate climate made life relatively easy for these early Oklahomans, who probably were members of America's first human family.

Natural shelter, provided by many overhanging rocks, ledges, and caves, was available in many parts of the state. Durable weapons made from hard stone, generally flint, were important to the prehistoric hunters. Several local surface deposits of this material, notably the flint of northeastern Oklahoma in present Ottawa County, were discovered and worked by early hunters. Archaeologists have identified two types of early people in Oklahoma by the projectile points, or spear points, they used. Clovis man was the first; Folsom man came later.

Near Stecker, Oklahoma, scientists uncovered a prehistoric site called Domebo mammoth kill site. They used the carbon-14 test to determine the age of the material they found. Clovis projectile points were found in the rib cage of an excavated mammoth skeleton. The carbon-14 test determines the amount of radioactive carbon present, and the amount of carbon in bones tells scientists how old they are. Archaeologists found that the Domebo mammoth kill site material is 10,243 to 11,061 years old. When the Pleistocene Age ended in Oklahoma, about eight thousand years ago, plants and animals found in that period became extinct, and there evolved an environment with climate,

11

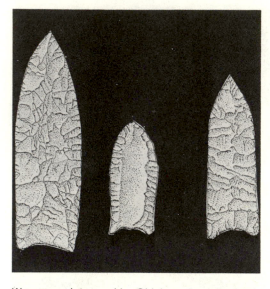

Weapon points used by Oklahoma's earliest settlers. Left to right—Clovis, Folsom, and Plainview.

the centuries left an accumulation of camp material and debris which collected in layers. From time to time, wind or water spread soil over these camp sites, separating one period of human use from another. In Oklahoma caves, archaeologists have found layers of remains that have built up nearly ten feet deep. Similar deposits have been dug up along many streams in the state.

Working through these sites, archaeologists have been able to follow the progress of early Oklahomans from the life of wandering hunters to the life of settled town dwellers and farmers. Diggings in caves and along creek and river sites have yielded spear points, stone knives and axes, grinders, bone fishhooks, animal bones, pottery, and corn.

The late prehistoric age in Oklahoma, which began about the time of Christ and ended near A.D. 1500, is called the moundbuilders epoch because during those years man-made mounds were built throughout the state. Some mounds were built to provide platforms for mud-and-wattle houses and for protection against floods. Many others, well over forty feet high, were for religious purposes. Some were solid; these probably served as open-air shrines. Others, built over cedar frames, were used as burial temples.

The Spiro epoch, A.D. 900 to 1450, marks the golden age of Oklahoma prehistory. During the late 1930s, workers discovered in eastern Oklahoma a man-made hill that they called the Spiro Mound. This archaeological find was a ceremonial pyramid and burial temple built of rot-resistant cedar logs and covered with thousands of tons of hand-carried earth. Although the Spiro people left no written record of their achievements, their story can be pieced together from the elaborate

plants, and animals such as are found today.

After the Pleistocene Age, Oklahoma's prehistoric age is easier to study because human signs are easier to find. Today concentrations of prehistoric evidence are found in the caves and ledges of the Ozarks of northeastern Oklahoma, the caves of the Oklahoma Panhandle (particularly near Kenton), and along the banks of many creeks and rivers across the state.

Scientists studying Oklahoma's prehistoric past after the environmental change found that early Oklahomans were still wandering hunters, but that they traveled one basic route year after year in search of food. Each season they camped at familiar sites on the banks of creeks and rivers, generally near springs and salt licks, and (especially during the winter) in caves or under ledges.

Stopping at these same sites through

Archaeologists at Spiro Mound.

burial goods found in Spiro Mound and housed today in Oklahoma museums.

Spiro-made goods taken from the burial chambers of this mound consist of elaborate ceremonial maces, finely decorated pottery vessels, cedar masks, human and animal effigies, human and animal heads sculptured from rock crystal, mother-and-child figures, clay and stone pipes, and pearl and shell beads.

Spiro household items include baskets and other woven items, fabrics made from vegetable and fiber cloth with geometric designs, and blankets and capes of buffalo hair, rabbit fur, and feathers. Also taken from the Spiro Mound were cane combs, polished stone tools and weapons, conch shells bearing sketches of Spiro history and ceremonials, decorated sheet copper shields, copper axes, and copper-covered ear spools.

The material remains of the Spiro people show that they were very advanced. They lived in thickly settled communities, and their life-style was based on agriculture. Spiro craftsmen developed special skills. They produced pottery, textiles, sculpture, and metal goods. They traded and commu-

13

Oklahoma Indian Tribes

Copper mask and ear spools excavated from Spiro Mound.

WE KNOW quite a lot about the Indian tribes of Oklahoma as a result of research on the Indian tribes of North America that has been carried out by archaeologists, historians, and anthropologists. Research in Indian languages has given a better understanding of the tribes generally and has explained more about Oklahoma's past on the eve of European exploration.

Scholars have found that although the life-styles of the more than two hundred separate tribes of North America were quite similar, their languages differed widely. Certainly no written language served the tribes of Oklahoma, let alone the United States generally. In 1816 scholars began an in-depth study of Indian languages, and in 1885 J. W. Powell finished a standard system for classifying Indian tribes by language. The Powell system for classification by language stock or family identifies fifty-one independent Indian languages spoken by tribes in the United States.

In recent times linguists (language scholars) and anthropologists have changed the Powell system of classifying the Indian tribes by language. They apply the genetic (or family) system of language classification to the study of Indian languages. Thus Algonkian, Iroquoian, Siouian, Caddoan, Athapascan, and Muskoghean, used in the Powell system, are kept, but several are changed. The Comanches, formerly in the Shoshonean language family, are now in the Uto-Aztecan, and the Kiowas, formerly in the Kiowan, are in the Tanoan group that includes the Taos Pueblo Indians.

From the Spiro period to the time of Coronado's expedition, Oklahoma was

nicated with other people. (Recovered grave goods include shells and pearls from the Gulf area, and copper from the upper Great Lakes region.) Although many authorities call this pre-Columbian period the Stone Age, it is important to note that the Spiro people were using metal in the making of goods.

Many archaeologists and prehistorians believe that the Spiro culture had vanished by the time European explorers entered the region in 1541. Other writers, however, suggest that warfare with the Plains Indians brought an end to the Spiro community. It was during the period A.D. 1200 to 1500 that the human setting was created for the discovery of Oklahoma by the Europeans.

the home of tribes representing possibly as many as three of the basic language stocks or families. For many years after the Louisiana Purchase, the area that is presently Oklahoma served the nation as Indian Territory. This was a special area to which Indian tribes were sent from all parts of the United States. The result is that today Oklahoma includes a greater number of tribes (sixty-seven) than any other state in the Union.

The tribes in Oklahoma represent many Indian cultures and languages. The principal language stocks and tribes present in Oklahoma at some time (most of them are still in the state) include those listed in the following table.

Language Affiliations of the Oklahoma Tribes

Language Stock	Tribes
Algonquian	Arapaho, Cheyenne, Delaware, Fox, Kickapoo, Miami, Potawatomi, Sac, Shawnee
Athapascan	Apache
Caddoan	Caddo, Pawnee, Wichita
Iroquoian	Cherokee, Wyandot, Seneca, Cayuga, Erie
Muskhogean	Choctaw, Chickasaw, Creek, Seminole
Uto-Aztecan	Comanche
Siouan	Osage, Quapaw, Kansa, Ponca, Missouri, Iowa
Tanoan	Kiowa

When Oklahoma was being explored by the Europeans, the Quapaws ranged along the Arkansas River into eastern Oklahoma. On the tributaries of the Red and the Arkansas rivers, the Caddoan-speaking peoples, ancestors of the present day Wichitas and Caddos, built villages, hunted the uplands, and farmed small patches of corn, squash, pumpkin,

Polished stone effigy excavated from Spiro Mound.

and melons. On the western border of Oklahoma roamed a fierce people called the Querechos, the Plains-Apaches.

The Querechos had no permanent houses. They used a buffalo-hide tipi, which they moved from place to place as they followed the buffalo herds. Dogs, used as beasts of burden, dragged the Querechos' simple belongings on a travois (a kind of sled made of poles laced with strips of hide). These Indians depended completely upon the buffalo. They used its skin for shelter and clothing, and they ate its flesh. They had no agriculture. The Querechos were the Indians that Coronado met in 1541.

15

Study Aids

Explain the significance of each term or phrase listed below:

1. Domebo
2. Spiro Mound
3. Cross Timbers
4. Clovis man
5. Querechos
6. Archaeology

On an outline map of Oklahoma locate the following places:

1. Black Mesa
2. Panhandle

3. 100th meridian
4. Kiamichi Mountains
5. Washita River
6. Great Plains

Use the suggestions below for study guides:

1. Outline Oklahoma prehistory.
2. Discuss Oklahoma's two drainage systems.
3. Describe Oklahoma's climate.
4. Distinguish between prehistoric and historic Oklahoma.
5. Explain the system for classifying Indian tribes.

For Further Reading*

BOOKS

Gould, Charles N. *Oklahoma Place Names.* Norman, 1933.

Leonhardy, Frank C., ed. *Domebo: A Paleo-Indian Mammoth Kill in the Prairie Plains.* Contributions of the Museum of the Great Plains, Lawton, Oklahoma.

Marriott, Alice. *The First Comers.* New York, 1961.

Morris, John W. *Oklahoma Geography.* Oklahoma City, 1961,

Wedel, Waldo R. *Prehistoric Man on the Great Plains.* Norman, 1961.

Wycoff, Don and Robert L. Brooks. *Oklahoma Archeology.* Norman, 1983.

ARTICLES

Bell, Robert E. "Recent Archaeological Research in Oklahoma, 1946–1948." *Chronicles of Oklahoma,* Vol. 27 (Autumn, 1949): 303–12.

Gibson, Arrell M. "Prehistory in Oklahoma." *Chronicles of Oklahoma,* Vol. 43 (Spring, 1965):2–8.

*Some of the titles listed under Further Reading throughout this text may not be available in either your school library or the local public library. To secure books that are not available at your local libraries, write to the Oklahoma Department of Libraries, 200 N. E. 18th Street, Oklahoma City, Oklahoma 73105, for information concerning their loan services to public or school libraries.

Chapter 2. OKLAHOMA: A BORDERLAND, 1541 TO 1820

Spanish Explorations

FROM 1541 to 1820 Oklahoma was important in the contest between Spain, France, and later the United States, for control of the Southwest. First to come were the Spaniards in 1541. Spain had conquered and settled the islands of the Caribbean and much of the mainland from Mexico south. Indians told the Spaniards that north of Mexico were rich kingdoms named Cale, the Gran Quivira, and the Seven Cities of Cibola.

Daring Spanish explorers called conquistadors were eager to visit the northern lands and search for these centers of wealth. One kingdom was reported to be greater in size than Seville, Spain's largest city. It was said that its outer wall was made of solid gold, and that the doors of the shops and houses were covered with turquoise. The conquistadors were excited by another story that told of a kingdom where there was so much wealth that the people wore hats of gold.

Several groups from Mexico went in search of Cale, the Gran Quivira, and the Seven Cities of Cibola. One of these groups was organized by Francisco Vasquez de Coronado. In February, 1540, he set out from Compostela (on the west coast of Mexico) leading an expedition with nearly fifteen hundred Spaniards and Mexican Indians. Coronado led his men across the present states of Arizona, New Mexico, and the Texas Panhandle, western Oklahoma, and into Kansas in search of the Gran Quivira, situated supposedly on the Arkansas River in south-central Kansas.

Quivira was not a city where the people ate from golden plates and made their weapons from silver. Women did not serve their men from golden pitchers. There were no tiny golden bells tinkling on the branches of shade trees; and children did not wear heavy gold bracelets on their arms and legs. Rather, Quivira was a humble settlement of dome-shaped, grass houses built by the Wichita Indians, who got their food

Artist's sketch of conquistadors from Coronado's column.

territory as a part of the Spanish empire. The Spanish flag had come to Oklahoma.

In this period, other Spaniards visited Oklahoma or the land surrounding it. Hernando de Soto explored parts of the lower Mississippi Valley at the same time Coronado was wandering across western Oklahoma. De Soto came no farther west than present Little Rock on the Arkansas River. But his claim, in the name of the Spanish crown, added to Spain's right to rule the territory north of Mexico.

After 1598, Spanish settlements were developed in New Mexico along the Rio Grande. Spanish explorers from the Rio Grande towns continued to search the territory to the east for the Gran Quivira and other centers of wealth. One of these expeditions from New Mexico in 1601, which explored western Oklahoma in the valley of the Canadian, was led by Juan de Oñate.

from their fields of corn, beans, squash, and pumpkins.

In disappointment, Coronado wrote to his king. "What I am sure of is that there is not any gold nor any other metal in all that country." Then he marched back to the Rio Grande and returned to Mexico. The important thing about Coronado's northern expedition is that for the first time Europeans visited Oklahoma. Their written reports of the land and people are a written record of Oklahoma. The prehistoric age had come to a close and the historic age had begun. Another reason why Coronado's exploration of western Oklahoma and the American Southwest is important is that, in the name of the Spanish king, he officially claimed this

French Claims in the Southwest

FRANCE soon challenged Spain for control of the Mississippi Valley. The Joliet-Marquette and the La Salle explorations of the territory along the Mississippi River were carried out before 1700 from French bases in Canada. These developed official French interest in the region. La Salle's 1682 expedition led to the French claim to all the land drained by the western watershed of the Mississippi River; this included Oklahoma. The French named this vast area Louisiana in honor of Louis XIV, king of France.

Beginning in 1699 with a permanent settlement at Biloxi on the Gulf of Mexico, Frenchmen began the development

18

of the new French province of Louisiana. Jean Baptiste Lemoyne, Sieur de Bienville, established New Orleans in 1718. From this base an army of French traders marched up the Red, the Arkansas, the Canadian, the Grand, and the Verdigris rivers to take advantage of the fur riches of Oklahoma and other sections of Louisiana.

The first Frenchman to visit Oklahoma was Juchereau de St. Denis. In 1714 he explored the region drained by the Red River hoping to trade with the Indian tribes. During 1719, Bernard de La Harpe led a group from New Orleans to the Indian towns on the Canadian River in eastern Oklahoma. In his journal, La Harpe described the wealth of these natives, the Wichitas and the Caddos, called "Taovayas" by the French.

La Harpe was impressed with the Taovayas' fields of corn, pumpkins, beans, and tobacco scattered on the fertile river bottoms about the villages. He noted that the Taovayas and other tribes on the Arkansas and Canadian rivers "cultivate prodigious quantities of tobacco which they press into flat loaves." These were used for trade. In addition to crops, the Indians raised good horses, and native craftsmen made fine saddles, bridles, and leather breastplates for the warriors. La Harpe was told that the Taovayas left their villages in October each year to hunt and returned in March to plant their crops. Their houses were built of sapling (young tree) frames to form domes and were covered with mats of woven straw and reeds.

La Harpe was favorably impressed with Oklahoma and recommended that French officials at New Orleans pay special attention to developing its fine fur resources. He wrote:

There is not in the whole colony of Louisiana an establishment more useful to make than on the branch of this river not only because of the mild climate, the fertility of the land, the richness of the minerals, but also because of the possibility of trade that one might introduce with Spain and New Mexico.

After La Harpe's visit to eastern Oklahoma, the French flag flew over the Taovaya villages on the Canadian and Arkansas rivers. Traders soon moved out over the waterways of Oklahoma and established trading posts among the Taovayas. These French traders, because they could adjust to life in the wilderness, lived in the Indian villages and married the native women.

From New Orleans, by small boats on the Arkansas and the Red rivers, they brought in many goods to trade. These included guns, ammunition, knives, beads, axes, hatchets, hoes, cloth, blankets, mirrors, and paint, which they traded to Indian hunters for pelts and buffalo robes.

Each year the traders took out of Oklahoma bales of beaver, otter, mink, and muskrat furs and beautifully tanned buffalo robes, all of which were in great demand in Europe. The main French settlements in Oklahoma were at Ferdinandina on the Arkansas River near present Newkirk, and Twin Villages (San Bernardo and San Teodoro) on the Red River in present Jefferson County.

Louisiana, and thus Oklahoma, became involved in European dealings and war in the middle of the 1700s. By an agreement called the Family Compact between the rulers of France and Spain, each was to support the other in its frequent wars against England.

France and Spain were defeated by Great Britain in the Seven Years' War (called the French and Indian War in North America), which ended by the Treaty of Paris, 1763. Spain demanded payment from France for the loss of Florida to England. And France, under the terms of the Family Compact, gave Louisiana, including Oklahoma, to Spain. Thus the Spanish flag returned to the country north of Red River.

For thirty-seven years Oklahoma was a frontier area in the Spanish province of Louisiana, ruled by the Spanish governors at New Orleans and San Antonio. During the second Spanish period, which lasted until 1800, officials at San Antonio and New Orleans attempted to control the trade in arms with the Comanches. This trade was based in remote Oklahoma trading towns and managed by outlaw French traders. Spanish engineers surveyed and built several wagon roads between Saint Louis and Santa Fe, and between San Antonio and Santa Fe. Sections of these roads crossed Oklahoma.

The Louisiana Purchase

As a frontier of Louisiana territory, Oklahoma continued to figure in international affairs. The Spanish flag, which had returned to Oklahoma in 1763 was again replaced by the flag of France after Napoleon Bonaparte, first consul of France, and the king of Spain signed the Treaty of San Ildefonso in 1800. The French, who were busy fighting wars in Europe, could not return to Louisiana with enough people to develop its resources. Thus, in 1803 American commissioners in Paris completed the bargaining with French offi-

cials that sold Louisiana to the United States. In 1803, through the Louisiana Purchase, Oklahoma became the southwestern territory of the United States.

Louisiana's western boundary was unmarked. The lack of a definite border in the southwestern portion of the new territory created conflict between the United States and Spain over where the authority of one nation ended and the other began. Many Americans believed that the principal rivers of the Southwest, particularly the Arkansas and the Red, could serve as boundaries to establish an international boundary separating the Spanish and the American territories. The part of Louisiana that became Oklahoma was an important border region for the two countries.

President Thomas Jefferson, whose vision and energy had brought about the purchase of Louisiana, was eager to have the new territory explored and mapped. Jefferson planned to use the knowledge gained from the explorations in bargaining with Spanish officials for a settlement of the international boundary in the Southwest. To accomplish this, he ordered the War Department to begin the exploration of Louisiana. This was carried on by other presidents until the boundary question was settled between 1819 and 1821. As explorers published reports on the Southwest, readers in the eastern United States first heard of the future Oklahoma. In 1806 two trips were made to find out where the Arkansas and Red rivers began. This resulted in the first official Americans being in Oklahoma.

During 1806 Captain Richard Sparks received orders from the secretary of war to trace the Red River to its source. He prepared to take twenty-four men and their equipment and supplies in two flat-bottomed boats and several pirogues (all light-weight craft) to Twin Villages on the upper Red River. There he hoped to trade for horses to take his party farther west. Departing from Natchitoches (a town in present Louisiana) on June 2, 1806, the Red River expedition proceeded slowly because the river channel was blocked for several miles by a great log jam called "the raft."

The American party reached the southeastern corner of present-day Oklahoma and landed their boats to eat the noon meal. Just as they did so, Spanish troops under Don Francisco Viana from the fort at Nacogdoches burst from the woods on the Texas side of the river. The Spanish commander charged that the Americans were trespassing on Spanish territory, and he offered Sparks a choice of turning back to the American settlements or of being arrested and jailed at Nacogdoches. Faced with superior numbers, Captain Sparks ordered his men to go to Natchitoches. Although the Red River expedition failed to trace the river to its source, it is remembered because Captain Sparks was the first official representative from the United States to visit Oklahoma.

Also in 1806 the United States War Department organized an Arkansas River expedition to the Rocky Mountains. Captain Zebulon M. Pike commanded the group. His second-in-command was Lieutenant James Wilkinson. Captain Pike's party of twenty-three men left Saint Louis during the summer of 1806. They traveled by boat up the Missouri River and then up the Osage River as far as they could go by boat. At the Osage villages Pike got horses to take his party across the plains.

Thomas Jefferson, the president responsible for bringing the Louisiana Territory and thus Oklahoma into the Union. *Painting by Rembrandt Peale.*

Pike led his men across the future state of Kansas to the great bend of the Arkansas River, where he ordered Lieutenant Wilkinson to take five men and follow the Arkansas River to its mouth. For his mission Lieutenant Wilkinson had two boats constructed, a pirogue cut from a cottonwood log and a light pole-framed craft covered with elkskin and buffalo hide.

On October 28, 1806, the Arkansas River expedition divided. Captain Pike rode west with his group toward the Rocky Mountains. Lieutenant Wilkinson and five men launched their boats into the Arkansas River and drifted

21

Zebulon M. Pike, commander of the expedition that brought Lt. James Wilkinson to Oklahoma.

south. They spent November and December in present Oklahoma.

Winter came early in 1806 and was very severe. Lieutenant Wilkinson's boats capsized several times, dumping his meager supplies into the water. Ice, sometimes reaching from shore to shore or drifting in huge chunks slowed the trip down the Arkansas. Finally, on December 31, 1806, the party passed the mouth of the Poteau River. On New Year's Day, 1807, they left present Oklahoma for the Mississippi River.

Lieutenant Wilkinson's journal of the trip down the Arkansas gave the the first American account of northeastern Oklahoma. He reported passing several Osage villages and a number of Cherokee and Choctaw hunting

camps. He referred to reports of rich lead mines northeast in the Osage country, and he mentioned meeting American trappers on the Poteau River and other streams.

The Sparks and Wilkinson explorations in Oklahoma during 1806 were followed by the Sibley expedition of 1811. George C. Sibley, Indian agent at Fort Osage, Missouri, along with fifteen Osage warriors, traveled to the buffalo plains during May, 1811. The expedition was out two months and ranged over present Kansas, Nebraska, and northern Oklahoma. The party entered Oklahoma along the valley of the Arkansas River, visited its tributaries, including the Salt Fork, the Cimarron, and the Chikaskia, and camped near present-day Blackwell. Sibley was particularly impressed by the Great Salt Plains, "glistening like a brilliant field of snow in the summer sun" on the banks of the Salt Fork River.

Major Stephen H. Long gets credit for the most extensive survey of Oklahoma in this early period of disputed boundaries between Spain and the United States in the Southwest. Major Long was an officer in the United States Corps of Topographical Engineers. He explored Oklahoma twice. In 1817 he was ordered by the War Department to select a site on the Arkansas River for a military post. He chose Belle Point, situated at the junction of the Poteau and Arkansas rivers. The post constructed there became Fort Smith. While in Oklahoma during 1817 he led a small party on a mission southwest from Fort Smith across the Kiamichi Mountains to the Red River.

In 1819 the War Department sent Major Long on another assignment in the West. His mission was to find the beginnings of the Arkansas and the Red rivers and to trace each stream back to the American settlements. Major Long took his party up the Missouri and the Platte rivers into the Rocky Mountains. During July, 1820, he ordered Captain John R. Bell and twelve men to follow the Arkansas River back to Fort Smith. Captain Bell's men suffered great hardship riding through the scorching August heat, but reached Fort Smith on September 9, 1820.

Major Long led his ten-man group south through the Rocky Mountains searching for the headwaters of the Red River. A five-day ride across eastern New Mexico brought the party to a deep creek that Major Long identified as the source of the Red River. Unknown to him at the time, this was the beginning of the Canadian River. As Major Long's party crossed the high plains, the streambed gradually widened until it became two miles wide in places.

On September 10, 1820, Major Long and his men suffered a great disappointment. They had arrived at the point where the Canadian and the Arkansas rivers flow together in eastern Oklahoma. It was only then that they were aware of their error. It was too late in the year for them to retrace their steps and search out the Red River; therefore, Major Long ordered his column to proceed on the Arkansas River. They arrived at Fort Smith on the thirteenth of September, 1820. They were welcomed by Captain Bell and his men who had traced the Arkansas River to Belle Point.

One other expedition into Oklahoma during this period should be noted because of the scientific information it produced. At the time that Major Long's

George C. Sibley, explorer of northwestern Oklahoma.

party was moving toward the Rocky Mountains in 1819, the world-famous botanist (a scientist who studies plants) Thomas Nuttall was traveling down the Arkansas River toward Fort Smith.

Arriving at the post in early spring, Nuttall spent several months collecting botanical specimens in eastern Oklahoma. He studied the plants and animals along the Arkansas, the Grand, the Verdigris, and the Cimarron rivers. He also crossed the Kiamichi Mountains to the Red River during his travels in eastern Oklahoma. Nuttall's experiences in Oklahoma are described in his *Journal of Travels into the Arkansas Territory*. This is one of the earliest scientific books on the plants and animals of Oklahoma.

Stephen H. Long, explorer of eastern Oklahoma and the Canadian River Valley. *From a painting by C. W. Peale.*

These expeditions across Oklahoma and the Southwest produced two important results. First, expedition leaders published books, articles, and official reports telling of their adventures and describing the region.

Much of the Southwest, including Oklahoma, they described as an arid wasteland. Major Long wrote that this dry wasteland was

providentially placed to keep the American people from ruinous diffusion. . . . We have little apprehension of giving too unfavorable an account of this portion of the country. Though the soil is in some places fertile, the want of timber, of navigable streams, and of water for the necessities of life, render it an unfit residence for any but a nomad population. The traveller who shall at any time have traversed its desolate sands, will, we think, join us in the wish that this region forever remain the unmolested haunt of the native hunter, the bison, and the jackall [coyote].

From these published descriptions of Oklahoma and the Southwest came the term the "Great American Desert." This image of the Southwest and much of Oklahoma to some degree continues to present times.

A second result of these expeditions across Oklahoma and the Southwest was, finally, the settlement of the southwestern boundary question with Spain. The Adams-Onís Treaty was written in 1819 and was signed two years later. It provided that the southern and western boundaries separating the American and the Spanish territories were established by a line that began in the Gulf of Mexico at the mouth of the Sabine River, and extended up the west bank of this stream to the 32nd parallel. From this point it moved due north to the south bank of the Red River, and west along the south bank of that stream to the 100th meridian. It then went north on that line to the south bank of the Arkansas River, and out that stream to its source. Last, it moved north to the 42nd parallel and out that line to the Pacific Ocean. The Adams-Onís Treaty therefore set the principal southern and western borders of the future state of Oklahoma.

Early Government in Oklahoma

OKLAHOMA as a part of the Louisiana Territory was governed in several different ways before it became the Indian Territory around 1820. Soon after the United States bought the Louisiana

24

Territory, Congress passed an act dividing the vast territory at 33° north latitude. This is the present boundary between Louisiana and Arkansas. Congress named the area south of that parallel the Territory of New Orleans. The area north of 33° north became the District of Louisiana and was popularly called Upper Louisiana. For purposes of government, Upper Louisiana was attached to Indiana Territory, which at that time extended to the Mississippi River. Its capital was at Vincennes. Since William Henry Harrison was governor of Indiana Territory in 1804, he also was governor of Upper Louisiana and Oklahoma.

In 1805, Congress separated Upper Louisiana from Indiana Territory and ordered that the area be governed from Saint Louis. General James Wilkinson served as governor. Seven years later Congress created the Territory of Missouri to include the future Oklahoma, with headquarters at Saint Louis. William Clark was appointed governor. Oklahoma remained a part of the Missouri Territory until 1819 when Congress created Arkansas Territory. This Territory included present Arkansas and Oklahoma.

Oklahoma stayed a part of Arkansas Territory until the 1820s when the western half of this territory was set aside for the Indian tribes who had been moved there from the East. Then it took on the name of Indian Territory, a name it retained, at least in part, until Oklahoma statehood in 1907.

Indian Tribes in Oklahoma

WHEN the United States took over Oklahoma as a part of the Louisiana Purchase, it was the home of a number of important Indian tribes. The Osages roamed the area from the Missouri River on the north to the Arkansas River on the south. This area included northeastern Oklahoma. The Osages were of Siouan language stock. They were a large tribe whose warriors were feared by other tribes for their courage and terrible fury in battle. There were about 4,500 in the tribe with 1,250 warriors. They were said to be at war with all tribes of the Southwest. By the terror they inspired, they drove several weaker tribes out of Kansas and Oklahoma into the Texas country.

The territory between the Arkansas and the Red rivers was the home of the Arkansas or Quapaws. They, too, were of Siouan stock, speaking a language similar to the Osages, but they were less warlike than the Osages. When the Americans bought the Louisiana Territory in 1803, the Quapaws, weakened by close contact with the French, numbered only about one thousand.

West of the area where the Osages and the Quapaws lived were the Wichitas and Caddos. From earliest historic times they had lived in Oklahoma. During the time of Spanish and French control, they had lived in northern Oklahoma. One of their main villages was built on a site along the Arkansas River near present Newkirk. La Harpe found several villages near the mouth of the Canadian River in 1719. Osage pressure forced the Wichitas and Caddos to settle along the Red River. Their settlements were next to the French trading posts of Twin Villages.

During the eighteenth and early nineteenth centuries, two fierce tribes from the north, the Comanches and the Kiowas, moved to the southern plains and

John Mix Stanley's painting depicting an Osage scalp dance. *Bureau of American Ethnology.*

spent much time on the western border of Oklahoma. These tribes played a major role in Oklahoma history in later times.

Each hunting season, small bands from the eastern tribes entered Oklahoma by way of the Arkansas and the Red river valleys to hunt buffalo. Local tribes resented this, and fights generally broke out each year between the outsiders and the warriors from the Oklahoma tribes. In 1807 the famous Choctaw chief Pushmataha led a band of warriors from Mississippi into Oklahoma on a hunting expedition. The Choctaws fought several battles with Osage warriors before returning to Mississippi.

In 1795 a group of Cherokees from Tennessee, led by a chief named The Bowl, found the country along the Arkansas River so attractive that it settled permanently in the West. Through the years, other eastern Cherokees joined The Bowl's band. They built villages along the Arkansas River and into northwestern Arkansas, and hunted on Osage territory in eastern Oklahoma.

The Osages fought against these raids on their game. A long and bloody border war took place between the defending Osages and the invading Cherokees. One example of this fighting occurred in October, 1817, when a large party of Cherokee raiders struck an Osage village near present Claremore. The contest, which resulted in the death of more than one hundred Osages, is known as the Battle of Claremore Mound.

The fury and destruction of the Osage–Cherokee border war threatened to spill over into the American settlements on the Missouri-Arkansas border. Settlers asked the national government for protection. In 1817 the United States army built its first post in the raw southwestern wilderness. Fort Smith was built where the Poteau

Artist's sketch of Fort Smith, mother post for the Southwest.

and the Arkansas rivers join. Military patrols from Fort Smith guarded the Oklahoma–Arkansas border against Cherokee invasions and Osage revenge raids, with the result that peace soon came to the region.

Early American Settlers

EVEN before the Louisiana Purchase in 1803, restless, daring Americans, "Long Knives" as they were called on the frontier, had entered the Trans-Mississippi country. When the United States gained control of this area, more and more American trappers and traders entered Louisiana. Oklahoma was one of the most appealing parts of Louisiana because of the rich commerce in furs already developed by French traders among the Osages, the Quapaws, the Wichitas, and other tribes. Also, the rivers and streams of Oklahoma pro-

vided a way to reach markets on the Gulf Coast.

Joseph Bogy and Pierre Chouteau were pioneer developers of the Oklahoma fur trade after the United States began governing the area. They built trading settlements and posts along the Grand and the Verdigris rivers and at Three Forks where the Verdigris, the Grand, and the Arkansas rivers merge. Their prosperity attracted others. By 1812, hunters and trappers were bringing in their families or marrying into Indian families. They began erecting log cabins, clearing farms, and raising livestock.

Tom Slover, an early-day Grand River hunter, brought in his family about this time and was reported to have developed "a good farm on a fine elevation on Grand River." Mark Bean settled on the Illinois River and was reported to have a "neat farmhouse with a considerable stock of cattle,

Artist's sketch of American explorers, sometimes called "Long Knives."

Thomas James, merchant explorer of western Oklahoma. *Missouri Historical Society.*

hogs, and poultry, and several acres of corn." Frontiersmen also built settlements on the Red River and prepared to organize a county in this part of southwestern Arkansas Territory.

More people brought a change in the goods shipped out by flatboat to markets on the Mississippi River and the Gulf of Mexico. The Indian trade continued. Each season the tribes brought to Three Forks bales of beaver, bear, panther, wolf, and otter skins, buffalo robes, elk and deer hides, and containers of much-sought-after bear oil. The Indians exchanged these items for earrings, twists of tobacco, pipes, rope, vermillion (a red dye), axes, knives, beads, cheap jewelry, bright-colored cloth, and guns and ammunition.

Each year, however, more of those cargoes bound for Gulf markets included grain, salt, bacon, lead, beeswax, leather, and pecans. Mark Bean was a typical trapper-settler. In addition to shipping furs and hides, he shipped loads of grain, bacon, and salt. On his farm was a salt water spring that flowed so heavily it would fill his salt kettles three days a week. (Fifty-five gallons of salt-water from Bean's spring produced a bushel of salt.)

Settlers came into the Trans-Mississippi West following a familiar pattern. The temporary camps of traders and trappers gave way to permanent settlement by farmers, craftsmen, and builders of towns. Just as other lands had first become territories and then states,

28

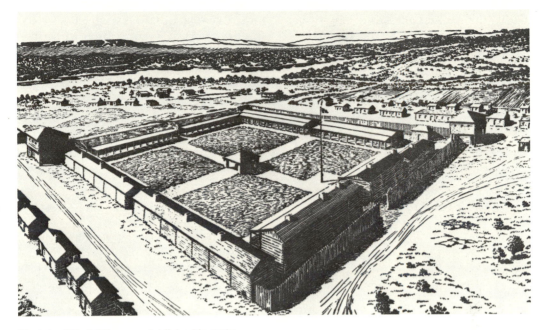

Sketch of Fort Gibson, established in 1824.

so too it seemed to be for Oklahoma. As trappers and traders blazed trails in the wilderness, settlements moved up the Arkansas and the Red rivers. Fort Smith was no longer a lonely outpost on the frontier; it had become a gateway to the West.

Because the new settlements west of Fort Smith needed protection from Indian attacks, the stockade at Fort Smith was temporarily closed in 1824. The garrison moved to the mouth of Grand River where Fort Gibson was established. In the same year Fort Towson was built near the mouth of the Kiamichi River to protect the growing settlements along the Red River.

These two new posts opened an area for settlement west of Fort Smith. Troops were stationed at these posts mainly to protect the settlers from the Indians. In 1824, Congress marked the western boundary of Arkansas Territory on a line from Fort Gibson south to the Red River. The Arkansas Territorial Legislature organized Lovely County in the north and placed the county seat on the west bank of Sallisaw Creek. Almost overnight a log town sprang up with the name of Nicksville. On the Red River another county, Miller County, was organized within present Oklahoma. Its main settlement was named Miller's Courthouse.

Oklahoma was well on its way to becoming a state, either in parts as an absorbed portion of Arkansas, or as a separate and distinct unit. Then federal officials decided to use Oklahoma for a different purpose. It was agreed that the area should serve the nation as Indian Territory. It would be a special settlement zone where the government could relocate the Indian tribes from

29

east of the Mississippi River. Those settlers living on lands in the two Arkansas counties in eastern Oklahoma were forced to move back into Arkansas, east of a line established in 1825, separating Arkansas Territory and Indian Territory. Because of this change, Fort Gibson and Fort Towson, which were created to protect the settlers from the Indians, became posts to protect the Indians from the settlers.

Study Aids

Explain the significance of each term or phrase listed below:

1. Taovaya
2. Family Compact
3. Twin Villages
4. Cale
5. Long Knives
6. Battle of Claremore Mound

Identify each of these persons:

1. Bernard de La Harpe
2. Richard Sparks
3. Stephen H. Long
4. Thomas Nuttall
5. The Bowl
6. Juchereau de St. Denis

On an outline map of Oklahoma locate the following places:

1. Fort Smith
2. Canadian River
3. Newkirk
4. Verdigris River
5. Great Salt Plains
6. Fort Gibson

Use the suggestions below for study guides:

1. Summarize European explorations of Oklahoma.
2. Show how the French used Louisiana, including Oklahoma.
3. Outline the role that Oklahoma played in foreign relations between 1764 and 1803.
4. Discuss Major Stephen H. Long's explorations of Oklahoma.
5. Describe the settlement of Oklahoma before 1820.

For Further Reading

BOOKS

Bolton, Herbert E. *Spanish Borderlands.* New Haven, 1921.
Foreman, Grant. *Pioneer Days in the Early Southwest.* Cleveland, 1926.
Morris, John W., Charles R. Goins, and Edwin C. McReynolds. *Historical Atlas of Oklahoma.* Norman, 1976.
Nuttall, Thomas. *Journal of Travels into the Arkansas Territory during the Year 1819.* Edited by Savoie Lottinville. Norman, 1980.
Thomas, Albert B. *Forgotten Frontiers.* Norman, 1932.

ARTICLES

Lewis, Anna. "La Harpe's First Expedition in Oklahoma, 1718–1719." *Chronicles of Oklahoma,* Vol. 2 (December, 1924):331–49.

Chapter 3. OKLAHOMA: THE INDIAN TERRITORY

Early Indian Colonization

BETWEEN 1820 and 1907, Oklahoma was shown on the maps of the United States as the Indian Territory. In this period it served the nation as a place for resettling tribes from other parts of the United States. Before Oklahoma's role as an Indian resettlement zone ended around 1889, it had received more than sixty tribes from the eastern United States, Kansas, Texas, Arizona, California, Idaho, and Washington. The federal government sent these tribes to Indian Territory so that others could have the Indian lands.

The first tribes to be resettled in Indian Territory were from the eastern United States. A voluntary removal to Oklahoma was under way long before Indian Territory was established. Bands of Kickapoos, Delawares, and Shawnees from north of the Ohio River were attracted by the abundant wild game and by expected freedom from the continu-ing influence of the American settlements. They migrated to the Canadian River and settled on the North Fork and other tributaries. Cherokee and Choctaw hunters also crossed the Mississippi and hunted in present-day Oklahoma at the time of the removal.

The Five Civilized Tribes

THE FORCED removal of the eastern tribes began soon after the War of 1812. Within twenty-five years most of the territory in present-day Oklahoma had been assigned to five Indian nations. The so-called Five Civilized Tribes from the southeastern United States were the Cherokees, the Choctaws, the Chickasaws, the Creeks, and the Seminoles.

The Cherokees numbered about 20,000 and occupied an area in parts of western North and South Carolina, eastern Tennessee, northern Georgia, and northeastern Alabama. Very early they came under the influence of traders from the

David Vann, Cherokee leader who supported removal to Indian Territory.

English coastal settlements. The traders brought firearms, trade goods, horses, cattle, hogs, and chickens, and frequently took Cherokee wives. This gave rise to mixed-blood families with names such as Rogers, Ward, Adair, Vann, Chisholm, Ross, Lowry, Reese, and Hicks, who came to play important roles in Cherokee affairs in the East and later in Oklahoma.

The mixed bloods, more like their fathers than their mothers, developed farms, plantations, ranches, and businesses in the Cherokee Nation, and became slaveholders. The full bloods continued to live in log cabins, farmed only a small patch of food crops, raised horses, excelled in the old tribal crafts of hunting and fishing, and now and then joined a war party for a raid on American settlements.

The Choctaws numbered about 22,000 and occupied an area from the central part of Mississippi south to the Gulf of Mexico. At the time of discovery by the Europeans, the Choctaws had an advanced village life based on agriculture, although the warriors were excellent hunters. Choctaw tribal government included a division of the nation into three districts or provinces, each ruled by a principal chief. A national council composed of leading men and warriors also had a voice in the Choctaw government.

The location of the Choctaws on the Gulf of Mexico brought them into more frequent contact with the Spanish, the French, and the British than with others of the Five Civilized Tribes. Undoubtedly this contact improved Choctaw skills in diplomacy, which their tribal leaders later used well in dealing with the United States government. The presence of French, Scot, and English agents and traders was reflected in the mixed-blood family names in the Choctaw Nation—LeFlore, McCurtain, Folsom, McKenney, Walker, Perry, Jones, and Locke.

The Chickasaws claimed as their territory the western parts of Tennessee and Kentucky, northwestern Alabama, and northern Mississippi. In tribal language and culture the Chickasaws were closely related to the Choctaws. There were about 4,500 Chickasaws at the time of discovery by the Europeans. They lived in villages, sustained themselves by agriculture, and had an advanced system of tribal government and religion. They were much feared by the other tribes because of their military power. Between 1720 and 1763 the French from Biloxi and New Orleans tried three times to invade and conquer the Chickasaws. Each attempt failed.

The Chickasaws had an alliance with

the British during this period. They provided important military assistance in the British drive to gain control of the Lower Mississippi Valley and the Gulf of Mexico. During the Revolutionary War the Chickasaws fought with the British. Many loyalists took refuge in the Chickasaw Nation during the war and became adopted Chickasaw citizens. Some of these English people survived until the removal period and went with the Chickasaws over their Trail of Tears to Indian Territory.

Residing between the Cherokees in the east and the Choctaws and Chickasaws in the west were the Creeks, who had vast lands in Georgia and Alabama. The Creek population exceeded twenty-thousand and was a mix of several tribes called the Muscogee Confederacy. It included the Creeks, a band of Natchez, and Alabamas, Koasatis, and Euchees. The Creeks had developed an advanced village life with productive agriculture, a stable government, and talent for dealing with other tribes. Traders from the English settlements, especially the Scots, came among the Creeks very early. The mixed-blood community in this tribe —McIntosh, Grayson, Stidham, and McGillivray—furnished important leadership.

The Creek Nation was divided into the Upper Creeks and the Lower Creeks. The leader of the Lower Creeks was William McIntosh. In the Creek system, each town was governed by a *micco* or king. A bicameral (two-part) national council, consisting of the House of Kings (representatives from the towns) and the House of Warriors (one delegate from every two hundred persons), made the laws for the Creek Nation.

The Seminoles, of Muskhogean language stock and thus speaking a lan-

Spring Frog, Cherokee leader who opposed removal to Indian Territory.

guage similar to the Creeks', Choctaws', and Chickasaws', numbered about thirty-five hundred and lived in Florida. They were closely related to the Creeks, and probably in earlier times many Seminoles had been a part of the Creek Nation. The hunting range of the Seminoles was Florida and southern Georgia and Alabama. Most of their settlements, however, were in Florida. The Seminoles did not come under United States jurisdiction until 1819 when Spain gave Florida to the United States.

The Seminoles were town dwellers and sustained themselves with agriculture and hunting. Their government consisted of a head chief and a council with moderate power. The nation was divided into bands, each named for the captain or chief of the band. Some of the leading band chiefs at the time of removal were Osceola, Alligator, Jumper, Coacoochee (Wildcat), and Micanopy.

33

Moshulatubbee, a Choctaw chief who signed the Treaty of Dancing Rabbit Creek, 1830, and who removed to Indian Territory.

United States Indian Policy

THE UNITED STATES government followed the British system in dealing with the Indian tribes by treating each tribe as an independent community. Thus each tribe was self-governing; its people were citizens of the tribe rather than citizens of the United States. Rather than individual members of tribes being subject to laws of Congress and the states and territories where they resided, they were subject to tribal law.

When a change in relations between a tribe and the United States was required, such as making peace, altering trading privileges, or giving up tribal lands, a treaty was negotiated (agreed to) by the president, through the agent living with the tribe. It was then ratified

by the United States Senate much like any of today's United States treaties with foreign nations. Most of the treaties negotiated by the government with the Indian nations during the 1820s and 1830s were agreements that provided for the Indians to give up their eastern lands and be removed to Indian Territory.

As the line of American settlement grew and moved west onto Indian lands, settlers demanded that the federal government take over Indian lands and permit the settlers to occupy the territory. Soon after 1800, in response to these demands, the federal agents began negotiating treaties with the Five Civilized Tribes.

These early treaties reduced the eastern lands of the Five Civilized Tribes to such an extent that by the 1820s these Indians were located on drastically reduced areas. For example, all that remained of the once vast Creek Nation was a small territory in Georgia and Alabama. The Cherokees had been stripped of their land in western North and South Carolina and eastern Tennessee, and were crowded into northwestern Georgia. The Seminoles were being forced to retreat in Florida. The Chickasaws had been forced to give up their lands in western Kentucky and Tennessee and most of their territory in Alabama. All that remained of their once great land was a reduced territory in northern Mississippi and a fragment of land in northwestern Alabama.

Colonizing Indian Territory

ONWARD the settlers came, demanding even the last of the eastern lands of the Five Civilized Tribes. The federal government gave in to these settler demands by applying great pressure on the five tribes to give up all their eastern lands and move to a new western settlement zone called Indian Territory. Tribal leaders generally opposed the removal and resisted government pressure for several years before finally moving west.

The first of the Five Civilized Tribes to accept a new home in Indian Territory were the Choctaws. For years government agents had urged the Choctaws to exchange their remaining eastern lands for a place in Indian Territory. Finally, in 1820, Pushmataha and other Choctaw chiefs met with General Andrew Jackson at Doak's Stand on the Natchez Trace in Mississippi to discuss the removal.

There followed the Treaty of Doak's Stand whereby the Choctaws, in return for giving up a part of their Mississippi land, received much land in Indian Territory. It was bounded on the north by the Arkansas and the Canadian rivers, on the south by the Red River, and extended from the western border of Arkansas Territory to the western limits of the United States.

To each Choctaw warrior who would move, the treaty required the United States government to supply a rifle, a bullet mold, a camp kettle, a blanket, enough ammunition for hunting and defense for one year, and payment for any improvements left in Mississippi. Pushmataha insisted that the treaty include a clause providing that fifty-four sections of eastern Choctaw land be surveyed and sold at auction. The proceeds were to go into a special fund to support schools for Choctaw youth in the new country.

Government officials hoped that the

Tukoseemothla, a Seminole chief who supported Osceola in his military resistance to removal from Florida to Indian Territory.

Choctaws would move at once, but the treaty made removal a voluntary matter. Thus only about one-fourth of the tribe moved west under the terms of the Doak's Stand Treaty. Most of the tribes remained in Mississippi on their reduced land. They put up with ten years of pressure by federal officials, settlers, and state officials in Mississippi before their leaders in 1830 signed the final removal treaty for the nation.

During 1830, Secretary of War John Eaton and General John Coffee met with the three Choctaw district chiefs, Greenwood LeFlore, Moshulatubbee, and Nitakechi, at Dancing Rabbit Creek council ground in the Choctaw Nation of Mississippi. This meeting produced the Treaty of Dancing Rabbit Creek

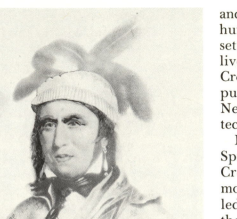

Opothleyaholo, Chief of the Upper Creeks.

and Georgia lands and move west. Land-hungry settlers helped the agents by settling on Creek lands, stealing Indian livestock, and starting fights with the Creeks. This created incidents that were publicized as savage Indian attacks. Neither state nor federal officials protected the Creeks from these attacks.

Finally, in 1825 at a council at Indian Springs, federal commissioners and Creek leaders sat down to discuss a removal treaty. A faction of Upper Creeks led by Opothleyaholo refused to sign the treaty and walked out of the council. William McIntosh, leader of the Lower Creeks, signed the Treaty of Indian Springs which gave up Indian title to Creek lands in Georgia in return for land in Indian Territory.

A little later, the Creek council met as a court of final judgment and tried William McIntosh on the charge of violating tribal law by signing the treaty without proper authority. The council found him guilty and ordered his execution. On April 29, 1825, a party of one hundred Creek warriors surrounded the McIntosh home near Milledgeville, Georgia. They set fire to the dwelling, and when the heat and flames drove McIntosh into the dooryard, they shot him to death.

In 1826 a Creek delegation headed by Opothleyaholo, and delegated full authority by the Creek council, went to Washington. There the Creeks signed the First Treaty of Washington. The treaty provided for the Creeks to give their lands in Georgia to the United States in exchange for land in the center of Indian Territory between the Arkansas and the Canadian rivers. During 1827 a portion of the Creek Nation migrated to Indian Territory. Most remained in Alabama.

whereby the Choctaw Nation signed over to the United States all lands east of the Mississippi River and agreed to move to the Indian Territory within three years.

The treaty said that the federal government would pay the cost of transporting and feeding the Choctaws, and would provide supplies for one year after removal to allow the Indians time to settle and adjust to the new country and to raise their first crop. The treaty contained the promise that the Choctaw Nation in Indian Territory would never be included in any state or territory, and that the Indians would have the right to make their own laws and to govern themselves.

The Creek Nation was the second Indian tribe to accept a new home in Indian Territory. Federal agents urged Creek leaders to give up their Alabama

A second removal treaty was required to erase Creek title to eastern lands. This agreement was negotiated in 1832 and is called the Second Treaty of Washington. Creek leaders met with federal officials in the nation's capital to negotiate this treaty. It required the federal government to pay the costs of removal and to pay to the Creek Nation $12,000 a year for five years, followed by a $10,000 annual payment for fifteen years. By this treaty the Creek Nation in the East was dissolved. Citizens of the Creek Nation had the choice of moving to the Creek Nation in Indian Territory or remaining in Alabama. Those who stayed had to accept parcels of land varying in size from 320 to 640 acres and become subject to Alabama law.

The Choctaw Nation received its land in 1820 and the Creek Nation received its land in Indian Territory in 1826. The Cherokees, the third tribe to be assigned a new domain in Indian Territory, received their western lands by a treaty negotiated in 1828. Cherokee bands, however, had been drifting west since the 1790s. They built their settlements in northwestern Arkansas south to the Arkansas River. By 1815 they numbered about three thousand. They were separate and distinct from those Cherokees living in Georgia and called themselves the Western Cherokees.

In 1817 these Western Cherokees signed a treaty with federal officials. This agreement confirmed their title to the land they occupied in northwestern Arkansas. The agreement promised each Indian equipment, living expenses, and payment for what was left behind. This encouraged the Cherokees in the East to migrate west to join those in Arkansas. Many Eastern Cherokees took advantage of this so that by 1820 the Western Cherokee community had increased to more than six thousand people.

Soon after the 1817 treaty had been negotiated, American settlers moved in on the Cherokee lands in Arkansas. They ignored Indian rights to the soil and timber, starting farms on tribal land and running their stock across Indian fields. The Americans hunted on Cherokee hunting lands, carelessly killing the game. They slaughtered the buffalo solely for tallow, and the stench of rotting carcasses carried even into the Cherokee towns.

To escape the pressure of the settlers, Western Cherokee leaders went to Washington and appealed to federal officials. The result was the 1828 treaty with the United States whereby the Western Cherokees gave to the government their lands in northwestern Arkansas in exchange for a new home in northeastern Indian Territory. Most of the Western Cherokees moved to their new home within a year after the treaty was signed. On the Illinois River tribal leaders set up a new capital for the tribal government. The people went to work clearing fields, establishing settlements, and opening the wilderness.

By the terms of the treaty between the United States and the Eastern Cherokees, signed in 1835, the Western Cherokees were required to take in all of the Eastern Cherokees. The Eastern Cherokees had made remarkable progress in the arts of civilization. They had established a modern capital at New Echota, Georgia. They were governed by an elected principal chief and a legislature guided by a constitution. Some of their best-educated men published a newspaper, the *Cherokee Phoenix*. Indian farmers had developed large farms with orchards, worked by slave labor,

Major Ridge, Cherokee leader who signed the Treaty of New Echota.

at New Echota in 1835, this group signed a treaty giving to the United States all Cherokee lands in Georgia and committing the Cherokee Nation to migrate to Indian Territory and join the Western Cherokees.

Most of the Cherokees, including Principal Chief John Ross, refused to attend the council. They denied that the Treaty of New Echota was valid since the Treaty party members had no authority to sign the agreement for the entire tribe.

Despite this denial of the treaty's validity by the elected leaders of the Cherokee Nation and their determination not to abide by it, the United States Senate ratified the treaty and prepared to carry out its terms. Among other things, the Treaty of New Echota required the Cherokees to move west and join the Western Cherokees within three years.

By the terms of the treaty, the Cherokees gave to the United States all tribal lands east of the Mississippi River in exchange for $5 million. The only new territory the Cherokees received in the West was a strip of 800,000 acres (the Cherokee Neutral Lands) located on the western Missouri border in present southeastern Kansas. The federal government was required to pay the Cherokees for improvements left in Georgia, to pay the expenses of removal, and to supply the tribe with a year's provisions.

By 1828 all of present Oklahoma except the Panhandle had been assigned to three tribes—the Choctaws in the south, the Creeks in the center, and the Cherokees in the north. The Seminoles were the fourth tribe to be assigned to Indian Territory. As mentioned before, the Seminoles first came under the jurisdiction of the United States in 1819

and stocked with large herds of cattle, hogs, and sheep. Cherokee youth were educated in local schools in the Cherokee Nation and in colleges in the North.

With their prosperity, they were understandably reluctant to migrate to the western wilderness. As in the case of the other tribes, great pressure was applied to the Cherokees by federal officials, by state agents in Georgia, and by settlers. Federal and state officials refused to honor treaties guaranteeing protection for the Cherokees. They refused to enforce United States Supreme Court decisions favoring the Cherokees in their contest with the state over jurisdiction in the Cherokee Nation.

Finally, the tribe began to divide into groups. One group, in despair, favored removal to escape the increasing trouble. Led by Cherokee mixed-bloods Elias Boudinot, John Ridge, and Stand Watie, this group came to be called the Treaty party. At a council with federal officials when Spain gave Florida to the United States. At once American citizens moved into Florida and began demanding that the government move the Seminoles and open their rich lands to settlement.

In 1823 the Seminoles signed their first pact with the United States. By the Treaty of Tampa they agreed to move into the swampy land in the center of Florida east of Tampa Bay. This satisfied the settlers only briefly. Soon they were demanding that the federal government remove the Seminoles altogether, claiming that the Indians stole their slaves and livestock and were a danger to the settlements.

Thus in 1832 federal officials and Seminole chiefs negotiated the Treaty of Payne's Landing, by which the tribe agreed to move to Indian Territory when a suitable home was found in that country. The Indians had three years to make the move, and the government agreed to pay the cost of removal and to provide living expenses to the Seminoles for one year after their arrival in Indian Territory. The federal government was also to pay the Seminoles $15,400 for the land given up in Florida, plus a $3,000 payment each year for fifteen years.

A group of Seminole chiefs traveled to Indian Territory in search of a new home for the tribe. Creek leaders invited the Seminoles to make their home in the Creek Nation. In February, 1833, Seminole chiefs signed the Treaty of Fort Gibson, which required their people to move to the Creek domain. The Seminole removal was carried out under the authority of the Treaty of Payne's Landing and the Treaty of Fort Gibson.

The last tribe of the Five Civilized Tribes to be relocated in Indian Territory was the Chickasaw. By 1832, be-

John Ross, Principal Chief, Cherokee Nation. *From a painting by John Neagle, Philbrook Art Center.*

cause of a long series of treaties, the Chickasaws had remaining as their tribal land only a portion of northern Mississippi and a piece of land in northwestern Alabama. Pressured and harassed as were the Choctaw and other Indian tribes to move, the Chickasaw Nation finally bowed to the great demands of the settlers and the government.

In 1832 at the Chickasaw council house on Pontotoc Creek in Mississippi, tribal leaders and government officials signed the Treaty of Pontotoc. By its terms the Chickasaws gave up their eastern lands and agreed to relocate in Indian Territory when a suitable home was found. Chickasaw lands in Mississippi were sold at auction, either as homesteads or common domain of the tribe. The money from these sales was paid to individual Chickasaws and into the treasury of the Chickasaw Nation.

For several years Chickasaw leaders explored Indian Territory searching for a home. The Choctaws invited the Chickasaws to join them. In 1837, Chickasaw and Choctaw leaders met at Doaksville in the Choctaw Nation in Indian Territory and signed the Treaty of Doaksville. By this treaty the Chickasaws agreed to settle in the Choctaw Nation. For this privilege the Chickasaws were to pay the Choctaws the sum of $530,000.

Obstacles to Removal

IT WAS ONE thing to get a removal treaty from unhappy tribal leaders. It was another to get the citizens of the Five Civilized Tribes to give up the land of their ancestors and move to Indian Territory. Federal officials found that Cherokees, Creeks, and other tribesmen objected to moving to Indian Territory for several valid and fair reasons.

Federal officials were pushed by settlers and state officials in Georgia, Alabama, and Mississippi to get the Indians out as quickly as possible. They worked hard to remove the causes of the Indians' objections to moving. Even then some Indians refused to leave their eastern lands. This state of affairs led the federal government to use military force to drive the Indians west to Indian Territory.

A major objection of leaders of the eastern tribes to moving west was the hazard to life and property posed by the tribes living in Indian Territory. Federal officials spent much time and effort in attempts to make the Indian Territory a safe place for the eastern Indians to settle. They negotiated treaties with the resident tribes in the territory, providing for the surrender of lands on which the eastern tribes could settle. In

1818 and 1825 the Osages signed treaties with United States commissioners giving up their claim to a vast tract of land between the Kansas and the Canadian–Arkansas rivers. By the 1825 treaty the Osages were assigned a reservation in southern Kansas.

In 1818 the Quapaws also signed away to the United States their claim to all their lands in Indian Territory between the Arkansas and Canadian rivers and the Red River. These treaties with the Osages and Quapaws cleared tribal title and freed the land in Indian Territory for assignment to the eastern tribes.

The Osages, however, did not move from their lands in Indian Territory. They continued to threaten the Cherokee towns in Arkansas and to prey on the American settlements in Missouri and Arkansas. Another threat to peace in Indian Territory was the Wichita, the Caddo, the Kiowa, and the Comanche tribes in the western part of the territory. Federal agents had never contacted these tribes officially, and no treaties existed between them and the United States.

President Andrew Jackson, determined to satisfy the people of Georgia, Alabama, and Mississippi by removing the Five Civilized Tribes from their midst, took several steps to complete the removal. Congress passed his Indian Removal Act in 1830. This law formalized the removal of eastern tribes and strengthened the authority of the federal government in carrying out the program.

The Stokes Commission

PRESIDENT JACKSON also appointed three commissioners and assigned them the task of traveling to Indian Territory to settle the problems that were delaying the removal of the eastern Indians. The commissioners appointed by President Jackson were Montfort Stokes, Henry L. Ellsworth, and John W. Schermerhorn. This official body was called the Stokes Commission from its chairman, Montfort Stokes, a former governor of South Carolina.

The Stokes Commission set up headquarters at Fort Gibson. Its work was aided by the important guests who accompanied the commission members to the Indian Territory wilderness. They included Washington Irving, the best-known American writer of that time; Charles J. Latrobe, an English writer; and Count Albert de Pourtales, a young Swiss nobleman. Descriptions of their travels west from Fort Gibson were published in Irving's *A Tour on the Prairies,* Latrobe's *The Rambler in North America,* and de Pourtales's *On the Western Tour with Washington Irving.*

The Stokes Commission first settled a problem involving a band of Seneca Indians. Once a member tribe of the great Iroquois Confederacy, they had lost population and land through the years. The Senecas lived at that time at Sandusky, Ohio. In 1831 their leaders made treaties giving to the United States their reservation of 86,000 acres in return for 127,000 acres west of Missouri. A new treaty by the Stokes Commission relocated them and a small number of Shawnees, who were with them between the Missouri line and the Grand, or Neosho, River in northeastern Indian Territory.

The Quapaws had ceded their lands to the United States in 1818, and were living on the south bank of Red River. The Stokes Commission assigned them

Washington Irving, popular American author and explorer of central Oklahoma.

a reservation of 96,000 acres east of the Grand River, next to the Senecas. The Stokes Commission also corrected the Creek-Cherokee boundary that had caused disputes between the two tribes.

Dealing with the Osages was not so simple. Several meetings between Osage leaders and the Stokes Commission failed to get the Osages to move to their new reservation in Kansas. It was the commission's recommendation that an increase in military strength at Fort Gibson and other Indian Territory posts would persuade the Osages to move to their assigned lands.

The Stokes Commission turned next to the task of contacting the tribes of western Indian Territory to get them to accept the Five Civilized Tribes as neighbors. To impress and perhaps to scare the tribes into peaceful relations with the United States, it was decided to send an army to their villages in the southwestern part of the territory.

The First Dragoon Regiment at Fort Gibson, commanded by General Henry Leavenworth and Colonel Henry Dodge, was assigned this mission. The summer heat took a heavy toll of both troops and horses. General Leavenworth and several score of the cavalrymen died on the way to the Wichita Mountains. Colonel Dodge led the survivors into the villages of the Wichitas and the Comanches and held a meeting with the chiefs. Leaders of these tribes agreed to come east and talk with American officials.

Accompanying the dragoon expedition was George Catlin, an artist from Philadelphia. He visited the Indian villages while Dodge was meeting with the chiefs and sketched the people and camp scenes. He also kept a daily journal. He later published both the journal and sketches in a two-volume work entitled *Letters and Notes on the Manners, Customs, and Condition of the North American Indians*.

During 1834 chiefs of the Comanches and the Wichitas came to Fort Gibson for a meeting with the leaders of the Cherokees, the Creeks, the Choctaws, and other immigrant tribes. In 1835 at Camp Mason on the Canadian River in present McClain County, representatives of the western tribes, the immigrant tribes, and United States officials signed a treaty of peace and friendship.

As added protection for the eastern tribes, federal officials put more troops at Fort Gibson and Fort Towson, reactivated Fort Smith, and built several military posts at strategic points in Indian Territory. These included Fort Coffee on the Arkansas River, twenty-five miles upriver from Fort Smith;

Camp Arbuckle at the mouth of the Cimarron; Camp Holmes at the mouth of Little River; and Camp Washita at the mouth of the Washita River. All of these military posts were established in 1834.

Fort Wayne was established on Spavinaw Creek in the Cherokee Nation in 1838. The troops at these posts were assigned the duty of keeping the peace in Indian Territory and thus making the area more attractive for the eastern Indians.

The Trail of Tears

REMOVAL of the Five Civilized Tribes was largely completed during the 1830s. The blacks, as slaves of Indian owners, performed much of the heavy work connected with removal. Some of their jobs were loading freight wagons and caring for livestock. Black workers cleared new trails and opened roads for the overland march. And because of their early arrival in Oklahoma, they are recognized as being among the pioneer settlers of this area.

Intense suffering seemed the common lot of all who moved. This was largely because of poor planning by government agents who supervised the removal. Many Indians and blacks were caught on the trail in midwinter with temperatures regularly at zero.

Several Choctaw parties had to march through six inches of snow. Transportation for the Choctaws was so limited that only the very young, the old and feeble, the sick and the blind were permitted to ride. Roads were nearly impassable; the wagons got stuck and slowed travel to fewer than five miles a day. Cholera, smallpox, and measles

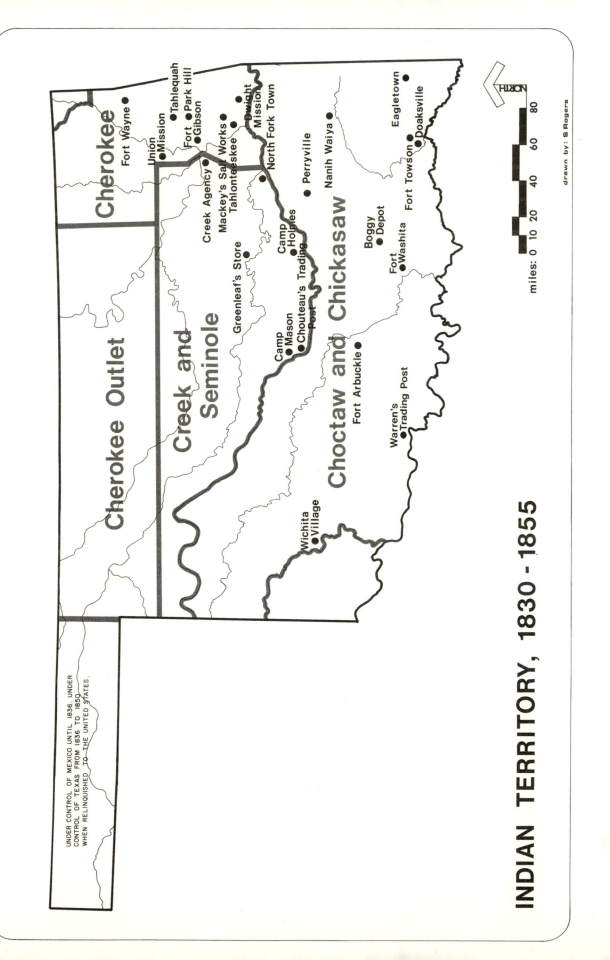

INDIAN TERRITORY, 1830 - 1855

miles: 0 10 20 40 60 80

drawn by: S Rogers

NORTH

UNDER CONTROL OF MEXICO UNTIL 1836. UNDER
CONTROL OF TEXAS FROM 1836 TO 1850
WHEN RELINQUISHED TO THE UNITED STATES.

Cherokee Outlet

Cherokee

Creek and
Seminole

Choctaw and Chickasaw

Fort Wayne
Union
Mission
Tahlequah
Park Hill
Fort
Gibson
Dwight
Mission
Mackey's Salt Works
Tahlonteeskee
North Fork Town
Eagletown
Doaksville
Creek Agency
Perryville
Nanih Waiya
Greenleaf's Store
Camp
Holmes
Chouteau's Trading
Post
Boggy
Depot
Fort
Washita
Fort Towson
Camp
Mason
Fort Arbuckle
Warren's
Trading Post
Wichita
Village

Cheyenne artist Dick West's painting of the Trail of Tears.

caused many deaths. The heavy casualties, possibly as high as one-fourth of the tribal population, certainly justify calling this mass relocation the Trail of Tears.

The Chickasaw removal was probably the most orderly. They were to pay for their removal from tribal funds, and tribal leaders directed the relocation. With a shorter distance to travel from Mississippi, they were able to collect most of their personal possessions and their slaves and livestock and move to Indian Territory on river steamers with a minimum of loss. Their trouble began after they arrived in the territory when cholera and smallpox swept through the camps.

The Cherokee removal was a heart-rending story. Only about two thousand Cherokees voluntarily moved west under the terms of the Treaty of New Echota. The remainder, led by Chief John Ross, refused to observe the treaty. The three-year period passed and these Cherokees had made no preparations to move to Indian Territory. United States troops under General Winfield Scott were ordered to the Cherokee Na-

tion to round up the Indians and forcibly relocate them in Indian Territory. They were assisted by the Georgia militia. An observer of the times wrote:

The troops were disposed at various points throughout the Cherokee country, where stockade forts were erected for gathering in and holding the Indians preparatory to removal. From these, squads of troops were sent to search out with rifle and bayonet every small cabin hidden away in the coves or by the sides of mountain streams, to seize and bring in as prisoners all the occupants. . . . Families at dinner were startled by the sudden gleam of bayonets in the doorway and rose up to be driven with blows and oaths along the weary miles of trail that led to the stockade. Men were seized in their fields or going along the road, women were taken from their spinning wheels and children from their play. In many cases, on turning for one last look as they crossed the ridge, they saw their homes in flames, fired by the lawless rabble that followed on the heels of the soldiers to loot and pillage.

After about five thousand Cherokees had been ruthlessly uprooted and marched to Indian Territory in this manner, Chief Ross appealed to General Scott to permit him and other Cherokee leaders to supervise the removal. With the army's permission, the Cherokees were organized into parties of one thousand persons each, and the removal proceeded in a more orderly and humane fashion. By 1839, most of the Cherokees had arrived in Indian Territory.

The Creek removal matched the Cherokee removal for suffering. Settlers invaded the Creek Nation before the Indians were ready to make the move west. The invaders drove off livestock, robbed homes, and burned cabins and barns. When the Creeks attempted to defend their homes and drive off their attackers, they were arrested by state officers for assault and disorderly conduct. Finally the Creeks united under Eneah Emothla and prepared to defend their country from further invasion by the attackers.

The settlers became alarmed and appealed for protection. United States troops were sent to Alabama to put down the so-called rebellion. The army captured nearly twenty-five hundred Creek leaders and warriors who were classed as hostiles and therefore dangerous. Bound in chains, they were forced to march to Fort Gibson during the bitterly cold winter of 1836–1837. One party of three hundred Creeks was taken down the Alabama River to the Gulf of Mexico, transported to the Mississippi River, then placed on a riverboat that had been condemned as unsafe. Upriver the rotting craft sank and all passengers were lost.

The Seminoles in Florida refused to abide by the Treaty of Fort Gibson. Osceola gathered several hundred warriors, and they pledged to fight to the death before they would move to Indian Territory and live among the Creeks. In 1835 army units entered Florida to enforce the treaty, and Osceola's warriors won several battles against the federal troops. The Seminole War lasted until 1842. Osceola was captured under a flag of truce and died in federal prison at Fort Moultrie, Charleston, South Carolina.

Wildcat and other Seminole leaders continued the war of resistance. Small bands of Seminoles were rounded up by troops and taken to Indian Territory where they were held for some time as prisoners of war. By 1842, three thousand Seminoles had been relocated in Indian Territory. In that year the federal government gave up its expensive attempt ($20 million spent and 1,500 soldiers killed) to remove the Seminoles, and permitted those bands still in hiding in the swamps of Florida to remain.

The Seminole removal brought to a close one of the blackest periods in American history. The Trail of Tears of the Five Civilized Tribes and other Indian groups, savagely uprooted to make way for the settlers, ranks with the saddest stories of the ages.

Study Aids

Explain the significance of each term or phrase listed below:

1. Western Cherokees
2. Stokes Commission
3. Treaty of Doaksville
4. Dragoons
5. Dodge and Leavenworth Expedition
6. Treaty of Fort Gibson

Identify each of these persons:

1. Pushmataha
2. William McIntosh
3. Washington Irving
4. Coacoochee
5. Opothleyaholo
6. George Catlin

On an outline map of Oklahoma locate the following places:

1. Grand River
2. Fort Towson
3. Camp Holmes
4. Illinois River
5. Fort Coffee
6. Camp Washita

Use the suggestions below for study guides:

1. Discuss the method used by the United States government to conduct relations with the Indian tribes.
2. Summarize the role of the Stokes Commission.
3. Explain the significance of the Dragoon Expedition.
4. Describe the removal of the Indian tribes as operated by the federal government.
5. Outline the removal treaties for the Five Civilized Tribes.

For Further Reading

Foreman, Grant. *The Five Civilized Tribes,* Norman, 1934.

Irving, Washington. *A Tour on the Prairies.* Norman, 1956.

Latrobe, Charles J. *The Rambler in Oklahoma.* Muriel H. Wright and George Shirk, eds. Oklahoma City, 1955.

Mathews, John J. *The Osages: Children of the Middle Waters.* Norman, 1961.

Pourtalès, Count Albert-Alexandre de. *On the Western Tour with Washington Irving: The Journal and Letters of Count de Pourtalès.* George F. Spaulding, ed., Seymour Feiler, tr. Norman, 1968.

Teall, Kaye M. *Black History in Oklahoma.* Oklahoma City, 1971.

Wright, Muriel H. *A Guide to the Indian Tribes of Oklahoma.* Norman, 1951.

Chapter 4. **OKLAHOMA ON THE EVE OF THE CIVIL WAR**

Adjustment to the New Land

A COMMON MISTAKE is to date Oklahoma's emergence as a settled community, with towns, schools, a constitutional government, commerce, communication systems, and other trappings of civilization, as very recent. This civilizing did not begin with statehood in 1907, nor did it begin with the opening of a portion of Indian Territory to homesteaders in 1889. This view gives all of the credit to the American settlers for planting the arts of man's progress in the Oklahoma wilderness. This is a fiction.

Many traits of civilization were carried to Oklahoma by Indians in the early part of the nineteenth century. The homesteaders did not tame the Oklahoma wilderness. This had been done nearly a century before by Cherokee, Choctaw, Creek, Chickasaw, and Seminole frontiersmen who migrated from their ancestral homes in the East to Indian Territory over the Trail of Tears.

The agony and suffering of the Trail of Tears and the shock of being uprooted and forced to the West had a serious effect on the citizens of the Five Civilized Tribes. The removal cost many lives because of bad food supplied by greedy government contractors who got rich at the expense of the Indians, and because there were epidemics of smallpox, measles, and cholera among them. It is said that the line of march to the West for the Cherokees was marked by the gravestones of those who died along the way.

The removal was particularly hard on the very young and the old. These age groups were nearly wiped out in the five tribes. This created a population imbalance of age groups in each tribe that was not restored until around 1860.

The removal ruined many wealthy people in the tribes. Their livestock,

47

tools, and other property had to be abandoned when they began the removal. Many of their belongings were lost, or, as was often the case, stolen. Many citizens of the Five Civilized Tribes had to start new lives in the Indian Territory wilderness, poor and with little to help them except their energy and intelligence.

The removal question also split several of the tribes into groups that disagreed with each other. The Cherokees and the Creeks, particularly, were divided over the move, and the argument continued after arrival in Indian Territory. It required good strong leaders in each tribe to deal with these groups and to unite the people for the task of taming the wilderness.

Recovery from Removal

THE CHOCTAWS probably had greater unity than any other tribe. This unity helped speed up their adjustment to the new land. By 1834 enough Choctaws had arrived in Indian Territory for tribal leaders to begin the organization of a new tribal government.

Because they had adopted a written constitution in 1826 while in Mississippi, the Choctaws were experienced in constitutional government. Choctaw leaders in 1834 met at a council on the Kiamichi River and drafted Oklahoma's first constitution. This document set up executive, legislative, and judicial departments. The ancient Choctaw practice of being governed by three chiefs was continued.

The settled portion of the Choctaw Nation was divided into three districts — Pushmataha, Moshulatubbee, and Okla Falaya (Red River) districts. The voters in each district elected a chief who served a four-year term. No chief could serve more than two terms.

The Choctaw National Council consisted of twenty-seven members, nine elected from each of the three districts of the nation. This body met yearly to conduct the legislative business of the nation. The judicial system included a supreme court of four justices and district courts. Eighteen light-horse police or rangers (six men in each district) were to enforce the laws of the national council and maintain the peace.

The Choctaw constitution contained a bill of rights that gave the right to have a jury trial. It also defined eligible voters as all male citizens aged twenty-one years or older. Following the 1837 Treaty of Doaksville which united the Chickasaws with the Choctaw Nation, the constitution was changed to create a fourth district for the Chickasaws. The national council membership was increased to forty to provide the Chickasaws with representation. The number of chiefs was increased to four, one of whom was to be a Chickasaw.

The Choctaw constitution of 1834, altered from time to time to meet changing conditions, remained in force until the Choctaw Nation was dissolved by Oklahoma statehood in 1907. The Choctaw national capital was first situated at Nanih Wayah, near Tuskahoma. In 1850 it was moved to Doaksville, and then to Boggy Depot, to Armstrong Academy or Chahta Tamaha (Choctaw City), and finally to Tuskahoma in 1884.

The government established by the Creeks for their nation in Indian Territory was similar to the system they used in the East. The nation was divided into two groups, the Upper Creeks and the Lower Creeks. The Upper Creeks were led by Opothleyaholo, the Lower Creeks by members of the McIntosh family. Roley McIntosh was the leader of this group at the time of arrival in the territory.

Each of the two divisions of the Creek Nation was divided into towns, and each town had its local chief and its council made up of leading warriors. Yearly the two national chiefs and the general council (which was all the representatives selected from the councils and chiefs of the towns) met at the national capital. This is when laws were adopted and business was conducted for the entire nation.

The Seminoles were part of the Creek Nation after 1833, subject to the government and laws of the Creeks. Scattered in settlements throughout the Creek Nation, the Seminoles were low in spirit from the military actions directed against them by the United States government to drive them to Indian Territory. Several years were required for them to recover enough to take an active part in government.

In 1859, Creek leaders drafted their nation's first constitution. It included a bill of rights and provided for a national council and five elective officials. These officials were a principal chief and an assistant chief for each of the two tribal divisions, and a speaker to preside over the national council. All men eighteen years old and older were permitted to vote.

In the first election under this constitution, Motey Kinnard and Jacob Derrisaw, both mixed bloods, were elected chief and assistant chief of the Lower Creeks. Echo Harjo and Oktarharsars Harjo won these offices for the Upper Creeks.

The Creek capital was at different locations at various times. Among the places was Council Hill (near present-day Muskogee), at a watering place called High Spring where there was a log council house. North Fork Town, Creek Agency near Fort Gibson, and Okmulgee served at various times as sites for the Creek national capital.

Establishing an orderly government for the Cherokee Nation was hard. Already the Western Cherokees had created a working government in Indian Territory. The arrival of the Eastern Cherokees, led by principal chief John Ross, caused problems. Ross claimed that the Western Cherokees were merely a part of the original tribe and that their government was temporary until the entire tribe was united. Ross proposed a new constitution that provided for the two divisions of the tribe to be joined.

Aware that Ross's group outnumbered them at least two to one, and that it would control elections and the proposed government, Western Cherokee leaders refused. They declared that the land in Indian Territory had been given to them alone and not to the whole tribe. They objected that they had been forced to divide their tribal domain with the larger part of the tribe without being asked about it or giving their consent.

The Western Cherokee leaders also stated that "the newcomers in coming into a territory which already had an organized government accepted that government; and accordingly, since the Western Cherokees had received and welcomed their brother emigrants, the two people were already united." Western Cherokee leaders argued that their people had been pioneers and had tamed the wilderness by driving out the Osages and other enemies and had made the area safe. Their government as already elected should continue in force.

Eastern Cherokee leaders believed that Western Cherokees were being advised by Treaty party leaders—Elias Boudinot, John Ridge, Major Ridge, and Stand Watie. Ross's followers held the Treaty party responsible for the Eastern Cherokees' suffering on the Trail of Tears. They also believed the leaders of the Treaty party were a roadblock to Ross's plan for uniting the parts of the Cherokee Nation. This problem was solved in part on June 22, 1839, when Major Ridge, his son John Ridge, and Elias Boudinot were killed by unknown parties. Stand Watie, also marked to be killed, escaped. These murders frightened Western Cherokee leaders and they gave in to the demands of the Ross group.

A national convention was held at Tahlequah on September 6, 1839. A constitution was written for the united Cherokee Nation. With minor changes adopted after the Civil War concerning slavery, this constitution led the Cherokee Nation until Oklahoma statehood in 1907.

The executive power of the nation was given to a principal chief, elected every four years. Legislative power was contained in a bicameral (two houses) national council, with the members elected from legislative districts for two-year terms. The Cherokee judicial branch consisted of a supreme court and lower courts set up by the national council.

The Cherokee constitution contained a bill of rights; it defined eligible voters as male Cherokee citizens, eighteen or more years of age. It named Tahlequah as the national capital. John Ross was

elected principal chief in the first election held under this constitution, and he was reelected to that office until his death in 1866.

Until 1855 most of present Oklahoma was divided into three semi-independent Indian republics. A map of the times would show the Cherokee Nation located in northeastern Indian Territory, with the Cherokee Outlet extending to the 100th meridian; the Creek-Seminole Nation in the central part of the territory; and the Choctaw-Chickasaw Nation in the southern part. Because of changes in tribal governments that were finished by 1856, this map of Indian Territory contained five semi-independent Indian republics. These changes came about in the manner described below.

The Chickasaws were a proud and independent people. They soon tired of their political connection with the Choctaws. Chickasaw leaders believed that the interests of their people were overlooked by the larger group of Choctaws. During the 1840s the Chickasaws, who had settled in a district in south-central Indian Territory assigned them by the Choctaws, began to work for an independent government. This finally came about in 1855 by a treaty that separated the Chickasaw and Choctaw nations.

By the terms of this agreement, the Chickasaws received land west of the Choctaw Nation in south-central Indian Territory. By this Choctaw-Chickasaw Separation Treaty of 1855, Indian Territory was now divided into four semi-independent Indian republics.

The year after separation from the Choctaws, Chickasaw leaders wrote a constitution that provided for an elected chief executive called the governor.

The elected council—the legislative body—was composed of a senate and a house of representatives. The judicial branch consisted of a supreme court and lesser courts.

The constitution contained a bill of rights, and eligible voters were defined as all male citizens nineteen years of age and older. Chickasaw voters elected Cyrus Harris governor in the first election held under this constitution. The Chickasaw national capital was located at Tishomingo.

The Seminoles, just as proud and independent in spirit as the Chickasaws, soon found their connection with the Creeks not to their liking. One problem was over land. The Creeks had promised the Seminoles a piece of land located near the mouth of the North Fork of the Canadian. When the Seminoles reached Indian Territory, they found this land already occupied by Creek settlers. Throughout the years Seminole leaders asked Creek officials and federal agents to grant them land separate from the Creeks. Finally, in 1856, Seminole and Creek leaders negotiated a treaty. By this agreement the Seminoles received a nation of their own, created from the western land of the Creeks. Its boundaries were the North Canadian and the Canadian rivers, and it extended from the 97th meridian to the 100th meridian.

The Seminoles moved to their new land and established a national capital near present Wanette in Pottawatomie County. Their government, without a written constitution, was based on towns, each ruled by a local chief and council. The general government of the Seminole Nation was headed by John Jumper, a famous warrior-chief in the Seminole War. The town chiefs and leading warriors of the Seminole Nation met once each year in general council to conduct the business of the nation. Thus, in 1856, Indian Territory had been divided into five semi-independent Indian republics.

Economic Recovery

LIKE pioneers on other parts of the American frontier, the Indian settlers of the Five Civilized Tribes on the Indian Territory frontier supported themselves by agriculture, hunting and fishing, and gathering nuts, berries, herbs, salt, wild honey, and other products from nature.

Indian settlers cleared fields and sawed logs from thick forests. They used the logs to build homes. These varied from single-room cabins to double-log houses connected by a passage (called the "dog trot") between, with porches on both sides of the structure. Back of the cabin were log stables, barns, corrals, and a kennel for hunting dogs. Later, the more successful farmers and stockmen replaced their log houses with large mansions that were furnished with carpeting, pianos, libraries, and other fixtures in the manner of fancy southern homes.

The Five Civilized Tribes kept their ancient system of holding their lands in common. In these times not a single acre of Indian Territory land was privately owned. All members of a tribe had equal rights to share in the tribal land. A tribal citizen could hunt, fish, and cut timber in all places not occupied by towns or farms.

The Five Civilized Tribes followed an open-range practice. Livestock, carrying the owner's brand or mark, grazed at large on the public lands. Cultivated land was surrounded by rail fences. In the period before the Civil War, with a total population of less than 100,000 and a land area of nearly 70,000 square miles, there were fewer than two persons per square mile. Because all of their land was public, they paid no taxes on it.

An Indian citizen could clear, improve, and farm as much land as he wished, provided he did not bother his neighbor. Tribal law allowed a citizen to sell his improvements (a house, for example) or pass them on to his children, but, of course, he could not sell or give away title (ownership) to the land where he lived. The full bloods in each tribe, generally with simpler tastes and needs, had small patches ranging from three to ten acres. Mixed bloods generally developed larger farms.

The biggest plantations in Indian Territory were in the Red River Valley where Choctaw and Chickasaw planters often farmed single fields of fifty or more acres of cotton or corn. Robert Love, a Chickasaw, operated two large plantations on Red River and owned two hundred slaves. Each autumn he traveled to New Orleans and chartered a steamship to carry out his crop of about five hundred bales of cotton. Robert M. Jones, a Choctaw planter and one of the richest men in the American West, owned five hundred slaves, five Red River plantations, and a fleet of river steamers that operated between Kiamichi Landing and New Orleans.

Economic activity in the Cherokee, Creek, and Seminole nations was more varied. Farms, plantations, and mines in these areas produced meat, hides, grain, salt, lead, and other products. While the farm and ranch holdings developed by Stand Watie (on Spavinaw Creek in the Cherokee Nation), Benjamin Perryman, a Creek planter (on the Verdigris River), and others, were large, they did not match the huge estates of their Choctaw and Chickasaw neighbors.

Markets for Indian Territory products were both local and on the Gulf Coast. The officials at the several military posts in the territory bought eggs, butter, meat, and vegetables each year to feed their soldiers. They also signed contracts with Indian farmers for grain and hay to feed the cavalry's horses.

Cotton, grain, hides, salt, lead, pecans, wild honey, and other products from Indian Territory farms, ranches, mines, and forests were collected at the river ports at Three Forks, Fort Gibson Landing, Kiamichi Landing, and Fort Smith. Loaded on flatboats, keelboats, and river steamers, these products were delivered to Natchez and New Orleans.

Steamboat travel on the Arkansas and the Red rivers had begun in the 1820s. In 1822 the steamer *Robert Thompson* reached Fort Smith, and in 1828 regular steamboat service between Fort Gibson Landing and the Gulf was begun by the arrival of the *Facility*.

Those frontier Indian Territory towns not located near river landings were served with wagon roads. The first road built in the territory was a 58-mile-long wagon road laid out in 1825 to connect Fort Smith and Fort Gibson. A military road between Fort Gibson and Fort Towson was cut through the Kiamichi Mountains in 1832.

Troops at Indian Territory military posts opened roads to guide the Indians from the East. These were later developed into major roads connecting Indian settlements after removal. Troops also built roads connecting the military posts in western Indian Territory. From

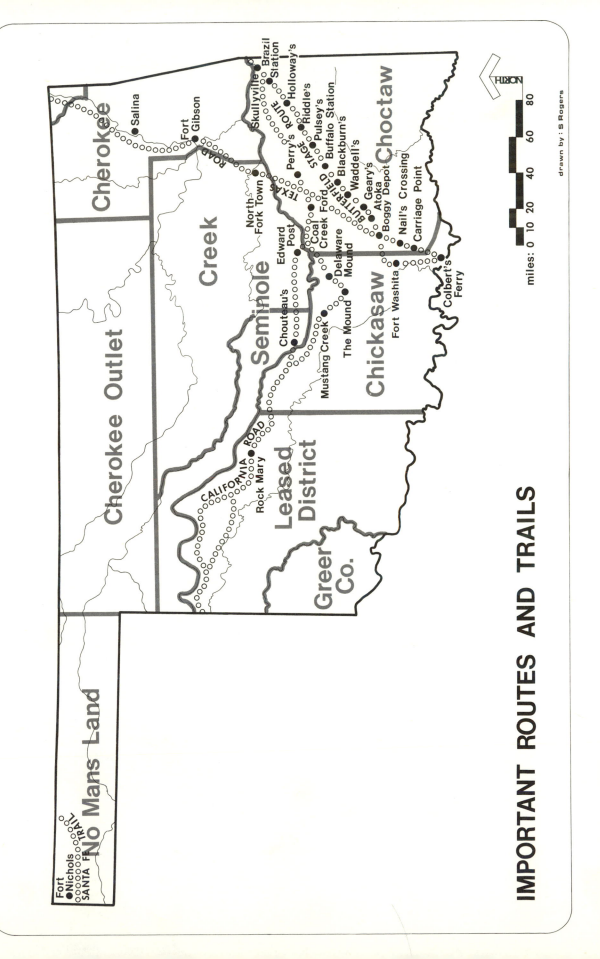

IMPORTANT ROUTES AND TRAILS

drawn by : S Rogers

miles: 0 10 20 40 60 80

NORTH

No Mans Land

Fort ● Nichols
SANTA FE TRAIL

Cherokee Outlet

Cherokee

● Salina

Fort Gibson

Creek

ROAD

North Fork Town

Skullyville

Brazil Station

Holloway's

Riddle's

Pulsey's

Buffalo Station

Blackburn's

Perry's ROUTE

STAGE

Waddell's

Geary's

Atoka

Boggy Depot

Choctaw

Nail's Crossing

Carriage Point

Seminole

Edward Post

TEXAS

Coal Creek

BUTTERFIELD

FORD

Delaware Mound

Chouteau's

Mustang Creek

The Mound

Chickasaw

Fort Washita

Colbert's Ferry

Leased District

CALIFORNIA ROAD

Rock Mary ●

Greer Co.

these roads other roads were constructed to connect Indian towns. Thus by 1845 central and eastern Indian Territory had a network of roads connecting towns, military posts, missions, and schools.

As the most remote frontier region of the United States, Indian Territory was a land bridge across which passed a number of national highways. An early road to Santa Fe, blazed by Josiah Gregg for the American traders doing business on the Rio Grande and into Chihuahua, Mexico, crossed the territory on a route along the Canadian River. The Texas Road followed the valley of the Grand River, crossed the Arkansas River at Three Forks and angled across the Choctaw Nation and the Chickasaw Nation, and crossed the Red River east of the mouth of the Washita. It was a well-traveled route for Texas-bound settlers.

One of the favorite routes to the California goldfields during the rush of 1849 crossed central Indian Territory by way of the Canadian River Valley. The fourth great highway to cross the territory in the period before 1861 was the Butterfield Overland Mail and Stage route. Stagecoaches provided mail and passenger service between Saint Louis and Memphis and on to San Diego and San Francisco. These entered the Indian Territory at Fort Smith. The route angled across the Choctaw and Chickasaw nations into Texas and and went southwest toward El Paso. Several important stage stations were located in Indian Territory.

While most Indian settlers in pioneer Indian Territory lived on farms and ranches, tribal, political, and business leaders developed towns. Therefore, the growth of towns that was happening in

other frontier regions of the United States was also happening in Indian Territory.

The leading towns in the Cherokee Nation were Tahlequah, Beatty's Prairie, and Fort Gibson. In the Choctaw Nation, Doaksville, Miller Courthouse, Perryville, Skullyville, Boggy Depot, and Eagleton were important trade and social centers. Leading towns in the Chickasaw Nation were Tishomingo and Oak Grove. Creek towns included Honey Springs, North Fork Town, Micco, Edward's Post, Shieldsville, and Creek Agency. Most important of the Seminole settlements was Wewoka.

These towns were linked with roads and stage lines; towns located on rivers had steamboat service. Newspapers such as the *Cherokee Advocate,* the *Choctaw Intelligencer,* the *Choctaw Telegraph,* and the *Chickasaw Intelligencer* kept the citizens of Indian Territory well informed on local, national, and world events.

Education in Indian Territory

JUST AS settlers on the Indian Territory frontier tamed the wilderness, began farms, plantations, and ranches, and built towns, they also worked at providing an education for their children. Most of the tribal money gained from the sale of eastern lands was set aside for the support of schools.

Each of the Five Civilized Tribes elected a commissioner of education. This person supervised the location and construction of school buildings, the training of teachers, the curriculum that was taught, and the general operation of tribal schools. The Choctaws and the Cherokees had public school systems that were better than the edu-

Cherokee Female Seminary, Park Hill, near present Tahlequah.

Spencer Academy, Choctaw Nation.

cation offered young people in the states and territories around the Indian Territory.

Tribal school systems included kindergarten through grammar school training, as well as special education for those with physical handicaps. Scholarships were given to the brightest students in each Indian nation to complete their education at famous schools like Yale and other eastern colleges and universities.

Missionaries, supported by eastern churches, established schools and churches among the Five Civilized Tribes. Presbyterian, Baptist, Methodist, and Moravian missionaries had worked among these Indians while they lived in the East. After removal, many missionaries traveled to Indian Territory and resumed their work among the tribes.

In some cases, as for the Cherokees, a public school system operated by Cherokee officials and a private school system operated by missionaries functioned at the same time. In other cases, as for the Chickasaws, Methodist missionaries signed a contract with the tribal government to operate the nation's schools on a mixed public-private basis. Tribal funds and church funds were used to support the same schools.

Among the Cherokees the most beloved missionary was Samuel Austin Worcester. Like the Cherokees, he was punished by settlers and state officials in Georgia and served a prison term for teaching the Cherokees. He came to Indian Territory with the Cherokees over their Trail of Tears. He settled near Tahlequah and began the town of Park Hill, which became famous over the Southwest as a center of learning.

Besides building a fine school, a church, and other settlement buildings, Worcester imported a printing press and started the Park Hill Press. The Park Hill Press imprint appeared on the annual *Cherokee Almanac,* the *Cherokee Primer,* and other textbooks, religious literature, and teaching materials. The Park Hill Press did a great volume of work for the Cherokees, numbering 14 million printed pages. Additional work came to Worcester from the Creeks, the Chickasaws, and the Choctaws. For the Choctaws alone, Park Hill Press published 11 million printed pages.

The Moravian and Baptist missionaries, along with the Congregationalists and the Presbyterians who supported Worcester, worked for years among the Cherokees in Indian Territory. The best known of the Baptist missionaries was Evan Jones. He was popular with the Cherokee full bloods. Like Worcester, Jones imported a printing press and type and provided his converts with reading material and hymn books. He also published the *Cherokee Messenger,* a sixteen-page paper that carried tribal and religious news. It was the first magazine published in Indian Territory.

The most active missionaries among the Choctaws were Presbyterian, supported by the American Board of Commissioners for Foreign Missions. The busiest of these teachers and preachers were Alfred Wright, Cyrus Byington, and Cyrus Kingsbury. Schools for the Choctaws that were supported by tribal and missionary funds included Spencer Academy, Wheelock, Goodwater, and Stockbridge.

Methodists and Baptists also worked with the Choctaws in Indian Territory. Alexander Talley was a favorite Metho-

Samuel Austin Worcester, ABCFM missionary teacher to the Cherokees.

Evan Jones, Baptist missionary teacher to the Cherokees.

dist teacher, and Isaac McCoy and Joseph Murrow were Baptist teachers to the Choctaws.

The first schools built for the Chickasaws were operated by the Methodists under a joint tribal-church arrangement. Wesley Browning, a Methodist educator, supervised the development and growth of the Chickasaw schools. Presbyterians also provided funds and missionaries for work among the Chickasaws. Important Chickasaw schools included Chickasaw Academy, Bloomfield, and Wapanucka Institute.

Baptist and Presbyterian missionaries served among the Creeks. The Baptists worked more at building churches and converting Creeks to Christianity than in setting up schools for tribal youth. David Lewis, H. F. Buckner, and Joseph Murrow were the best-known Baptist missionaries who worked with the Creeks. Presbyterian

Cyrus Byington, ABCFM missionary teacher to the Choctaws. *Oklahoma Historical Society.*

John Jumper, Chief of the Seminole Nation.

chief, Osceola. The Presbyterians supported Bemo's efforts to set up schools and churches among the Seminoles. Presbyterian missionary John Lilley joined him, and their work included beginning the Oak Ridge School for Seminole youth near present Holdenville.

James R. Ramsey, also a Presbyterian missionary, worked among the Seminoles before the Civil War. Joseph Murrow, the Baptist missionary who had earlier worked among the Choctaws and Creeks, entered the Seminole Nation in 1857. He began several Baptist churches for the Seminoles and counted Chief John Jumper as one of his converts (a person who changes his religion).

missionaries began both churches and schools for the Creeks. The Creek Council each year set aside funds to help support the mission schools.

William S. Robertson was to the Creeks in education what Samuel A. Worcester was to the Cherokees. As an educator, Robertson wrote educational materials for Creek youth and began several schools, including the most important school in the Creek Nation — Tullahassee.

The Methodists later entered the Creek Nation to build schools and churches. In 1850 a Methodist missionary, Thomas B. Ruble, began the Asbury Manual Labor School near North Fork Town.

A pioneer educator among the Seminoles was John Bemo, a converted Seminole and nephew of the great war

Work in Indian Languages

MISSIONARIES had to teach and preach with the help of others who could translate their words until tribal youth learned the English language. Teaching the English language to Indians was a slow process, but two language developments eased the teaching and learning process for the Five Civilized Tribes.

One of these developments came from the Cherokees who, like other Indian tribes, had no written language. Their spoken tongue, of the Iroquoian language family, was very complex. A Cherokee mixed blood, George Guess, better known as Sequoyah, invented an alphabet that he used to put the Cherokee language into written form. This invention was remarkable because Sequoyah had never attended school; he could not read or write and could not speak English.

A hunting accident in his youth crippled him for life, and to support his family he became a skilled silversmith. He was impressed with learning and with the work of the missionaries; he liked their schools and their books, which he called "talking leaves." He dreamed of finding a way to give his Cherokee-speaking people a written language.

In twelve years of study, Sequoyah identified eighty-five consonant and vowel sounds and a hidden sibilant sound in the Cherokee spoken language. Each of these he refined and gave a symbol, so that his world-famous alphabet had eighty-six characters. He was reported to have first tried the alphabet on his young daughter and other children in the community. Using them, he gave a demonstration before the Cherokee National Council. Tribal leaders were impressed, and they adopted Sequoyah's alphabet as the official written language for the Cherokee tribe.

Soon books and a newspaper were published in the Cherokee language. In 1822, Sequoyah came to live with the Western Cherokees in Arkansas, and he introduced his system to this part of the tribe. He moved to Indian Territory under the terms of the Cherokee Treaty of 1828. Through his invention, the Cherokee Nation could read almost overnight. Sequoyah's people were the best-informed Indians in America, probably better read than the settlers who were trying to take their land. Worcester and other Cherokee missionaries adopted Sequoyah's alphabet and published textbooks and other teaching materials in the Cherokee language.

Another language development that

Sequoyah (George Guess), creator of the Cherokee syllabary.

Sequoyah's Cherokee syllabary of eighty-six characters.

made teaching Indian youth simpler came from the work of Cyrus Byington and Cyrus Kingsbury. They changed the Choctaw spoken language to written form by using English alphabet letters. Textbooks and other teaching materials in the Choctaw language were widely used in the schools of the Choctaw Nation. Creek and Seminole missionaries used the Byington-Kingsbury system to change the Creek and Seminole spoken language to written form.

Population of Indian Territory

THERE were less than 100,000 people in Indian Territory before the Civil War. Indian Territory was largely Indian, both full blood and mixed blood. At this time there were also several hundred whites living in the territory; they were federal agents to the Indian tribes, missionaries and teachers, traders, intermarried citizens, and soldiers at the military posts. There were also about 5,000 blacks, who were slaves of tribal citizens.

As was pointed out earlier, blacks rank among Indian Territory's earliest settlers. They had come with their Indian owners over the Trail of Tears. It was their labor that helped tame the wilderness, open farms and plantations, and develop the country. Unfortunately, their influence, aside from labor, was slight because of their status as slaves.

In pre–Civil War times, the Seminoles were the only tribe to give any status to blacks. Many of the slaves could read and write. They served the Indians as clerks and interpreters. As a general rule, Seminole slaves lived in separate villages, free to come and

go. They were expected to furnish an annual payment of grain, meat, or other products or services to their owners.

Each of the Five Civilized Tribes adopted a special slave code to control their blacks. The Choctaw, the Cherokee, the Creek, and the Chickasaw slave codes were strict, especially about hiding runaway slaves and teaching abolitionism (doing away with slavery). These black codes provided that if a slave killed an Indian, the death penalty was the result. If an Indian killed a slave, he was required to pay the owner the value of the slave or suffer death. If a slave killed another slave, the killer received a severe lashing, and his owner was required to pay one-half the value of the dead slave.

Intermarriage between slave and Indian was forbidden and was punishable by public whipping for both parties. If an Indian or slave helped a slave escape, the sentence was a fine and public whipping. A slaveholder could free his slaves if he took them out of the nation. An addition to the slave codes in the 1850s shows that the movement to abolish slavery had reached Indian Territory. Before hiring missionaries and teachers, tribal officials were to decide whether the candidates were against slavery. If they were abolitionists, they could not be hired.

Relations with the United States

ALTHOUGH the five Indian tribes in Indian Territory were self-governing republics, they maintained close relations with the United States government. By the removal treaties, the federal government had to make annual payments to the tribes from the income earned by the funds due from the sale of their eastern lands. These funds were held by the federal government in trust for the Indians and invested, usually in state and federal bonds. In several instances, the federal government had agreed to pay the Indians for their loss of property during the forced removals.

To take care of these duties, as well as to look after the general interests of the federal government in Indian Territory, the president of the United States appointed an agent for each tribe. The Cherokee Agency was situated near Fort Gibson; the Creek Agency was located about forty miles northwest of Fort Gibson at a site called Creek Agency; the Choctaw Agency was near Fort Coffee; the Chickasaw Agency was at Fort Washita; and the Seminole Agency was near Wewoka.

The agent served as a commissioner to each of the tribes. Frequently the agent was asked to represent the government in treaty negotiations with the tribes and to advise the Indians in conflicts between tribes. Each year the agent distributed the funds due the tribes and reported to the president about things happening in Indian Territory.

The federal government's interest in Indian Territory was shown by the expansion of its military frontier across the territory. The United States War Department built Fort Washita in 1842 in the heart of the Chickasaw Nation. Located on the east bank of the Washita River about twenty-two miles above its mouth, the fort was founded by a future president of the United States, General Zachary Taylor.

In 1851, Captain Randolph B. Marcy

Jesse Chisholm, Cherokee mixed-blood trader who maintained several posts in central and western Oklahoma.

directed the building of Fort Arbuckle on Wild Horse Creek in present Murray County. This fort was to serve as a checkpoint to keep western tribes out of the Chickasaw Nation. In 1859 the War Department directed the building of a post near the Washita River. Named Fort Cobb, its troops attempted to keep peace on the troubled southern plains.

In 1855 the federal government signed an agreement with the Choctaws and the Chickasaws providing for a lease of the territory south of the Canadian River and extending from the 98th meridian to the 100th meridian. This area became known as the Leased District. For the use of this area, the federal government paid the Choctaws and the Chickasaws

Black Beaver, Delaware Indian guide for army expeditions in western Oklahoma.

$800,000. The Leased District was to be used as a reservation for settling the Kiowas, the Comanches, the Wichitas, the Caddos, and certain other bands of Indians in Texas.

This relocation program in western Indian Territory began moving many different tribes into the territory. Because of the differing cultures, their presence enriched the ethnic variety of Oklahoma. Although the Indians of the Five Civilized Tribes in the eastern part of Indian Territory and the Indians of western Oklahoma were similar physically, great individual and tribal differences existed among them. The differences surfaced on such matters as the role of the individual in tribal society, religion, and attitudes about accepting or rejecting Anglo-

American civilization. Those tribes settled on Indian Territory's western borders were especially unhappy about having to become farmers. Most of them preferred to roam the plains, to hunt buffalo, and to raid American settlements in Texas.

Kiowa and Comanche bands had raided the Texas settlements from the earliest days of the Texas Republic. During 1858 a Texas Ranger force led by Captain John Ford, chasing a raider band of Indians from southwestern Indian Territory, crossed the Red River and fought several battles with the tribes of that area.

Also in 1858, a United States cavalry force commanded by Major Earl Van Dorn set up a base of operations on Cache Creek which he named Camp Radziminski. Van Dorn's cavalry roamed the Leased District searching for hostile bands of Kiowas and Comanches. On October 1, 1858, he made a surprise attack on a Comanche camp in the southeastern corner of the Leased District at a place called Rush Springs. The Battle of Rush Springs resulted in the killing of many of this band of Comanches.

While United States troops were threatening the tribes of the Leased District, the federal government set up an agency near Fort Cobb, called Wichita Agency. During 1859, Robert S. Neighbors, agent for the Texas tribes on the Brazos River Reserve, sent to the Leased District fifteen hundred Texas Indians—Wacos, Tonkawas, Anadarkos, Tawakonis, Ionis, Keechis and Caddos, and some Comanche bands. The line of white settlements in Texas had reached the edge of the reservation of these tribes and the Texans were demanding that the Indians be removed.

The conflict on Indian Territory's western borders during the 1850s was but a prelude to the destructive fury that raged across all of the territory during the following decade as it was swept into the American Civil War. The progress of the Indian Territory's five Indian republics was shattered by their ill-fated alliance with the Confederate States of America.

Study Aids

Explain the significance of each term or phrase listed below:

1. Light-horse police
2. *Facility*
3. Butterfield Overland Mail
4. Park Hill Press
5. Tullahassee
6. Syllabary

Identify each of these persons:

1. Roley McIntosh
2. Cyrus Harris
3. John Jumper
4. Robert M. Jones
5. Josiah Gregg
6. Evan Jones

On an outline map of Oklahoma locate the following places:

1. Tuskahoma
2. North Fork Town
3. Tishomingo
4. Wanette
5. Tahlequah
6. Doaksville

Use the suggestions below for study guides:

1. Show how the people of the five Indian nations supported themselves.
2. Summarize missionary work among the Five Civilized Tribes.
3. Explain the creation of the Leased District.
4. Outline the formation of tribal governments in the Indian Territory.
5. Trace the national roads that crossed Indian Territory and show the importance of each.

For Further Reading

Bass, Althea. *Cherokee Messenger*. Norman, 1936.

Debo, Angie. *The Road to Disappearance*. Norman, 1936.

————. *Rise and Fall of the Choctaw Republic*. Norman, 1934.

Franklin, Jimmy. *The Blacks in Oklahoma*. Norman, 1980.

Gibson, Arrell M. *The Chickasaws*. Norman, 1971.

McReynolds, Edwin C. *The Seminoles*. Norman, 1957.

Woodward, Grace. *The Cherokees*. Norman, 1963.

Chapter 5. **WAR AND PEACE IN INDIAN TERRITORY**

The South Versus the North

DURING 1861, the nation was torn apart when eleven southern states left the Union (seceded). Leaders of this section of the country declared their states free of the United States and formed a government for their new nation, first at Montgomery, Alabama and later at Richmond, Virginia. This new nation was called the Confederate States of America.

The federal government at Washington was unwilling to permit this action. President Abraham Lincoln thought it was his highest duty to preserve the Union. Lincoln prepared to use military action to force the seceding states to return to the Union. Leaders of the Confederate States of America prepared to defend their nation against invasion by the United States. Their defense plans included Indian Territory as a Confederate province.

Farms and plantations of the South produced much cotton, sugar, and tobacco, but grains, meat, salt, and other food had been imported from north of the Ohio River. The war would close this source, and foreign markets were cut off when Union ships blocked the southern ports. Confederate planners decided to expand their area of power to the west to meet the economic needs of the South.

The Indian Territory played an important role in this plan. The Indian Territory, with its abundant cattle and horse herds, could furnish beef, hides, and mounts for troops. Grain from Indian farms figured in Confederate planning also. In northeastern Indian Territory, lead deposits were expected to provide enough refined lead to supply the total musket, rifle, and pistol needs for all Confederate troops. Added to this was the abundant supply of salt available from Indian saltworks.

Indian Territory was important as a land bridge connecting the confederacy with areas farther west. Across a friendly territory, Confederate agents could attempt to bring New Mexico, Arizona, and California into the Confederacy. The Indian Territory also was basic to Confederate military strategy in the West. First, it was a buffer for Confederate Texas to protect it against invasion from the Union state of Kansas; and second, it was a base for launching armies into Union states and territories west of the Mississippi River.

Pressure on Indian Territory's five Indian republics to join the Confederacy came from both state and national sources. Delegates from the new Confederate states of Arkansas and Texas, as well as representatives of the Confederate national government, paid several visits to the capitals of the Five Civilized Tribes during early 1861, urging Indian leaders to join the Confederate cause.

Except for the Cherokees, the mixed bloods, many of whom were slaveholders, dominated the tribal governments. In the case of the Cherokees, the full bloods, few of whom were slaveholders, were in power through the shrewd management of their leader, Chief John Ross. The Cherokee mixed-blood community, politically a minority in the nation, consisted largely of slaveholders.

Indian slave owners particularly were attentive to the words of Confederate state and national representatives who warned that the victorious Republican party and its President Abraham Lincoln were committed to the abolition of slavery. Such action would result in a heavy economic loss to Indian slave owners.

All citizens of the five Indian republics, both mixed bloods and full bloods,

paid special heed to the warning by the Confederate agents that the Republican party planned to take the land of the Five Civilized Tribes and open it to settlers. All Indians realized that their economic ties were with the South. Markets for the products of Indian Territory farms, ranches, and plantations were the lower Mississippi River towns and ports on the Gulf of Mexico.

Certainly a major factor in persuading the tribal citizens of Indian Territory to join the Confederacy was the action taken by the federal government in clearing out military posts in Indian Territory. All the troops had been ordered east, in effect abandoning the people of the territory. This created great anxiety among tribal leaders. Not only did it violate treaty promises, but it left the region exposed to possible invasion from Confederate Texas and Arkansas.

The Pike Mission

LEFT OUT by the federal government and very close to the strong Confederate states of Arkansas and Texas, Indian Territory's five Indian republics were open to Confederate talks. These came officially during the spring and summer of 1861. The Confederate States of America commissioned Albert Pike of Arkansas as its special representative to attempt to negotiate treaties of alliance with the tribes of Indian Territory.

Pike arrived in the Cherokee Nation in late May, 1861. He urged Chief John Ross to sign a treaty committing the Cherokee Nation to the Confederate cause. Ross refused. He declared that treaties between the Cherokees and the United States required his people to remain loyal to the Union.

Albert Pike, Confederate emissary to Indian Territory and later commander of Confederate Indian troops.

Turned down by the Cherokees, Pike went to North Fork Town in the Creek Nation. There he successfully negotiated treaties of alliance (agreement) with the Creek Nation and with the Choctaw and Chickasaw nations with delegates from Doaksville and Tishomingo, who had traveled north to meet him.

On August 11, Pike finished negotiations with the Seminoles. He then went to Wichita Agency in the Leased District and held council with the tribes of that area. In late summer he signed a treaty with the chiefs of the Wichitas and other tribes of the Leased District that committed them to the Confederate cause.

After his Wichita Agency council, Pike went to Arkansas. On the way, he was stopped by Cherokee messengers who told him that Chief Ross was ready to discuss placing his nation in the Confederacy. Ross's change in attitude perhaps was brought about by the Battle of Wilson's Creek in southwest Missouri.

At Wilson's Creek, General Sterling Price's Confederate army had won a smashing victory over General Nathaniel Lyon's Union army. It appeared that the Confederate cause in the West would win. Ross found his people surrounded on three sides by Confederate states and Confederate Indian nations, and no effort was being made by the federal government to support the Cherokees. Thus when Pike returned to the Cherokee capital at Tahlequah in October, 1861, Chief Ross signed a treaty with him, committing the Cherokee Nation to the Confederate cause.

The Confederate treaties of alliance with the Five Civilized Tribes were similar. These agreements gave the Indians the same title to their lands in Indian Territory and other rights they had acquired in treaties with the United States. The Confederate government agreed to pay money due the tribes by the United States and to do the things for them that the federal government had done. The Indian nations were expected to raise armies to help defend their country against invasion. No Indian troops were expected to serve outside of Indian Territory. Among other benefits of membership in the Confederacy, the Five Civilized Tribes were promised the right to send delegates to represent them in the Confederate Congress.

Trans-Mississippi Department

INDIAN Territory became a part of the

Trans-Mississippi Department of the Confederate army. Confederate troops from Arkansas, Louisiana, Texas, and Indian Territory for service on the southwestern border were under the command of General Ben McCulloch of Texas. The local commander of Indian Territory troops was Colonel Douglas H. Cooper, a former agent for the Choctaws and Chickasaws.

Mixed units of white and Indian troops were to man the border posts, which included Fort Smith, Fort Wayne, Fort Coffee, Fort Gibson, Fort Washita, Fort Arbuckle, Fort Towson, and Fort Cobb.

The Indian governments were permitted to form four regiments: one regiment of Choctaws and Chickasaws, one regiment of Creeks and Seminoles, and two regiments of Cherokees. One Cherokee regiment was composed of mixed bloods under the command of Colonel Stand Watie and was called the First Cherokee Mounted Rifles. The other Cherokee regiment, made up of full bloods commanded by John Drew, was called the Second Cherokee Regiment.

Most of the Indian troops of the four regiments, numbering about five thousand men, were organized as cavalry. They were supported by units from McCulloch's border army of Louisiana, Arkansas, and Texas troops that were organized as infantry (foot soldiers), artillery (heavy weapons), and cavalry. The Indian troops were to be armed and equipped by the Confederacy. However, because of the shortage of war supplies in the Confederacy, and the distance supplies had to travel, the Indian Territory fighting men were equipped with great difficulty. Most Indian troop supplies came from local sources.

Stand Watie, Confederate Cherokee and only Indian to achieve the rank of general in the Civil War.

The Neutral Indians

THE FIRST battle in Indian Territory during the Civil War resulted from combat between two Indian factions. Opothleyaholo, leader of the Upper Creeks, refused to recognize the treaty that bound his nation to the Confederacy. He urged that all the people of Indian Territory should stay out of the conflict (be neutral), warning that this was a foolish white man's war. His stand appealed to many persons, especially Creeks and Seminoles. Soon, more than six thousand men, women, and children joined Opothleyaholo at a camp on the Deep Fork River, bringing with them livestock and personal possessions loaded in wagons.

The threat of attack by Confederate forces caused Opothleyaholo to lead his band of neutral Indians to a remote location near the mouth of the Cimarron River at Round Mountain. Colonel Douglas Cooper, at the head of a 1,400-man column of Confederate Indian cavalry, found Opothleyaholo's secret camp on November 19, 1861. He sent his men against the neutral Indians, but the Confederates were driven off. The Battle of Round Mountain was the first military clash of the Civil War in Indian Territory.

Opothleyaholo's victory allowed him to lead his followers to a safer place. He chose a site on Bird Creek, known as Chusto Talasah or Caving Banks, north of the Creek settlement of Tulsey Town (Tulsa). Cooper's army found this hiding place and struck with repeated fury. For a second time the Confederate Indians were defeated by Opothleyaholo's warriors.

Opothleyaholo moved his followers a third time to a place called Chustenalah on the eastern edge of the Cherokee Outlet. Cooper fell back to Fort Gibson for supplies and more men and prepared for a third fight against the neutral Indians. His scouts located the camps at Chustenalah on the day after Christmas, 1861.

Confederate troops circled the camps and at the signal swept like a tide over the neutrals. The neutral Indians fought bravely as before. But with their bullets running low because of the two earlier battles, and with no sources of supply, they could not defend their position. The Confederate troops stormed through the camps, capturing most of the wagons, equipment, and livestock.

Opothleyaholo's people scattered over the wooded hills. A fierce snowstorm swept over the countryside on the night after the battle, causing great suffering

among the survivors of Chustenalah. They eventually reached safety in Union Kansas. The Confederate victory at Chustenalah brought to a close the first phase of the Civil War in Indian Territory.

Union Drive in the Southwest

DURING 1862, Union commanders in the West began to drive the Confederates out of Missouri and to conquer the Arkansas-Indian Territory border. They planned to open a pathway for the conquest of Confederate Texas. Early in March, 1862, a Union army commanded by General Samuel Curtis moved through southwestern Missouri into northwestern Arkansas. Confederate General Sterling Price fell back with his troops and prepared to stop the Union advance in the rough country of northwestern Arkansas at a place called Elkhorn Tavern on Pea Ridge.

Confederate armies commanded by General Earl Van Dorn and General Ben McCulloch joined Price for what they hoped would be another Confederate victory. Although not forced to do so by the terms of the Confederate alliance, the two Cherokee regiments rode to Pea Ridge and took up positions. Fighting began on March 6 and lasted for two days. The Union forces won; they caused many deaths in the Confederate army and captured large amounts of arms and supplies.

Colonel Stand Watie's Cherokee Mounted Rifles won one of the few minor victories claimed by the Confederates in this fiercely fought battle. They captured a Union artillery battery that had rained death and destruction on the Confederate ranks until the

Cherokees silenced it. Also, Watie's men held their position on the broad Confederate line; they were among the last to retreat and helped cover the general Confederate withdrawal.

The Confederate defeat at Pea Ridge had far-reaching effects on the Confederate cause in the West, especially in Indian Territory. First, the disaster at Pea Ridge resulted in such a dreadful loss of troops, weapons, and supplies to the Confederacy that afterwards it lacked the means to help protect the Indian Territory as guaranteed by the treaties of 1861. The Five Civilized Tribes were required to protect themselves.

Union leaders, aware of the weakened Confederate position in the West, once again tried to regain Indian Territory. During the spring of 1862, Union commanders in Kansas organized a force known as the Indian Expedition. This force consisted of two brigades of men from Wisconsin, Ohio, and Kansas, an artillery troop from Indiana, and two Indian regiments recruited from the refugee camps of Opothleyaholo's followers in Kansas.

The Indian Expedition entered the Cherokee Nation in early June, 1862. It marched down the valley of Grand River. Stand Watie's cavalry troubled the Union troops throughout its march, finally making a stand at Locust Grove on July 3. The Confederate defenders fought well and stopped the Union advance until the Union artillery was brought up. Bursting shells broke the Confederate ranks, and the Union army scattered Watie's men. The Confederate defeat at the Battle of Locust Grove opened Tahlequah and Fort Gibson to Union attack.

Tahlequah was defended by Colonel Drew's full-blood Cherokee regiment.

Upon the approach of the Union army, they deserted en masse (all together). On July 12, Tahlequah fell to the northern army. Chief John Ross was taken into protective custody, and with his family traveled to Philadelphia where he stayed for the remainder of the war. Shortly thereafter, through his agents, he organized a strong Union movement among the Cherokees.

A quarrel among the officers in charge of the Indian Expedition led to the Union forces pulling back into Kansas. Confederate Cherokees returned to Tahlequah and other northern Cherokee settlements. Stand Watie raided for several weeks, striking fear into the border settlements of Kansas and Missouri. His lightning attacks went as far north as Fort Scott, Kansas, and Neosho, Missouri.

The Union Reconquest

DURING September, 1862, Union General James G. Blunt was ordered to retake and hold the Indian Territory. Blunt divided his forces into two groups as he prepared to carry out his assignment. One group, commanded by Colonel William A. Phillips, was to drive down the Arkansas-Indian Territory border. The second group, under Blunt's command, was to enter the Cherokee Nation on the route followed earlier by the Indian Expedition invasion force.

Union forces occupied the upper part of the Cherokee Nation by February, 1863. Colonel Phillips spent much of the winter contacting Union Cherokees, most of them full bloods. He resettled them on the land his troops conquered. During February, 1863, with Phillips's encouragement, Union Cherokees met

General James G. Blunt, commander of Union troops in Indian Territory.

at the Cowskin Prairie in the northeastern corner of the Cherokee Nation.

Guarded by Union troops, these Union Cherokees elected Thomas Pegg as acting chief. They withdrew from the Confederate alliance and declared John Ross their chief. They further declared Stand Watie and his Confederate followers outlaws and confiscated their property. They also abolished slavery in the Cherokee Nation. The Cowskin Prairie Council set up a temporary government to govern the Union Cherokees until Chief Ross could return.

After the Cowskin Prairie Council, the Cherokee Nation had two governments—the recently created Union government and the Confederate government headed by Stand Watie. He had been elected principal chief after Ross's capture and exile in Philadelphia. Union forces stepped up their drive to retake the Cherokee Nation during the spring of 1863. By April, Union troops had driven through to the Arkansas River and captured Fort Gibson. Colonel Phillips renamed it Fort Blunt and it served as Union headquarters in Indian Territory for the rest of the war.

Douglas Cooper regrouped his Confederate Indian troops and prepared to drive the Union invaders back to Kansas. In July, 1863, he moved on Fort Blunt. General Blunt led three thousand Union troops out of the post to meet Cooper. Twenty miles southwest of Fort Blunt, at Honey Springs, the two armies collided. The Battle of Honey Springs resulted. The Union's superior weapons and the Confederates' faulty gunpowder turned the tide in favor of the Union army.

Following his victory at Honey Springs, Blunt continued his pressure on the Confederates. His scouts reported a Confederate buildup near Perryville in the Choctaw Nation. From his base at Fort Blunt, the Union general had his soldiers travel in wagons to move them more quickly and rushed into enemy territory. On August 22, he arrived at Perryville to find that Cooper and Watie had withdrawn their units toward Boggy Depot. A small Confederate force had been left at Perryville to guard the vast supplies gathered there. Blunt's men scattered the defenders and burned the depot in a fight known as the Battle of Perryville.

The Confederate retreat southwest of Perryville opened the roads to Fort Smith. Blunt marched east and easily took this post on September 1, 1863. The fall of Fort Smith to Union forces ended the major battles in Indian Territory. Colonel Phillips, with 450 mounted troops and one cannon, made one more daring move into the Choctaw and Chickasaw nations as far south as the

Middle Boggy River. He captured corn and other food, but his operation had little effect on the region. Thereafter until the close of the war Union forces held the country north of the Arkansas and Canadian rivers, while the Confederates controlled the southern half of Indian Territory.

From the fall of Fort Smith in September, 1863, to the Confederate Indian surrenders in the early summer of 1865, the Civil War in Indian Territory reached a standstill. Guerrilla (hit and run) warfare happened often. One kind of guerrilla warfare was led by Colonel William Quantrill, a Confederate raider known for his destruction of Lawrence, Kansas. From time to time the Quantrill gang roamed the Indian Territory, spreading destruction and slaughter among the Five Civilized Tribes.

Another kind of guerrilla activity was carried out by groups called "free companies." These raider bands were outcasts from the Five Civilized Tribes who stole cattle and horses and burned both Union and Confederate Indian communities.

A third kind of guerrilla activity during this period of military standstill was carried out by Stand Watie. He raided only military objectives. His men destroyed dwellings or barns only if they were used by the enemy for headquarters, for keeping troops, or for storing supplies. His favorite target was the Union supply line between Fort Scott in Kansas and Fort Blunt. Watie preyed on this lifeline not only because of the military aspects of such an operation, but because the things he collected in his raids could be distributed among Confederate refugees. Their camps were scattered along the Red River in the Choctaw Nation and in North Texas.

Colonel William A. Phillips, Union officer who called for the Cowskin Prairie Council.

During the spring of 1864, the Confederate War Department reorganized its Indian units, creating the First and the Second Indian Cavalry brigades. Stand Watie was placed in command of the First Brigade and promoted to brigadier general. Colonel Tandy Walker, a Choctaw, was placed in command of the Second Brigade. Because of the military standstill in Indian Territory, most of the Indian troops were released to clear fields and to grow crops for their families and the Confederate refugees.

Watie's troops, however, remained active to the end of the war. From his base south of the Canadian River, he sent squads of cavalry into Union territory to raid. Federal troops sent out to cut hay for the thousands of cavalry mounts at Fort Blunt were always in danger. Finally, to feed the starving animals, Union officers sent, under heavy guard, great horse and mule herds to graze the prairie around the

71

Artist's sketch of the Battle of Honey Springs.

post. Watie's raiders regularly swooped down to drive the animals across the river, with the result that cavalrymen at Fort Blunt became foot soldiers.

Feeding the troops and the sixteen thousand Cherokee, Creek, and Seminole Union refugees who had collected at Fort Blunt, was a serious problem for Union officials. Watie threatened the soldiers and refugees with starvation by causing damage and at times by cutting the post's lifeline—the military road that ran from Fort Scott to Fort Blunt.

Union officers attempted to supply the post by sending supply steamers up the Arkansas River. During June, 1864, Watie's scouts discovered the slow-moving *J. R. Williams* moving toward Fort Blunt Landing on Grand River. Near Pleasant Bluff, in shallow water, the colorful Watie, with a cavalry charge, swept from ambush and captured the boat. Great quantities of food, uniforms, and medical supplies fell to the Confederates by this move.

Watie's greatest stroke of the war occurred during September, 1864, at the crossing on Cabin Creek in the Cherokee Nation. A supply train of three hundred wagons and heavy military guard, traveling from Fort Scott to Fort Blunt, was attacked and captured by the Cherokee general. By a skillful trick, he escaped Union troops from Fort Blunt. He then drove his prize into Confederate territory where the food, medical supplies, clothing, and blankets were distributed among the Confederate Indian refugee camps.

This did no good, however, for Confederate fortunes continued to decline in the East and in the West. General Robert E. Lee surrendered to General Ulysses S. Grant at Appomattox Court House on April 9, 1865. Several western Confederate commanders surrendered their commands in May.

Before surrender occurred in Indian Territory, Creek leaders sent out a call for a council where Confederate Indians could make plans for presenting a united front to the victorious Union. The meeting was to be held at Council Grove.

When Union forces threatened to

break up this meeting, the Confederate delegates of the Five Civilized Tribes met with representatives of the Plains tribes at Camp Napoleon near Verden on the Washita River. Delegates at the Camp Napoleon Council adopted a compact of peace among all Indian tribes. They prepared themselves to present a united front against the United States in the forthcoming negotiations.

The Camp Napoleon Council was a prelude for official surrender of Confederate forces in Indian Territory. Choctaw commanders surrendered at Doaksville on June 19, 1865. Stand Watie, the last of the Confederate generals to surrender, gave up his sword in surrender to Union commissioners at Doaksville on June 23.

Indian Territory Reconstruction

BY THE TIME of the Confederate surrender, the United States government had already worked out plans whereby the Confederacy and its satellite, the Indian Territory, could retake their former places in the American Union. In American history, the plan for accomplishing this is called Reconstruction.

The Reconstruction plan for Indian Territory had been created by the two United States senators from Kansas—James Lane and Samuel Pomeroy. Their plan for reconstructing Indian Territory showed the anger that Kansans held toward the Five Civilized Tribes for joining the Confederacy. Their view was that the secession was treason, that Indian Territory was a conquered province, and that the people must submit to the terms set by the conqueror.

The action of the Five Civilized Tribes in going with the Confederacy

gave the Kansans an excuse to carry out a long-hoped-for plan. Some of the best land in Kansas was held by Indian tribes. Until 1854, Kansas had been the northern half of the Indian Territory. A score of tribes from east of the Mississippi River had been moved there. Kansas settlers wanted these Indian lands and demanded the removal of the tribes to Indian Territory so that the Kansas reservations could be opened to settlement.

Therefore, the joining of the Five Civilized Tribes with the Confederacy provided a convenient excuse for taking land from them and for moving the Kansas tribes to Indian Territory. Thus the Lane–Pomeroy Reconstruction plan for the Indian Territory was introduced into Congress in 1862. It authorized the president to suspend treaties with the Five Civilized Tribes, to take over certain parts of their lands, and to move the tribes from Kansas to Indian Territory.

The Lane-Pomeroy plan, as a part of the larger Reconstruction settlement for Indian Territory, was first presented in 1865 to the tribes of the territory at the Fort Smith Council. In attendance was a federal commission headed by Commissioner of Indian Affairs D. N. Cooley. He called the leaders of the territory's tribes to meet with him. The council started on September 8 at the military post of Fort Smith. The meeting lasted thirteen days. Commissioner Cooley told the Indian delegates that by joining the Confederacy they had forfeited all rights under treaties with the United States. He also said that each tribe must consider itself at the mercy of the United States.

Before each tribe could once again

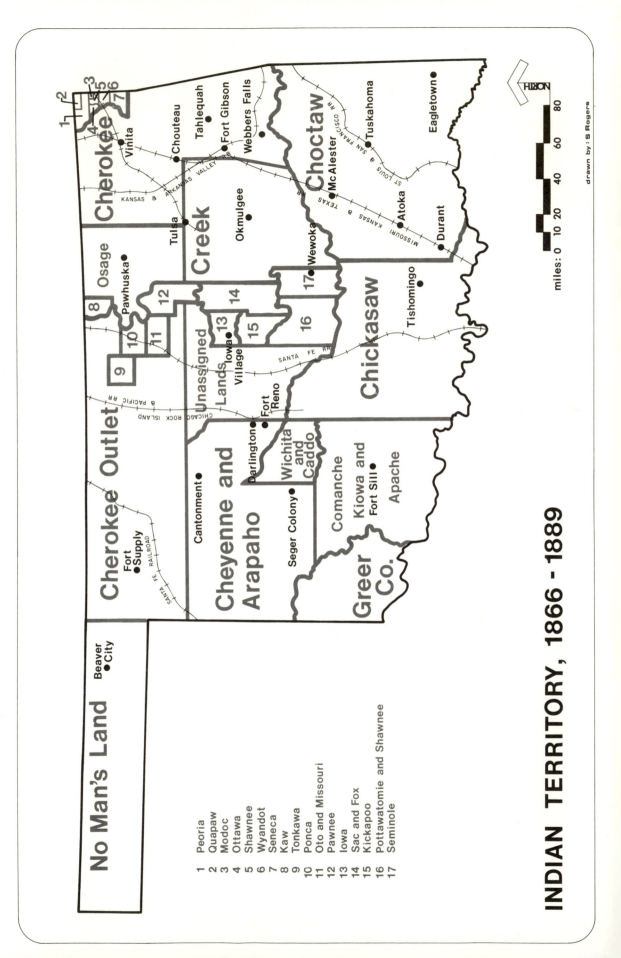

INDIN TERRITORY, 1866 - 1889

No Man's Land

Beaver City

Cherokee Outlet

Fort Supply

SANTA FE RAILROAD

Cherokee

Vinita
Chouteau
Tahlequah
Fort Gibson
Webbers Falls

KANSAS &
ARKANSAS VALLEY RR

Creek

Tulsa
Okmulgee

Osage

Pawhuska

8

10
9
11
12

13
14

15
Iowa Village

16

17

Wewoka

Unassigned Lands

Fort Reno

Santa Fe RR

SANTA FE

CHICAGO ROCK ISLAND & PACIFIC RR

Cheyenne and Arapaho

Cantonment

Darlington

Seger Colony

Wichita and Caddo

Comanche

Kiowa and Apache

Fort Sill

Greer Co.

Choctaw

McAlester
Tuskahoma
Atoka
Durant
Eagletown

ST LOUIS & SAN FRANCISCO RR

MISSOURI KANSAS & TEXAS RR

Chickasaw

Tishomingo

NORTH

miles: 0 10 20   40   60   80

drawn by : S Rogers

1   Peoria
2   Quapaw
3   Modoc
4   Ottawa
5   Shawnee
6   Wyandot
7   Seneca
8   Kaw
9   Ponca
10 Tonkawa
11 Oto and Missouri
12 Pawnee
13 Iowa
14 Sac and Fox
15 Kickapoo
16 Pottawatomie and Shawnee
17 Seminole

have normal relations with the United States, its leaders must sign a treaty providing for permanent peace with the United States and abolish slavery and incorporate the freed blacks into the citizenship of the tribe. They also had to surrender portions of the tribal lands to the United States for resettling tribes from Kansas and elsewhere. Each tribe must also agree to the policy of uniting all tribes of the Indian Territory into a single government. Tribal representatives objected to these terms and deliberately delayed proceedings.

When he discovered that he would be unable to negotiate Reconstruction treaties at Fort Smith, Cooley dismissed the council and called for a meeting at Washington the following year. Cooley thought that the tribal delegations could be more easily managed if they were removed from the influence of their fellow tribesmen. Before the Fort Smith Council closed, however, Cooley did negotiate a simple treaty of peace with the tribes. Through this, allegiance to the United States was restored and the Confederate treaties were dissolved.

During 1866 leaders of the Five Civilized Tribes went to Washington and worked out Reconstruction treaties for their people. Since the Choctaws and the Chickasaws signed a joint treaty, only four agreements were written. In most ways the treaties were similar. Each treaty contained a clause abolishing slavery. They also granted tribal citizenship to the freedmen with the same rights as Indians, and they provided for them with land and other benefits.

Each tribe agreed to grant railroad rights-of-way to allow railway companies to construct lines across Indian Territory. Each tribe agreed in principle to supporting a single government for Indian Territory. The Choctaw–Chickasaw Reconstruction Treaty provided that the name of this single Indian community would be "The Territory of Oklahoma." Allen Wright, a Choctaw delegate, was credited with proposing this name.

Each of the four Reconstruction treaties also contained clauses providing for turning over tribal lands to the United States as a sort of war debt payment. The Seminoles surrendered all of their land (2,170,000 acres) to the United States for fifteen cents an acre. They purchased a new territory of 200,000 acres on the western border of the reduced Creek Nation for fifty cents an acre.

The federal government took the western half of the Creek Nation, paying the tribe thirty cents an acre for the 3,250,000 acres taken. The Choctaw-Chickasaw Treaty provided for giving up the Leased District for $300,000. The Cherokees ceded the Neutral Lands, situated in southeastern Kansas. The federal government also insisted on the right to settle tribes from other parts of the United States in the Cherokee Outlet.

The seeds for the destruction of Indian Territory's five Native American republics were sown by the Reconstruction treaties. These brought new ways and new things to the territory, including the railroads. In fewer than twenty-five years, a network of railroad lines laced the Indian nations. This brought the cattleman, the boomer (a person who came in before the opening), then the homesteader. The process of dissolving the Indian nations, begun in the 1830s, was completed by 1907 with Oklahoma statehood.

Study Aids

Explain the significance of each term or phrase listed below:

1. Confederacy
2. Indian Expedition
3. Camp Napoleon
4. Reconstruction
5. Fort Smith Council
6. Freedmen

Identify each of these persons:

1. James G. Blunt
2. Douglas Cooper
3. William A. Phillips
4. John Drew
5. James Lane
6. D. N. Cooley

On an outline map of Oklahoma locate the following places:

1. Tulsey Town
2. Chustenalah
3. Locust Grove
4. Wichita Agency
5. Cowskin Prairie
6. Perryville

Use the suggestions below for study guides:

1. Explain the pro–South attitude among the people of Indian Territory.
2. Discuss the Confederate treaties of 1861.
3. Describe the Union reconquest of Indian Territory.
4. Describe the change in warfare tactics following the fall of Fort Smith.
5. Summarize the terms of the Reconstruction treaties of 1866.
6. Name five men who, in your opinion, played the most important roles in the history of the Civil War in Indian Territory. Explain your choice.

For Further Reading

Abel, Annie H. *The American Indian as a Participant in the Civil War.* Cleveland, 1919.
———. *The American Indian under Reconstruction.* Cleveland, 1925.
Anderson, Mabel W. *Life of General Stand Watie.* Pryor, 1915.

Britton, Wiley. *Civil War on the Border.* 2 vols. New York, 1899.
Franks, Kenny A. *Stand Watie and the Agony of the Cherokee Nation.* Memphis, 1979.
Monaghan, Jay. *Civil War on the Western Border.* Boston, 1955.
Teall, Kaye M. *Black History in Oklahoma.* Oklahoma City, 1971.

Chapter 6. INDIAN TERRITORY IN THE POSTWAR PERIOD

Postwar Problems

MANY DRASTIC CHANGES occurred in Indian Territory during the period of 1865 to 1889. One of these was territorial change. The Reconstruction treaties contained sections that redrew the map of Oklahoma. In 1861 the Five Civilized Tribes held title to almost all of present Oklahoma except the Panhandle. These treaties reduced the lands of the five Indian republics.

The western half of Indian Territory was taken by the United States government to relocate the tribes from Kansas and other states and territories. The process of moving these various tribes was difficult and at times bloody because many tribes resisted. Thus there was a great difference between events occurring in the peaceful eastern part and the disordered western part of Indian Territory.

Among other things, Oklahoma history for the period of 1865 to 1889 lacked unity. To have a clear understanding of this period, one must look at eastern Indian Territory and western Indian Territory separately.

In the eastern half of the territory the Five Civilized Tribes, on their reduced lands struggled mightily to recover from the ruin of war. The conflict had scattered the citizens of the five Indian republics. Most male Indians of military age had served in either the Confederate or the Union armies. Invading armies and guerrilla raiders had scattered the civilian population. The Creeks, the Seminoles, and the Cherokees of Union or neutral viewpoint lived in camps in southern Kansas and near the protection of Fort Gibson (Fort Blunt was again called Fort Gibson after the Civil War) and Fort Smith. Confederate refugees lived in camps along the Red River in northern Texas and in the Choctaw and Chickasaw nations.

The war had reduced the total population of the Five Civilized Tribes by 25 percent. Smallpox, measles, and cholera epidemics regularly swept through both Union and Confederate refugee camps. Hundreds of Indian soldiers had died of wounds and disease.

The Cherokee, Creek, and Seminole nations, located north of the Arkansas–Canadian river line of conquest, were wastelands. Raiding Union and Confederate armies and guerrilla bands had burned and destroyed towns, churches, schools, and homes. Most of the livestock, grain, tools, and personal property of any value had been taken by the armies or stolen by the guerrillas.

The antebellum (pre–Civil War) prosperity had been replaced by poverty. The countryside was in ruins. All that the people from this part of Indian Territory had left was the land. The Choctaw and Chickasaw nations had largely escaped invasion and the destruction of the war. Most of the livestock and food resources of that region, however, had been taken to feed the Confederate armies and refugees.

Just as there was personal poverty, so was there public poverty. Before the war the Five Civilized Tribes had efficient governments that protected the rights and property of their citizens. These governments were largely financed by investments on the money received from the sale of their eastern lands. The federal government held these funds in trust and made annual payments, called annuities, to each tribe. Treaties with the Confederacy had cut off this source of income.

The Reconstruction treaties provided for beginning the annuity payments again, but the federal government was slow in doing this. As a result, the tribal governments hardly functioned at all.

Because of the poverty of the Indian governments, there was almost no law enforcement by the light-horse police and the tribal courts. This lack of law enforcement in Indian Territory attracted all sorts of outlaws. They used Indian Territory as a base from which to rob banks, stores, and stagecoaches, to steal cattle and horses, and to commit other crimes in surrounding states and territories. Many well-known criminals used Indian Territory as a hideout. These included Belle Starr, the Younger brothers, and Ned Christie, the Cherokee bandit.

The leaders of the Five Civilized Tribes, unable to deal with this lawlessness, asked the federal government for help in restoring law and order to Indian Territory. Federal officials responded by setting up a Federal District Court on the western border of Arkansas, first at Van Buren and later at Fort Smith.

Isaac Parker was the most famous judge to preside over this court with jurisdiction in Indian Territory. From the Fort Smith court, squads of deputy United States marshals roamed the Indian Territory in a great outlaw round-up. By 1896 when Judge Parker's service as federal judge ended, nearly nine thousand accused criminals had been tried in his court. Parker became known around the world as the "hanging judge of Fort Smith." Eighty-eight convicted criminals were hanged on the gallows at Fort Smith.

The Federal District Court at Fort Smith had jurisdiction in all criminal matters where one or both parties were non-Indian, and in all cases where non-Indians and Indians were charged with violation of federal laws. As the Indian nations recovered from the ruin of war and Reconstruction, each reorganized its government and appointed Indian officials to enforce tribal laws. Indian offenders were then tried in tribal courts.

The Five Civilized Tribes also had to face Reconstruction as a required step in taking their former place in the American Union. Besides having to surrender large areas of their western lands to the federal government as a penalty for supporting the Confederacy, Reconstruction for the five Indian nations included undergoing a temporary military occupation. For a short time federal troops were stationed in eastern Indian Territory to guard against any outbreak by former Confederate Indians.

Agents of the federal Freedmen's Bureau, as a part of the Reconstruction process, worked among the former slaves, issuing them food, clothing, blankets. They required the reconstructed governments of Indian Territory to grant blacks those rights guaranteed by the Reconstruction treaties. This included requiring each of the Indian governments to add to their tribal constitution an amendment abolishing slavery and repealing the black codes and other tribal laws that pertained to slavery.

The separation of the races (segregation) was common throughout the Confederacy after the Civil War. It had also begun quite early in Indian Territory. The Indian governments required the former slaves to live in settlements apart from the Indian towns. This accounts for the presence of many all-black towns in Oklahoma today, such as Boley, Foreman, Red Bird, and Rentiesville. Segregation in education was also adopted in that the tribal governments had laws requiring separate schools for Indian children and black children.

Judge Isaac Parker, the "Hanging Judge" of Fort Smith.

Factions within the Tribes

RECOVERY FROM the Civil War was slowed by political divisions in certain tribes of Indian Territory. The Choctaws and Chickasaws were largely for the Confederacy and always supported the Confederate cause. Thus neither of these tribes was divided on the Civil War issue. The Cherokees, Creeks, and Seminoles, however, were still seriously divided in 1866. Several years went by before a unified leadership emerged in each of these tribes.

In the Cherokee Nation, the split between Union and Confederate groups took on many of the features of the old Ross party–Watie party division over removal to Indian Territory. John Ross returned from exile in Philadelphia to Indian Territory in 1865 and resumed

Cherokee national capitol, Tahlequah.

his position as principal chief of the Cherokee Nation. He died in 1866, and his nephew, William P. Ross, was elected principal chief. He too was very bitter toward the Watie Confederate faction and this increased the problem of unity in the Cherokee Nation.

Certain leaders of the old Ross political machine, including the Baptist missionary Evan Jones, were anxious to unite the divided nation. They refused to follow the harsh policies of William P. Ross toward the Watie group. Instead, they formed a new political party, which included members of the Watie party, and called it the Union party. In 1867 the Union party elected its candidate, Lewis Downing, principal chief of the nation.

With two exceptions, the Union party elected all chiefs during the remaining years of the Cherokee Nation. The exceptions were when William P. Ross and his National party returned to power when he served as appointed chief a

short time after the death of Chief Downing in 1872, and when Dennis Bushyhead won election twice, in 1883 and 1885, as the National party candidate. The new party structure united the nation, and by 1872 it was reported that the bitterness of the war had almost disappeared.

The Creeks had a long and stormy period of political and revolutionary disorder. This nation was split between Union Creeks who had joined Opothleyaholo in 1861 and the southern Creeks who had supported the Confederacy during the Civil War. The Union Creeks were very bitter over the loss of the western half of their land area to the United States. They blamed the Confederate Creeks and their alliance with the South for causing this.

Oktarsars Harjo, or Sands, the leader of the Union Creeks, ran for the office of principal chief in elections held under the revised Creek constitution of 1867. Samuel Checote, a former Creek Confederate officer, won the election. This angered Sands. He gathered a band of followers and roamed the Creek Nation, raiding settlements of those Creeks who supported Checote.

In 1870, Sands tried to overthrow the Creek government by invading the capital at Okmulgee, capturing the capital building, and naming certain of his followers officials of the Creek Nation. Federal Agent F. S. Lyons stopped the activity and restored the Checote government. Sands continued to harass the Creek government until his death in 1872.

The Sands followers then came under the leadership of Isparhechar. Mild resistance continued against the government of the Creek Nation until 1877 when, because of pressure from the

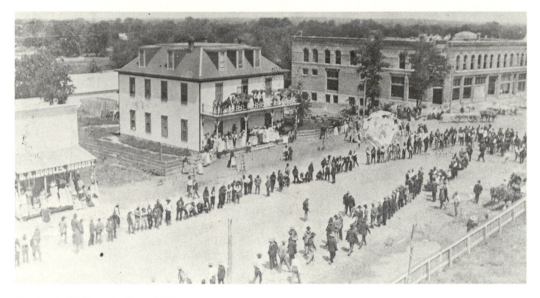

Seminole Nation election, 1898.

Checote government to disband, Isparhechar led about one thousand of his
followers to the Wichita Agency in the
Leased District. Federal troops from
Fort Sill forced them to return to the
Creek Nation. Shortly after that, federal officials, Chief Checote, and Isparhechar met at Muskogee and agreed to
a special election to settle the question
of leadership for the Creek Nation.

Checote, Isparhechar, and J. M. Perryman were candidates for the office of
principal chief. Isparhechar claimed
victory and took over leadership of the
Creek government until federal officials decided against him and installed
Perryman. This ended violence in the
Creek Nation, but mild resistance to
both the Creek government and the federal government and its policies continued among the full bloods of the
Creek Nation until Oklahoma statehood
in 1907.

The Seminoles were more harshly
treated during Reconstruction than any
of the other Five Civilized Tribes. Their
prewar nation was taken from them by
the federal government. They were
forced to develop a new nation on a
small piece of land on the western edge
of the reduced Creek Nation.

Like the Creeks, the Seminoles were
divided into two groups. One group,
numbering about twelve hundred people and led by John Chupco, had gone
to Kansas with Opothleyaholo and his
Creeks in 1861. Many of the warriors
had returned to Indian Territory as
Union soldiers. The Confederate group
of the Seminoles, led by John Jumper,
also numbered about twelve hundred.
Both groups settled in the new Seminole domain but lived apart. The Union
group followed Chupco's leadership,
and the Confederate group followed
Jumper.

Gradually the strong feeling growing
out of the war passed. The Jumper and
the Chupco bands joined during the
1880s and formed a single unified na-

Chickasaw Council House, Tishomingo.

tion. They elected John F. Brown to the office of principal chief, or governor, as he was called.

Improvements in Education

WITH STABLE governments set up again and law and order present, the tribal governments turned to restoring the school systems that had been strong before the war.

In the Cherokee Nation, Presbyterian, Baptist, and Moravian missionaries returned to the nation soon after the war and reestablished churches and schools. The Cherokee government also organized sixty public schools for 2,200 Indian students. Three public schools were organized for the children of former slaves, and special schools for orphans, the blind, the deaf, and the insane were in operation.

In the Creek Nation, Tullahassee, Asbury, and other educational centers had been used as Confederate barracks and

hospitals and were in ruins. The Creek government restored these institutions of learning early in the Reconstruction period. By 1896 the Creeks were supporting seventy public schools, six boarding schools, and separate schools for the children of former slaves. Seminole schools were reopened, largely as the result of Presbyterian and Baptist missionaries. The Seminole government also set aside funds for the construction and operation of both male and female seminaries.

Choctaw leaders, with the help of missionary educators, reopened the academies and built a new system of neighborhood public schools. Tribal government and missionary funds also went into the building of primary schools for the children of former slaves.

The Chickasaw government reopened four academies for advanced education and established fourteen public neighborhood schools where elementary work was offered. Baptist missionaries opened a school for the children of the former slaves in the Chickasaw Nation.

The Economic Recovery

INDIAN business leaders went to work to restore their trading, banking, and transportation enterprises. Indian Territory towns were rebuilt and expanded. Indian farmers cleared old fields, opened new fields, and restocked the ranges with livestock. Soon there was a flow of cargoes of grain, hides, lead, salt, and timber products that was loaded on flatboats and river steamers at the river landings in the territory, bound for the Lower Mississippi Valley and the Gulf markets. Herds of horses, mules, and cattle from Indian Territory ranches

Cherokee Female Seminary at Tahlequah, completed in 1888.

Jones Academy, Choctaw Nation.

reappeared in the livestock markets of Arkansas and Missouri.

The renewed business life in Indian Territory was shown at Muskogee in 1873 when tribal leaders held the first International Indian Territory Agricultural Fair. It was held each year after that under Indian leadership until 1907. It was heavily attended, with Indian farmers and craftsmen exhibiting handiwork, agricultural products, livestock, and crafts. The program included musical and educational entertainment, as well as horse races and other sporting events. The fair became the most popular event in Indian Territory each year.

Indian Territory's economic rebirth from the ruin of war was accomplished by the energy and hard work of the citizens of the Five Civilized Tribes. It was based largely on agriculture and trade. Other developments during the postwar period that sped recovery and brought even greater prosperity to Indian Territory were railroad building, mining, the short-lived buffalo hide industry, and the range-cattle industry.

In 1870 the Missouri, Kansas, and Texas Railway Company, called Katy or MKT, began building in Indian Territory. By February, 1871, trains were running into Muskogee, and before the end of the year had crossed Red River into Texas. The Frisco Railroad entered the Cherokee Nation by way of Seneca, Missouri, in 1871 and reached the Katy tracks at Vinita before the end of the year. Ten years later, the Frisco extended west to Tulsey Town (Tulsa), providing service to that part of the territory by 1882.

Other railroad lines building across Indian Territory in this period included the Fort Smith and Western and the Choctaw and Gulf railways. The Santa Fe and Rock Island lines crossed central and western Indian Territory with tracks by 1895. With the railroads came the telegraph line and related businesses. The Indian Territory towns along these lines became important commercial centers. People traveling through Indian Territory on these railroads saw the land and realized the great possibilities for development.

Rich coal mines were developed in the Choctaw Nation in 1871 by J. J. McAlester, a Confederate veteran who operated a store at the Cross Roads. This tiny village on the Texas Road was later named McAlester. Most of the early coal mines in the Choctaw Nation fell under the control of the railroads. The mining companies paid the Choctaw government a royalty of ten cents per ton for the right to mine the vital fuel. Between 1882 and 1897, two companies alone paid out more than $2 million in royalties. The income from coal royalties allowed the Choctaw government to finance its public schools and to provide other services for Choctaw citizens.

The railroads encouraged commercial buffalo hunting. The rail lines brought professional hide hunters to Indian Territory and the West, and transported the hides and meat, consisting of hindquarters, tongues, and "jerked" or dried meat, to eastern markets. The industry became more competitive and the number of hunters increased during the 1870s. The hide hunters then slaughtered the beasts for the harvest of hides, leaving the carcasses to rot. Soon the prairies of central Indian Territory were littered with the bones of countless buffalo. Famous hunters, such as Buffalo Bill Cody, Pawnee Bill Lillie, Wild Bill Hickok, Pat Garrett, and Billy Dixon, hunted buffalo

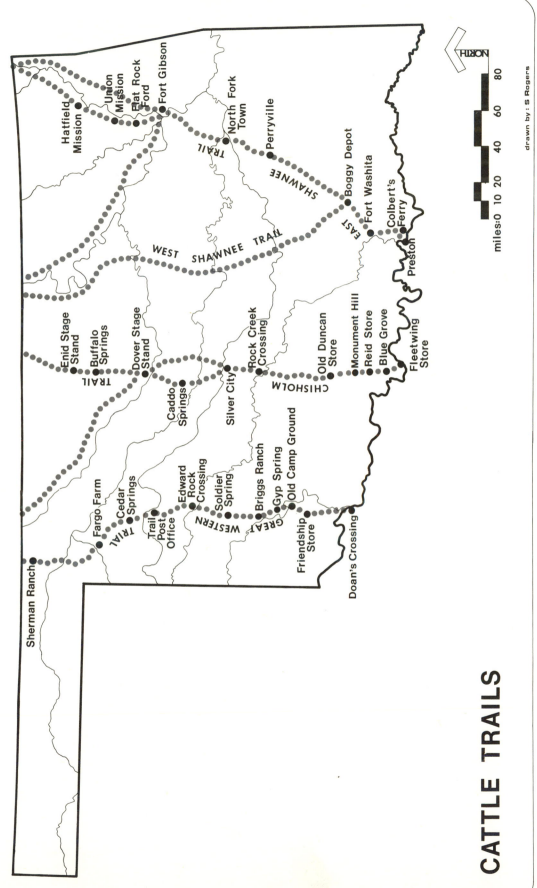

CATTLE TRAILS

drawn by : S Rogers

miles: 0 10 20 40 60 80

NORTH

Sherman Ranch

Fargo Farm
Cedar Springs
Trail Post Office

Hatfield Mission
Union Mission
Flat Rock Ford
Fort Gibson

Enid Stage Stand
Buffalo Springs
Dover Stage Stand
Caddo Springs

Edward Rock Crossing
Soldier Spring
Briggs Ranch
Gyp Spring
Old Camp Ground
Friendship Store

Silver City
Rock Creek Crossing
Old Duncan Store
Monument Hill
Reid Store
Blue Grove
Fleetwing Store

North Fork Town
Perryville
Boggy Depot
Fort Washita
Colbert's Ferry
Preston

Doan's Crossing

SHAWNEE TRAIL

WEST SHAWNEE TRAIL

EAST

CHISHOLM TRAIL

GREAT WESTERN TRAIL

Buffalo hunters camp. Skinners processing hides and tongues.

on the territory's western lands in this period.

Hunters received from one to four dollars for each cured hide. One hide hunter in 1874 killed 2,173 buffalo in a period of slightly over a month. A herd of 40,000 buffalo was reported on the North Canadian River near Fort Supply in 1877. Two years later the herd numbered less than one hundred animals.

The killing off of the buffalo on the prairies and plains had a drastic effect on Indians living in western Indian Territory. The disappearance of the buffalo also opened the vast grasslands of central and western Indian Territory for the cattlemen. Their entry from Texas involved the territory in America's first billion-dollar industry—the range-cattle industry.

The Range-Cattle Industry

AFTER THE WAR, the Texas ranges, largely untouched by invading armies, were crowded with beef animals locally worth about four dollars each. Beef was scarce in the North and the East, and a steer there was worth about forty dollars.

During 1866, some Texas cattlemen drove their herds northward to take advantage of these favorable market conditions. They crossed Indian Territory and this began the territory's first cattle highway—the East Shawnee Trail. This trail entered Indian Territory at Colbert's Ferry, located in the eastern part of the Chickasaw Nation, and followed the Texas Road to Baxter Springs, Kansas. Texas trail drivers had trouble as their herds passed through the towns of southern Kansas and southwestern Missouri. Their herds stampeded and they lost many animals in the rough Ozark mountain country.

Joseph McCoy, an Illinois stock raiser, solved this problem by setting up a cattle market on the railhead of the Kansas Pacific Railroad at Abilene, Kansas. He advertised the market among Texas cattlemen, and during 1867 thirty-five

Freight line serving Indian Territory settlements before the coming of the railroads.

thousand head of cattle reached Abilene, the first of the Kansas cow towns. The next year, seventy-five thousand head were delivered.

The cattle trail that crossed central Indian Territory and connected Texas ranches with markets in the Kansas cow towns was named Chisholm Trail for the frontier trader Jesse Chisholm, who blazed it before the Civil War. The Shawnee Trail branched at Boggy Depot in the Choctaw Nation and ran northwest to the Kansas cow towns.

A fourth cattle highway, which crossed Indian Territory and connected Texas ranches with the last of the cow towns at Dodge City, was the Dodge City or Great Western Cattle Trail. This trail crossed Red River at Doan's Store into the Leased District, then curved northwest across western Indian Territory to Dodge City.

As the tribes on Indian Territory's western boundaries were defeated and forced to move onto reservations, cattlemen entered the western section of the territory and leased grazing land from the tribes. Here they built great ranching empires. Thus Oklahoma is sometimes called the cattleman's last frontier.

Two ranching groups that for several years controlled millions of acres of Indian Territory's grazing land were the Cheyenne–Arapaho Stock Growers Association and the Cherokee Strip Livestock Association. The Cheyenne–Arapaho Stock Growers Association was formed in 1882. Begun by seven cattlemen, this organization leased 3 million acres of grasslands from the Cheyenne and Arapaho tribes in western Indian Territory and grazed 200,000 head of cattle on this land.

In 1883 a combine of stock raisers organized the Cherokee Strip Livestock Association. This group leased 6 million acres of grassland in the Cherokee Outlet from the Cherokee Nation for the sum of $100,000 per year. In 1888 the lease payment to the Cherokee Nation was increased to $200,000 per year. Association members grazed more than

Livery stable, El Reno, Oklahoma Territory, showing the transportation of the times.

300,000 head of cattle on the Outlet ranges.

Intertribal Government Attempts

BEFORE leaving the land of the Five Civilized Tribes and studying the history of western Indian Territory, there is one other matter that should be discussed concerning the progress of the five Indian republics in Reconstruction. By the treaties of 1866 the five tribes were required to work toward a single unified government for their territory. Nothing permanent ever came of their requirement, but some preliminary steps were taken by the leaders of the tribes.

The first council was held at Okmulgee in the Creek Nation during September, 1867. When the council meeting began, only the Cherokees, the Creeks, and the smaller tribes of north-eastern Indian Territory were present. A second meeting, better attended, was held at Okmulgee in December, 1869. From the council meetings a committee of twelve men was appointed to prepare a constitution for Indian Territory.

The committee prepared a document that proposed a government in which the tribes would be represented by population. The plan of government for Indian Territory produced by the Okmulgee Council was voted on by tribes of the territory during 1870. The Chickasaws defeated the plan by refusing to ratify the proposed constitution. Leaders of this tribe objected because the plan of government for Indian Territory did not give the smaller tribes fair representation.

No further attempt was made to produce a plan for governing a united Indian Territory. The tribes continued to send delegates to Okmulgee for an annual council where mutual problems

"On the Great Trail," by A. Castaigne.

were discussed. The experience in working together provided an important base for Indian Territory politicians when Oklahoma statehood was seriously considered after 1900.

Western Indian Territory Tribes

As EXPLAINED earlier, during the period of 1865 to 1889, two totally different streams of history were emerging in Indian Territory. One was in the future Sooner State's eastern half populated by the Five Civilized Tribes. The other was in the western half, the domain of the Plains Indian tribes and various other Indian groups. In order to understand this interesting but complex period, one must study the historical growth of each region separately. The western half of Indian Territory was taken from the Five Civilized Tribes as a part of the Reconstruction settlement. The fed-eral government intended to use the area as a settlement zone to move Indian tribes from Kansas and other states and territories.

In the postwar Indian concentration in western Indian Territory, some tribes were peaceful and settled quietly. Others were fierce and warlike and had to be subdued by military force before they settled to reservation life. During the Civil War, bands of Kiowas, Comanches, Cheyennes, and Arapahos had attacked towns and cut telegraph lines in Kansas, Colorado, and New Mexico. They were a threat to the postwar development of the West. The federal government was eager to confine them to limited reservations and to open their former lands for settlement.

While the Fort Smith Council for the Five Civilized Tribes was in progress in 1865, leaders of the Plains tribes met with federal commissioners at the mouth of the Little Arkansas River near pres-

89

ent Wichita, Kansas. The chiefs signed treaties of peace with the United States and gave to the government (ceded) claim to all land north of the Arkansas River. By the Little Arkansas treaties the Cheyennes and Arapahos and the Kiowa-Apaches were assigned a large reservation between the Arkansas and Cimarron rivers in southwestern Kansas and northwestern Indian Territory. The Kiowas and Comanches accepted a reservation between the Cimarron and Red rivers extending across western Indian Territory and the Texas Panhandle.

Soon it was clear that the lands given these tribes by the Little Arkansas treaties would have to be reduced to satisfy the land hunger of homesteaders, some of whom were settling on the reservations. Hunters were slaughtering the wild game upon which these tribes depended. There also was a heavy flow of traffic across the reservations. The tribes threatened war, so to keep the peace federal commissioners called a second council in 1867. During October of that year they met on Medicine Lodge Creek in southwestern Kansas with Kiowa, Comanche, Cheyenne, and Arapaho leaders to negotiate a new agreement.

By the Medicine Lodge treaties, the Cheyennes and Arapahos were given a smaller reservation in west–central Indian Territory. The Kiowas, Comanches, and Kiowa-Apaches were given a reservation in southwestern Indian Territory. In 1872 the Cheyenne and Arapaho land was reduced by 600,000 acres when the federal government set up a reservation on the Washita River for about eleven hundred Wichitas, Caddos, Absentee Delawares, and the remnants of Texas tribes brought into the old Leased District before the Civil War. The Texas tribes included Keechis, Anadarkos, Ionis, and Wacos.

Anticipating trouble from the Plains tribes, federal troops built several military posts in western Indian Territory. Fort Supply was constructed in 1868 at a point where Wolf Creek and Beaver River join to form the North Canadian River, on the northern edge of the Cheyenne-Arapaho Reservation. Fort Sill was built in 1869 in the Wichita Mountains in the heart of the Kiowa-Comanche Reservation. Fort Reno was built on the North Canadian River in the center of the Cheyenne-Arapaho country in 1874.

An agency was set up near Fort Sill to serve as headquarters for the federal agent assigned to administer the affairs of the Kiowas, Comanches, and Kiowa-Apaches. The Cheyenne-Apache Agency was built at Darlington near Fort Reno. Additional agencies were set up as more tribes were moved to western Indian Territory, following the government's policy of tribal concentration.

The Osages ceded their reservation in southern Kansas to the United States government in 1865. By 1872 the tribe had moved from its northern lands and settled on a reservation between the 96th meridian and the Arkansas River in the eastern part of the Cherokee Outlet. At the time of removal, there were more than fifteen hundred Osages. In 1872 the Osages were joined in Indian Territory by the Kaws, who were closely related to the Osages by language and culture. In return for their reservation in Kansas, the Kaws received a 100,000-acre tract in the northwest corner of the Osage reservation on the Arkansas River. Numbering about five hundred, they settled on their new reservation

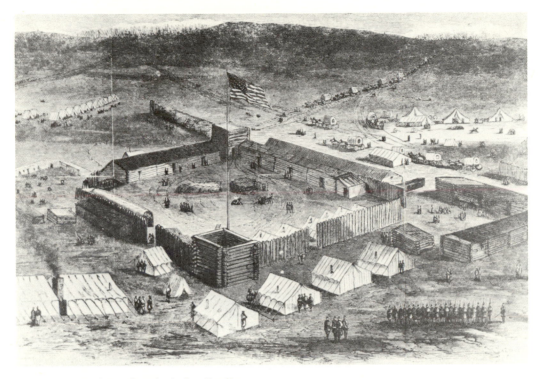

Artist's sketch of Fort Supply, Indian Territory.

home during 1873. The Osages and Kaw tribes were under the supervision of the Osage Agency at Pawhuska.

In central Indian Territory, on land taken from the Creeks by the Reconstruction treaties, the federal government colonized the Sac and Fox Tribe. Most of these Indians came from Kansas, although a few scattered bands were brought in from Iowa. The Sac and Fox move began in 1867 and was finished by 1869. Next to the Sac and Fox Reservation, on the west, the federal government resettled 450 Potawatomis from Kansas, the Absentee Shawnees, 250 Iowas formerly living on the Kansas-Nebraska border, and the Mexican Kickapoos.

These fierce Kickapoos, originally from the Old Northwest, had moved west and south ahead of American settlement until, during the Civil War, a large part of the tribe settled in the north Mexican state of Coahuila. The Mexican government welcomed the Kickapoos and gave them a reservation home and complete freedom from governmental interference. In return, the Kickapoos were required to protect the north Mexican frontiers from raids by Kiowas, Comanches, and Apaches. Kickapoo warriors did this well and also raided into Texas.

Their raids on south Texas towns and ranches were so serious during the early 1870s that Texas officials appealed to the federal government for help. The result was an invasion of Mexico during 1873 by Colonel Ranald Mackenzie and the Fourth United States Cavalry.

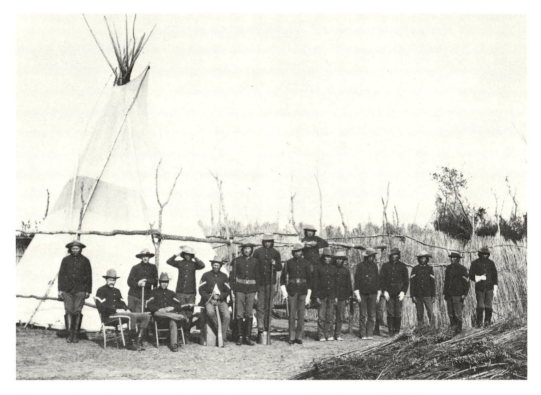

Cheyenne-Arapaho scouts attached to United States cavalry columns at Fort Reno.

Mackenzie's troopers crossed into Mexico, smashed the Kickapoo villages near Nacimiento, and forced more than three hundred Kickapoos to return as prisoners of war to the United States and accept a reservation in Indian Territory.

The Mexican Kickapoos were assigned land between the Deep Fork and the North Canadian rivers. The Sac and Fox, the Potawatomi, the Iowa, the Absentee Shawnee, and the Kickapoos tribes were placed under the control of the Sac and Fox Agency near present Stroud.

From Dakota Territory came the Poncas, a Siouan-speaking people who lived briefly in Nebraska. Numbering almost seven hundred, the Poncas moved to Indian Territory in 1876 and received a reservation in the Cherokee Outlet between the Chikaskia and the Arkansas rivers. The Otoes and the Missouris, also Siouan-speaking Indians, numbering together about four hundred, had been living on a reservation on the Kansas and Nebraska border. Their relocation in the Indian Territory took place between 1880 and 1883 on a reservation in the Cherokee Outlet south of the Poncas.

The Pawnees, numbering about two thousand, had occupied a reservation in Nebraska. Of the Caddoan language family, the Pawnees were assigned a reservation between the Arkansas and Cimarron rivers. Their lands contained a portion of the Cherokee Outlet and territory given up by the Creeks in 1866.

From the Pacific Northwest came the Nez Perces. Miners and settlers had invaded their lands after the Civil War. The Nez Perces, led by the great Chief Joseph, resisted the invasion and a bloody and extended war followed. The Nez Perces gave up in 1877, and 431 of this tribe were brought under military guard to Indian Territory and settled in the Cherokee Outlet on the Chikaskia River.

The Nez Perces protested their treatment, and finally in 1885 the federal government allowed them to return to their homeland in the Pacific Northwest. Their place in the Cherokee Outlet was taken by the Tonkawas, a Texas tribe relocated in the Leased District in 1859. The Tonkawas numbered about one hundred when, in 1885, they were settled on lands in the Cherokee Outlet. The Poncas, Pawnees, Otoes, and Missouris, for a time the Nez Perces, and the Tonkawas were administered by the Ponca Agency.

In the far northeastern corner of Indian Territory, between the Neosho River and the Missouri border, the Quapaws, Senecas, and a small band of Shawnees had resided since the Stokes Commission assignment in 1832. Following the Civil War, the federal government took a part of the lands belonging to these tribes to establish homes for those remaining of the tribes being relocated from the Kansas reservations. These tribes included the Wyandots, Peorias, Miamis, and Ottawas brought to Indian Territory under treaties negotiated during 1867.

In 1873 the federal government moved to this area a party of 153 Modocs. The Modocs had been making war on the California settlers. They were being punished by forced surrender of their lands in northern California and exile to Indian Territory as prisoners of war. The Shawnees, Senecas, Quapaws, Wyandots, Peorias, Miamis, Ottawas, and Modocs were administered by the Quapaw Agency.

Besides setting up reservations for tribes on the land obtained from the Five Civilized Tribes by the treaties of 1866, the government also settled tribes on lands that still belonged to these five tribes. A band of Delawares numbering about one thousand moved from northern Kansas in 1867 to the Cherokee Nation and settled in the northern Verdigris River valley. For this right to settle, the Delawares paid the Cherokees $280,000. This was not a separate reservation.

The goal of the government was to change the Indians, to erase tribal background and native customs, and to convince the Indians to accept the white man's civilization. The Indians were to become like the settlers around the reservations, supporting themselves by farming and stock raising. Schools to instruct the Indian children in the ways of civilization were established by federal agents and the missionaries.

Most of the Indians were peaceful and gave their agents no trouble other than for their efforts to continue their old ways. They visited with other tribes, gambled, attended horse races, feasted and danced, observed their traditional religions, and avoided farming and other civilizing programs forced upon them by the agents and missionaries.

The Kiowas and the Comanches, and the Cheyennes and Arapahos, however, refused to submit to reservation life. They continued to leave their assigned area to hunt buffalo and to raid the settlements. Determined to succeed in

Quanah Parker, Quahada Comanche war chief.

its reservation policy, the federal government carried out a fierce and extended campaign of military conquest against these tribes. Between 1867 and 1874, western Indian Territory was the scene of much bloodshed. This was the result of battles between federal troops and Indian warriors.

During 1868 the tribes of western Indian Territory had been slow in settling on their reservations assigned by the Medicine Lodge treaties. Some warrior bands had raided settlements on the border. To punish these Indians, the Seventh Cavalry, led by George Armstrong Custer, rode out of Fort Supply in late November, 1868. At daybreak on November 27, Custer and his troops reached the Washita River and made a surprise attack at Black Kettle's Cheyenne camp. The Seventh Cavalry killed more than one hundred warriors and took fifty women and children as prisoners. The soldiers burned the village and captured a large herd of horses.

Chief Black Kettle was among the dead. The Battle of the Washita was more of a massacre than a battle. It was the first of a series of actions against the Plains Indian tribes that eventually forced these Indians to remain on their reservations.

Between 1868, the year of the Battle of the Washita, and the final surrender of the warrior bands in 1874, troops from Fort Supply, Fort Sill, and other posts on the southern plains kept constant pressure on the tribes. Troops patrolled their reservations and watched the warriors.

Despite the vigilance of the patrols, small bands of warriors slipped by the troops on foot; they raided ranches and farms in Texas and Kansas for horses and arms, then slashed and burned the settlements. These raids had become so widespread by 1874 that the War Department decided to end for all time the war-making potential of the Plains tribes of western Indian Territory.

General Nelson A. Miles was placed in command of a large force of cavalry, infantry, and artillery. His forces combed western Indian Territory and the Texas Panhandle and kept pressure on the tribes. Most of the warrior bands came in and surrendered voluntarily. Some fought to the death.

The Cheyenne and Arapaho bands came to Darlington Agency and surrendered. Kiowa and Comanche bands surrendered at Fort Sill. The last hostile band, the Quahada Comanches led by Quanah Parker, surrendered on June 1, 1875, to officers at Fort Sill. As each band surrendered, the troops at Fort Sill, Fort Reno, or the other posts, disarmed the warriors, took their horses, and arrested their leaders. Seventy-two raider chiefs were placed in irons and taken under heavy guard to the military prison at Fort Marion, Saint Augustine, Florida.

Another band of hostile Indians, followers of the Apache leader Geronimo, consisted of nearly four hundred men, women, and children. They surrendered in Arizona during 1886. The War Department first sent the Apaches to Fort Marion military prison. During 1888 the Apache prisoners were moved to Mount Vernon Barracks in Alabama. Tuberculosis killed so many Apaches that in 1894 the 296 survivors were re-

settled on the Kiowa-Comanche Reservation under the guns of Fort Sill. Their status as prisoners of war of the United States continued until 1913.

Peace had come to Indian Territory. The Indians had been conquered. The warriors of the Plains tribes were now leaderless, disarmed, and afoot. Their horses had been confiscated and shot or sold to ranchers at auction by military authorities. The tribes were completely conquered. With sadness and anger, they settled down to the dull routine of reservation life.

Study Aids

Explain the significance of each term or phrase listed below:

1. Guerrilla
2. Battle of the Washita
3. Segregation
4. Freedmen's Bureau
5. Union Agency
6. Katy

Identify each of these persons:

1. William P. Ross
2. Samuel Checote
3. John F. Brown
4. J. J. McAlester
5. Joseph McCoy
6. Lewis Downing

On an outline map of Oklahoma locate the following places:

1. Okmulgee
2. Fort Supply
3. Fort Sill
4. Fort Reno
5. Colbert's Ferry
6. Chisholm Trail

Use the suggestions below for study guides:

1. Compare the tribes of eastern and western Indian Territory.
2. List the Indian agencies in Oklahoma and the tribes assigned to each.
3. Summarize the purpose and operation of the Federal District Court at Fort Smith.
4. Discuss the status of the blacks in postwar Indian Territory.
5. Outline early railroad construction in Indian Territory.

For Further Reading

Berthrong, Donald J. *The Southern Cheyennes.* Norman, 1963.

Dale, Edward E. *The Range Cattle Industry.* Norman, 1930.

Gibson, Arrell M. *The Kickapoos: Lords of the Middle Border.* Norman, 1963.

Leckie, William H. *The Military Conquest of the Southern Plains.* Norman, 1963.

———. *The Buffalo Soldiers.* Norman, 1968.

Masterson, V. V. *The Katy Railroad and the Last Frontier.* Norman, 1953.

Chapter 7. **EMERGENCE OF OKLAHOMA TERRITORY**

Homesteaders Versus Indians

THE THEME of two streams of history emerging on the Oklahoma scene continued after 1889, but with a difference. Between 1889 and 1907, the two different streams of history were controlled by the homesteaders and the Indians, and by the continued presence of Indian Territory and the birth of Oklahoma Territory. All this was taking place within the limits of present Oklahoma.

By the 1870s most of the land that was good for farming in the American West had been homesteaded. Oklahoma as the Indian Territory was reserved for the Indians, but settlers wanted its rich farming lands. Their desire to settle in Indian Territory at last was satisfied. It took several years of hard work and intense pressure on the federal government before they succeeded.

The settlers' efforts to open Indian Territory to homesteading were aided by the railway companies that had constructed lines across Indian Territory. The MKT, Frisco, Rock Island, and Santa Fe lines crossed the Indian country, and linked the Missouri and Kansas trade centers with the greater Southwest. The thinly settled Indian nations and reservations made small use of these railway lines except in the mining and timber regions of eastern Indian Territory. One railroad official commented that his company was the first railroad in history to construct a line "two-hundred and fifty miles through a tunnel." The railway companies wanted the territory more thickly settled, with a farmer on every quarter section and thriving towns developing along the tracks.

The Rise of the Boomers

THE PERMISSION that would allow settlement in Indian Territory had to come from the United States Congress. Railroad companies operating in the territory tried for years to get Congress to remove the ban on settlement in the Indian country. They were joined by settler and farm organizations. From this campaign to open Indian Territory to settlement came a group of professional promoters called "Boomers." The most active of the Boomers, those men who promoted the opening of the territory to settlement, were Elias C. Boudinot (son of Elias Boudinot of the New Echota Treaty), Charles C. Carpenter, David L. Payne, and William L. Couch.

Boudinot was a Cherokee attorney practicing law in Washington, D.C. He knew well the postwar treaties that had assigned lands to various tribes in Indian Territory. In February, 1879, he published a letter in the *Chicago Times* in which he said that millions of acres of land in Indian Territory, taken from the Five Civilized Tribes by the Reconstruction treaties, were properly a part of the public domain of the United States and thus open to settlement under the Homestead Act. He called attention to a two-million-acre tract in central Indian Territory that was taken from the Creeks and the Seminoles by the 1866 treaties. No tribe had been settled in this area and it was called the Unassigned Lands. Boudinot's published letter caused much interest across the United States. He continued to write letters and pamphlets and to make speeches in the East describing the Indian Territory and the possibility of settlers homesteading there.

Charles C. Carpenter, a man who liked to look like Buffalo Bill Cody, complete with buckskin-fringed hunting jacket and long flowing hair, organized the Oklahoma Colony in 1879 in several Kansas towns. He collected his

Elias C. Boudinot, Cherokee, who introduced the idea of opening the Unassigned Lands to settlement.

followers at the towns of Independence and Coffeyville, Kansas, and prepared to lead them into Indian Territory where each would select a 160-acre homestead. The leaders of the Five Civilized Tribes learned of the plan to invade their country and protested to federal officials. The secretary of war answered by placing troops on the border. Carpenter was warned by army officials not to enter the territory. The invasion was called off.

Next on the scene as professional promoter for opening Indian Territory to settlement was David L. Payne, called the "Prince of the Boomers." Born in Indiana, Payne came to Kansas in 1858. As a frontier guide and scout he became acquainted with much of the Southwest. During 1879, Payne arrived in the Kansas towns to organize the homeseekers.

David L. Payne, leader of the "Boomers."

Payne used his time in the courtroom to make popular the cause of homesteading in Indian Territory. In addition, on each Boomer raid into the territory he allowed newspapermen to accompany the group. Their stories published in the eastern press increased interest in Indian Territory as the homesteaders' last frontier. More than anything else, the Boomer raids can be regarded as demonstrations — protest movements — against the barriers to settlement in Indian Territory.

Payne died at Wellington, Kansas, in 1884. One of his followers, Captain William L. Couch, took over the leadership of the Oklahoma Colony. Couch led several Boomer raids into Indian Territory. His most famous entry occurred in December, 1884. The Oklahoma colonists started a town on Stillwater Creek. Army troops found the location and forced the intruders to return to Kansas.

He began a string of Boomer camps at Arkansas City, Caldwell, Hunnewell, and other border towns. These camps were called "Payne's Oklahoma Colony." He regularly visited the camps, made speeches, and kept his followers excited by publishing a newspaper called the *Oklahoma War Chief.*

Payne received his greatest fame from the Boomer raids he led into Indian Territory. His most publicized entry was made in 1880 when he led a column of settlers to central Indian Territory and started a settlement on the North Canadian River on the present site of Oklahoma City. United States cavalry from Fort Reno moved in; they burned the town, forced the settlers to return to Kansas, and arrested Payne and took him to Fort Smith for trial.

Opening Oklahoma to Settlement

THE BOOMER campaign to popularize the Indian country and to win support for removing the barriers to settlement finally met with success in 1889. On March 3 of that year Congress adopted an amendment to the Indian Appropriation Act. Called the Springer Amendment from its author, Congressman William Springer of Illinois, it provided for the opening of the Unassigned Lands to settlers under the Homestead Act. On March 23, President Benjamin Harrison issued a proclamation that declared that the Unassigned Lands could be entered by eligible settlers on April 22, 1889.

Up to this time there had been a sur-

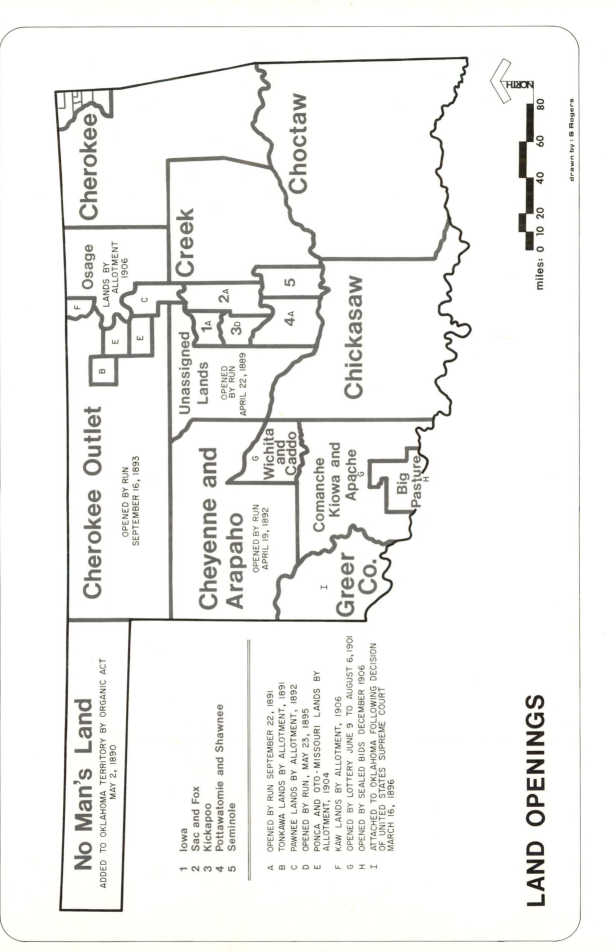

LAND OPENINGS

No Man's Land

ADDED TO OKLAHOMA TERRITORY BY ORGANIC ACT
MAY 2, 1890

1   Iowa
2   Sac and Fox
3   Kickapoo
4   Pottawatomie and Shawnee
5   Seminole

A   OPENED BY RUN SEPTEMBER 22, 1891
B   TONKAWA LANDS BY ALLOTMENT, 1891
C   PAWNEE LANDS BY ALLOTMENT, 1892
D   OPENED BY RUN, MAY 23, 1895
E   PONCA AND OTO-MISSOURI LANDS BY
    ALLOTMENT, 1904
F   KAW LANDS BY ALLOTMENT, 1906
G   OPENED BY LOTTERY JUNE 9 TO AUGUST 6, 1901
H   OPENED BY SEALED BIDS DECEMBER 1906
I   ATTACHED TO OKLAHOMA FOLLOWING DECISION
    OF UNITED STATES SUPREME COURT
    MARCH 16, 1896

Cherokee Outlet

OPENED BY RUN
SEPTEMBER 16, 1893

Cherokee

Osage

LANDS BY
ALLOTMENT
1906

Creek

Choctaw

Unassigned Lands

OPENED
BY RUN
APRIL 22, 1889

Chickasaw

Cheyenne and Arapaho

OPENED BY RUN
APRIL 19, 1892

Wichita and Caddo

Comanche Kiowa and Apache

Big Pasture

Greer Co.

miles: 0 10 20 40 60 80

NORTH

drawn by : S Rogers

Arrested for entering Oklahoma Territory before the designated day for the land opening, these "Sooners" are being ejected.

plus of desirable land in the American West for homeseekers and the settlement rate had been moderately slow. By 1889, however, most of the good land had been settled. The Boomers had made Indian Territory well known across the nation, and it was expected that the land opening would draw many more people seeking homesteads than the number of homesteads and town lot claims available in the Unassigned Lands.

So that all could have a chance, it was decided to settle the area by a land run. Homeseekers began gathering on the four borders of the Unassigned Lands three days before the run. Government surveyors had laid out the area into townsites and 160-acre homesteads. The townsites became the urban centers of Guthrie, Kingfisher, Oklahoma City, and Norman. Homeseekers could rush for a 160-acre farm or for a city lot in the townsites.

Troops patrolled the borders of the Unassigned Lands for several days before the opening, watching for early entry by homeseekers. Despite their efforts, several persons, called "Sooners," did enter the settlement zone before April 22 and staked out choice homesteads.

An estimated fifty thousand homeseekers thronged the borders of the Unassigned Lands on April 22, 1889. At noon troops along the line gave the signal and Oklahoma's first land run was begun. Homeseekers walked, ran, rode swift horses or wagons pulled by thundering spans of horses or mules, pedaled bicycles, and rode the trains. The Santa Fe Railway had completed its north–south line across Indian Territory in 1887. It crossed the approximate center of the Unassigned Lands. On April 22, trains from the north and the south waited on the line, overflowing with passengers; some rode on the "cowcatchers," an iron grill on the front of the trains' engines. By dark on April 22, 1889, most of the Unassigned Lands had been staked by homeseekers.

Nearly a thousand blacks were in the Run of 1889. Most of them had been recruited from the South. Certain black leaders who dreamed of establishing an all-black state on the Indian Territory frontier convinced them to come. Many black homeseekers were successful in gaining homesteads in the territory. Most of them settled east of Guthrie. Langston was an all-black town established by these black pioneers.

Congress had made possible the settlement of the Unassigned Lands, but it had failed to provide for a territorial government. Thus, for more than a year after the land run, the settlers kept some measure of law and order by following basic rules of government and by enforcing laws themselves (vigilante actions). In each town the citizens organized local government, usually consisting of an elected mayor and a town marshal. Citizen boards settled disputes over land claims, and they organized schools. These early schools were supported by subscription (tuition). Local groups of citizens asked Congress to provide the authority to form a territorial government.

The Oklahoma Organic Act

FINALLY, on May 2, 1890, Congress passed the Oklahoma Organic Act. This became one of the most important laws for Oklahoma because from this law came the present Oklahoma state government. In addition, the Oklahoma Organic Act marked the beginning of a training period during which the

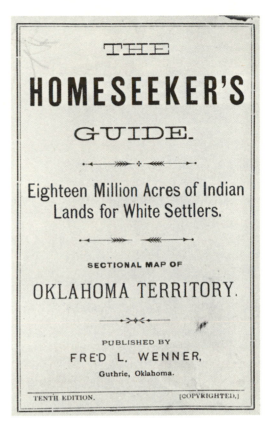

THE
HOMESEEKER'S
GUIDE.

Eighteen Million Acres of Indian Lands for White Settlers.

SECTIONAL MAP OF
OKLAHOMA TERRITORY.

PUBLISHED BY
FRE'D L. WENNER,
Guthrie, Oklahoma.

TENTH EDITION. [COPYRIGHTED.]

Sample of Boomer literature.

people of Oklahoma Territory gained practice in self-government in preparation for statehood.

The Oklahoma Organic Act provided for a territorial governor and a supreme court of three judges (later increased to five, then to seven as the territory grew) who also served as district judges. All of these officials were appointed by the President of the United States. A bicameral legislative assembly (the house to contain twenty-six members, the council, thirteen members), and a delegate to Congress were to be elected by the people of the territory.

The laws of Nebraska were to be used in Oklahoma Territory until the assem-

101

Land Rush opening the Cherokee Outlet, 1893.

bly adopted an Oklahoma code of laws for the territory. County and township governments were to be organized. The Oklahoma Organic Act contained an important provision for the growth of Oklahoma Territory in that all reservations in western Indian Territory, when opened to settlement, were automatically made a part of Oklahoma Territory.

The Oklahoma Organic Act provided for seven counties to which the citizens of each gave the following names: Logan, Oklahoma, Cleveland, Canadian, Kingfisher, and Payne in the Unassigned Lands, and Beaver in the Panhandle. The Panhandle was later divided into Cimarron, Beaver, and Texas counties. The Organic Act named Guthrie as the capital of Oklahoma Territory.

The Organic Act attached No-Man's Land to Oklahoma Territory. This rib-bon of land had been a sort of geographic orphan. Its territory evolved from incidents of national history. Its eastern boundary was established at 100° (degrees) west longitude by the Adams-Onís Treaty in 1819. The southern boundary came when Texas was annexed (became a state) in 1845 and with the Compromise of 1850, which cut off Texas at 36° 30' north latitude because it was a slave state. The western boundary at 103° west longitude came from the Mexican War conquest, the Treaty of Guadalupe-Hidalgo in 1848, and the organization of New Mexico Territory in 1850. The northern boundary was established by the organization of Kansas Territory in 1854 with a southern boundary at 37 degrees north latitude.

Called No-Man's Land because it was not attached to any state or territory, Oklahoma's Panhandle had other names—Public Land Strip, Cimarron

Downtown Oklahoma City, April 30, 1889.

Territory, and Robbers' Roost. This last name came about because, free from law enforcement by any state or territory, after the Civil War the strip of land became famous throughout the American West as a haven for outlaws, cattle rustlers, gamblers, and other kinds of lawbreakers.

During the 1880s cattlemen and nesters (illegal homesteaders) began settling in No-Man's Land. They organized vigilante committees and freed it of outlaws; then they organized Cimarron Territory. Representatives of the six thousand settlers in No-Man's Land met in convention at Beaver City during 1887. They formed a government for the area and elected a governor and a territorial delegate. Congress chose not to recognize this action, but solved the question of its status by making No-Man's Land a part of Oklahoma Territory.

Oklahoma territorial government began during the summer of 1890 when President Harrison's choice for territorial governor, George W. Steele of Indiana, arrived in Guthrie. Oklahoma Territory elected its first legislative assembly during August, 1890. That body met at Guthrie during the same month and began adopting the required laws to begin governing the new territory.

Besides passing civil and criminal laws for the territory, the assembly adopted legislation providing for a system of public schools and higher education for Oklahomans. Bills passed during the first legislative session provided for the establishment of the territorial university at Norman, the territorial agricultural and mechanical college at Stillwater, and the territorial normal, or teacher training, institution at Edmond.

The governors of Oklahoma Territory.

The Growth of Oklahoma Territory

PROBLEMS in Oklahoma territorial government were caused by the rapid growth of the territory, both geographically and in population. The Springer Amendment had provided for the appointment of a commission to negotiate two matters with the tribes of western Indian territory. The first was to terminate common or tribal ownership of Indian lands. The second matter was to assign each Indian resident a tract of land (allotment) in fee simple (private ownership). After each Indian man, woman, and child in each tribe had been given an allotment, generally about 160 acres, the surplus land on each reservation was to be purchased from the tribe by the federal government and opened to homesteading.

President Harrison appointed three men to this commission—David H. Jerome, former governor of Michigan, Warren G. Sayre of Indiana, and Alfred M. Wilson of Arkansas. The commission was called the Cherokee Commission or the Jerome Commission after its chairman. The Jerome Commission went to work at once, and during the early 1890s most of the tribes of western Indian territory agreed to these terms.

The first Indians to be allotted and their surplus lands readied for settlement were the Sac, Fox, Potawatomi, Shawnee, and Iowa tribes. Their surplus lands were opened to settlement by land run on September 22, 1891. More than twenty thousand persons, three times the number of claims available, made the run for homesteads in the Sac and Fox country. Payne, Cleveland, and Logan counties were expanded from portions of this addition to Oklahoma Territory, and two new counties, Lincoln and Pottawatomie, were created from the rest.

On April 19, 1892, the surplus lands of the Cheyenne-Arapaho tribes were opened to homesteaders by land run. About twenty-five thousand persons participated in this race for claims. The following year on September 16, more than a hundred thousand settlers made the race for homesteads in the Cherokee Outlet. The final land run was held in 1895 when the Kickapoo Reservation was opened to settlement. Soonerism, or unlawful entry before the appointed time for the run, had become widespread by 1895. It was charged that possibly one-half the claims in the Kickapoo country were filed by Sooners. To thwart the Sooners, the federal government decided to use the lottery in future openings.

The lottery was used in the Kiowa-Comanche opening in 1901. Before this occurred, though, Oklahoma Territory received another addition of territory by a decision handed down by the United States Supreme Court in 1896—the *Greer County Case.* Early government surveys and maps indicated that the North Fork of Red River was the southwestern boundary separating Indian Territory and Texas. In 1860 the state of Texas

Fox woman weaving.

organized Greer County out of the area bounded on the north by the North Fork of Red River and on the west by the 100th meridian. The Oklahoma Organic Act of 1890 contained a provision ordering the federal government to file suit in the United States Supreme Court to determine whether the North Fork or the South Fork of Red River was the true Texas boundary. In 1896 the High Court held that the South Fork was the main stream and thus the true boundary of Texas. Therefore, Greer County, containing 1½ million acres, was assigned to Oklahoma Territory. This area was settled under the land laws of Texas and the federal Homestead Act.

In August, 1901, the Kiowa, Comanche, Wichita, Caddo, and Apache surplus lands were opened to settlement. For this opening the federal government used the lottery. About 165,000 homeseekers registered at Fort Sill and

Geronimo, wearing a horned headdress, 1897.

any large quantity of surplus land after allotment. The remaining 51,000 acres were sold to settlers. The Osage reservation was allotted in 1906. Each tribal citizen received about 500 acres and there was no surplus for settlers.

Life in Oklahoma Territory

By 1906, the western half of present Oklahoma had been combined into Oklahoma Territory. Settlers had changed the prairie-plains wilderness into tidy farms and bustling towns. Most of the settlers were poor and they suffered in this new land until they adapted themselves and their farming methods and crops to it.

Money was scarce and the settlers on the Oklahoma Territory frontier used barter (trading) to meet many of their needs. They exchanged butter and eggs for salt, sugar, and coffee. They commonly traded a horse or a cow for a year's supply of flour. Men gathered buffalo bones on the prairie and sold them to fertilizer companies for seven dollars a ton. Settlers cut cedar posts and sold them to ranchers at two cents each. After the crops were in, many men followed the wheat harvest north to Kansas to earn money to stock and equip their frontier farms.

The kinds of dwellings used on the Oklahoma Territory frontier showed the people's adjustment to the environment. Immediately after each land run, the homesteader used a tent or a canvas-covered wagon box for shelter. If there was a timbered canyon on his claim, or if he had settled in the Cross Timbers, the settlers cut logs and built cabins. Most of the country in central and western Oklahoma Territory was grassland.

Fort Reno for the drawing to distribute 15,000 homesteads.

Large tracts in this area had been reserved from settlement. These included the Fort Sill Military Reservation of 56,000 acres; the Wichita Mountain Forest Reserve of 58,000 acres; and the Big Pasture Reserve of 480,000 acres, a grazing area reserved for the benefit of the Kiowas and Comanches. In 1906 the Big Pasture was sold at public auction, and ownership passed to private hands. The area, parts of Comanche and Tillman counties, came under the jurisdiction of Oklahoma Territory.

The small Indian reservations in north–central Indian Territory were all used up by the allotment process. The Ponca, Oto, Missouri, and Kaw reservations were allotted and assigned to Oklahoma Territory in 1904. Only the Oto and Missouri reservations had

Using a sod plow to ready the plains for crops.

Faced with the lack of suitable construction timber, settlers made dugouts in hillsides or built sod huts.

The sod house was the most common type of early dwelling. Its walls were constructed of sod blocks cut from the ground on the homesteader's claim with a special sod plow. Occasionally the settler used split cedar posts to construct the walls of his frontier dwelling. Placed up and down rather than sideways as was usual in building log cabins, this structure was called the picket-wall house. Early-day school buildings and churches on the territory's frontier also were constructed of logs, picket walls, or sod blocks. The labor was donated by the settlers.

Oklahoma settlers overcame the lack of wood for cooking and heating fuel by using cow chips (dried buffalo or cattle dung) gathered up about the claim. Pioneer Oklahomans had to be self-reliant and self-sufficient to survive. Preparing fields for wheat, cotton, and other cash crops took time and much labor to clear the thick, deep-rooted grass sod. Each farm was a food factory in that gardens and orchards yielded essential foods. Game was everywhere and the pioneer had to be a hunter, too. Wild turkey, prairie chicken, quail, deer, and rabbit were relied upon for meat by many families in the early survival period of establishing and developing a homestead in the Oklahoma Territory wilderness.

The Economic Development

OKLAHOMA Territory was largely agricultural and rural, but urban (city) development kept apace. Expanding railroad lines tied the new territory towns to the markets and sources of supply across the nation. The territory's wealth (its economy) began to grow.

The Santa Fe Railway Company, the first major line to cross Oklahoma Territory, was joined by the Rock Island Railway in 1890 when that company's north–south line was completed in the western part of the territory. The Choc-

Oklahoma dugout, a family's home.

A pioneer's sod house on a prairie claim.

taw, Oklahoma and Gulf line (later part of the Rock Island) extended from El Reno to Oklahoma City. It was completed eastward in 1895 to connect those towns with McAlester. A year later the Frisco completed the Vinita-to-Tulsa line to Oklahoma City and southwest to Quanah, Texas. On the eve of statehood, Oklahoma Territory had 2,872 miles of completed railway service.

Guthrie, Oklahoma City, Norman, Enid, Woodward, and other towns on the railroads became regional trade centers. Grain, cotton, lumber, and livestock products were marketed in these towns. Banking, farm and ranch supply, and other businesses developed and expanded as the territory grew. Guthrie, the territorial capital with nearly six thousand people, was the largest town in Oklahoma Territory.

The Political Development

OKLAHOMA Territory's economic development was matched by its political development. Republican, Democratic, Populist, and Socialist parties were active in Oklahoma Territory. The strongest parties were the Republican and Democratic. On occasion the Democratic and Populist parties joined to elect their candidates to political office. On the surface, Oklahoma Territory appeared to be moving in the direction of Republican party domination. Many of the early settlers, coming from the North and the East, were Republican. They were able to elect candidates to local and territorial offices in most of the elections held in Oklahoma Territory between 1890 and 1906.

All territorial governors appointed by the president were, with one exception, Republican. Oklahoma territorial governors in order of service were:

George W. Steele (1891)
Robert Martin (1891–92)
Abraham J. Seay (1892–93)
William C. Renfrow (1893 to 1897)
Cassius M. Barnes (1897 to 1901)
William M. Jenkins (1901)
William C. Grimes (1901)
Thompson B. Ferguson (1901 to 1906)
Frank Frantz (1906–1907)

All of these men were Republicans except Governor Renfrow, a Democrat appointed by Democratic President Grover Cleveland.

An important elected official serving Oklahoma Territory in Washington, D.C. was the congressional delegate. His function was to watch for and to promote and protect the interests of the people of the territory. He did this by speaking on the floor of Congress on matters pertaining to Oklahoma Territory and by writing and introducing bills to improve the welfare of Oklahomans and the territory.

An important example of the work of the territorial delegate to Congress in caring for the interests of Oklahomans is found in the Free Homes Bill promoted by Oklahoma Congressional Delegate Dennis Flynn. Settlers were expected to pay for their homesteads in Oklahoma Territory at the rate of about $1.25 per acre. Most Oklahomans were poor. Drought and other disasters in the early years of settlement prevented production of large cash crops of cotton and corn. The settlers had little cash, and few were able to pay the federal government for their homesteads. Flynn obtained Congress's approval of the Free Homes Bill in 1901, which excused Oklahoma homestead-

Oklahoma City in 1906. Downtown.

ers from paying the required fee to the federal government.

Those representing Oklahoma Territory in the Congress during the period were David A. Harvey (1890 to 1893), Dennis Flynn (1893 to 1897), James Y. Callahan (1897 to 1899), Dennis Flynn (1899 to 1903), and Bird S. McGuire (1903 to 1907). All congressional delegates elected from Oklahoma Territory were Republican except James Y. Callahan. He was elected in 1896 by the uniting of the Populist and Democratic parties on one ticket.

The Oklahoma territorial legislature was also dominated by the Republican party for most of the period. It had a particularly difficult task because of the piecemeal growth of Oklahoma Territory. Nearly every year an area of land was added to Oklahoma Territory, and the legislature had to extend territorial government for it by creating local courts, organizing counties, and providing for schools and other essentials for the orderly development of the new area. The overwhelming interest of the territorial legislature, the governor, and the public at large was statehood for Oklahoma Territory.

Every year from 1889 to 1907, statehood conventions were held in towns over the territory. A territory-wide convention was held at Oklahoma City on December 16, 1891. The delegates adopted resolutions urging Congress

Making sorghum at a sorghum mill in Indian Territory.

to grant Oklahoma Territory immediate admission to the Union. These resolutions were presented to Congress, and on January 25, 1892, an Oklahoma statehood bill was introduced in Congress. Final action was put off on this proposal, however, and in each Congress thereafter the territorial delegate reintroduced this Oklahoma statehood bill until passage of the Oklahoma Enabling Act in 1906.

Congress held up action on the proposed Oklahoma statehood bill for several sound reasons. One of these concerned the ability of the territory to support itself as a state. Much of the revenue for state and local government support in those times came from taxes on land. Most of the land in Oklahoma Territory produced no tax income for the territorial government because, under federal law, homesteads were nontaxable until title to the land passed to the settler. Before this could occur, the settler had to live on and improve his land for a period of from three to five years. Also, much of the land in Oklahoma Territory was held by Indians as allotments. Most of this land was nontaxable for at least twenty-one years.

Another roadblock to early statehood for Oklahoma Territory was its neighbor, Indian Territory, the land of the Five Civilized Tribes. Many political leaders in Oklahoma Territory and in Washington, D. C. were of the opinion that the best solution to the Oklahoma statehood issue was to join the two territories into a single state.

Out of the debate on the question of Oklahoma statehood came five different proposals; four of them would have resulted in the admission of Oklahoma to the Union. One Oklahoma statehood proposal urged joining the Twin Territories (Oklahoma Territory and Indian Territory) into a single state. Another proposal favored creating two states out of the Twin Territories. This sometimes was called the "double statehood proposition."

A third proposal, advanced by Oklahoma Congressional Delegate Dennis Flynn, was known as the "piecemeal absorption plan." This plan called for immediate statehood for Oklahoma Territory and for the new state of Oklahoma to absorb each portion remaining of Indian Territory as it became prepared for statehood.

The fourth plan called for statehood for Oklahoma Territory with Indian Territory left under its tribal governments. This plan was popular in Indian Territory where many of the people were opposed to joining with Oklahoma Territory to form a single state.

There was a fifth plan, favored by politicians in Washington, D. C., which amounted to taking no action at all on either of the Twin Territories. Most of the important political offices in the territory were filled by appointment by the president and his political party, not by election by the people of the territory. Having control of the appointments in the territory was important to both the Republican and the Democratic parties.

These statehood plans, and the interests each represented—political, economic, and personal—made the Oklahoma statehood issue more complex and delayed the Sooner State's entry into the American Union. The biggest problem in the statehood issue was the future of Indian Territory. Until that question was settled, it appeared that no action would be taken on Oklahoma statehood. While these five statehood plans were being debated, steps were being taken to prepare the land of the Five Civilized Tribes for statehood in some form. More than likely it would be part of Oklahoma Territory or a separate Indian state.

Study Aids

Explain the significance of each term or phrase listed below:

1. Vigilante
2. *Oklahoma War Chief*
3. Oklahoma Organic Act
4. No-Man's Land
5. Jerome Commission
6. *Greer County Case*

Identify each of these persons:

1. Elias C. Boudinot
2. George W. Steele
3. Dennis Flynn
4. Charles C. Carpenter
5. James Y. Callahan
6. William L. Couch

On an outline map of Oklahoma locate the following places:

1. Stillwater
2. Vinita
3. Guthrie
4. Norman
5. El Reno
6. Edmond

Use the suggestions below for study guides:

1. Summarize the work of the Boomers, noting their special role in opening western Indian Territory to settlement.
2. Outline the geographic growth of Oklahoma Territory from 1889 to 1906.
3. Give the terms of the Oklahoma Organic Act and show how it met the political needs of Oklahoma Territory.
4. Describe the work of the Oklahoma territorial delegate to Congress from 1890 to 1906.
5. Describe the different Oklahoma statehood plans.

For Further Reading

Alley, John. *City Beginnings in Oklahoma Territory.* Norman, 1939.

Constant, Alberta. *Oklahoma Run.* Oklahoma City, 1982.

Gittinger, Roy. *Formation of the State of Oklahoma.* Norman, 1939.

Rainey, George. *The Cherokee Strip.* Guthrie, 1933.

Rister, Carl Coke. *Land Hunger: David L. Payne and the Boomers.* Norman, 1942.

Stewart, Dora Ann. *Government and Development of Oklahoma Territory.* Oklahoma City, 1933.

Teall, Kaye M. *Black History in Oklahoma.* Oklahoma City, 1971.

Chapter 8. **LAST YEARS OF INDIAN TERRITORY**

Economic Development

THE EARLY SURGE of economic growth in Indian Territory that sped the recovery of the Five Civilized Tribes from the Civil War and Reconstruction continued during the period before statehood.

The older towns of Indian Territory were joined by railroads with markets and business centers in the North, the South, and the East. New towns grew up along the railroads' rights-of-way. The principal Indian Territory railroad lines—MKT, the Frisco, the Choctaw and Gulf (later Rock Island), and the Santa Fe (across the Chickasaw Nation)—were joined by five shorter lines. These were the Iron Mountain Railway, from Fort Smith up the Arkansas River valley to Coffeyville, Kansas; the Denison and Washita Railway, from Denison, Texas, to Lehigh and Coalgate in the Choctaw Nation; the Split Log Railway in northeastern Indian Territory; the Midland Valley Railway from Mus-

kogee to Arkansas City; and the Fort Smith and Western Railway that served much of the Choctaw Nation.

One reason for the construction of these railway lines was to serve the rapidly developing mineral and timber resources of the Indian nations. Oklahoma's first commercial coal mines were opened and developed by J. J. McAlester in 1871 on the Texas Road in the Choctaw Nation. As noted earlier, the town that grew up around these early mines was called McAlester. Several businessmen joined with J. J. McAlester to form Oklahoma's first coal mining company, the Osage Coal and Mining Company. Coal seams were discovered running in all directions from McAlester. Additional companies were formed to mine and market the coal. Many new towns grew up around the coal pits. These included Krebs, Hartshorne, Alderson, Wilburton, Lehigh, Coalgate, Midway, Savannah, Dow, Gowen, Blanco, and Haileyville.

More rich coal seams were found so

rapidly that a large labor supply was required. Few Choctaw Indians were interested in working as miners in the pits, so the mining companies brought in skilled coal miners from Pennsylvania to develop the mines. Still more miners were needed, so the mining companies turned to Europe. Workers were recruited from Italy, Poland, Russia, Germany, Belgium, France, and Great Britain, and especially from Wales, which had many miners. By 1907 more than eight thousand foreign workers had been imported to Indian Territory. Most of the miners brought their families and became permanent settlers. They brought their languages, their customs, and their folkways. All of these added richness and color to the culture of the future Oklahoma. Their settlements include the present towns of Krebs, Hartshorne, and Haileyville.

Coal deposits were also found in the Cherokee and Creek nations, and development similar to the Choctaws' occurred there. In those days, the working conditions were harsh and dangerous in the coal mines. The men worked underground ten to twelve hours daily, six days a week, for an average wage of two dollars a day. Each day the workmen faced sudden death in the coal pits. Multiple deaths and injuries at a time were common, caused by explosions, gas, cave-ins, and underground flooding. These poor working conditions led to Oklahoma's first labor union movement.

The first labor organizer in Oklahoma was Pete Hanraty. He was an immigrant from Scotland who worked in the Indian Territory coal mines. On several occasions he led the workers out on strike in protest against working conditions. He established a unit of the United Mine Workers of America in Indian Territory and served as its president. The labor movement, through the leadership of Pete Hanraty, was powerful on the eve of statehood. Its voice was heard in the Oklahoma Constitutional Convention. Hanraty was elected to be a delegate to that convention in 1906 and served as its vice-president.

Lead and zinc mining was another important business in Indian Territory. Mining these minerals had been going on across the border in southwestern Missouri and southeastern Kansas for some time. Shallow lead mines had been worked in northeastern Oklahoma before 1891, but in that year commercial large-scale mining began with the discovery at Peoria, in present Ottawa County.

Within a month after the lead discovery, Peoria was changed from a small community with a post office, a general store, and a school to a booming mining camp with fifteen hundred miners. Prospectors followed the ore beds west of Peoria, regularly finding new and richer lodes of zinc and lead. By the time of Oklahoma statehood, Ottawa County was a maze of mining camps—Tar River, Commerce, Hattonville, Douthat, Saint Louis, Hockerville, Quapaw, Sunnyside, Lincolnville, and Century.

This part of Indian Territory prospered from these mining operations. But the large-scale mining for which Ottawa County became world famous as a part of the Tri-State District grew out of a lead and zinc discovery made in 1914 by a prospect driller working for the Picher Lead Company of Joplin, Missouri. In that year the miner made a rich find in a farming area northeast of Commerce. Almost overnight a new camp named Picher developed. A billion dollars worth of lead and zinc ores was mined in the Tri-State District between 1900 and 1950. Most of this was produced in Oklahoma's part of the rich mineral zone.

Oklahoma's greatest fame as a mineral producer has come from the petroleum industry. Oklahoma's modern oil industry had its beginnings in Indian Territory times. Signs of oil were found in Oklahoma in early times, appearing as a slick on the water in springs, creeks, and rivers. In the 1800s crude oil was believed to be medicine, especially for diseases like rheumatism and dropsy. Oil springs in the Chickasaw Nation were developed as health resorts or spas, and people with certain ills came from all over the Southwest to bathe in these oil-coated waters. Before cars became common, the chief use of crude oil was for grease as a lubricant and for lighting, using kerosene or coal oil in lamps and lanterns.

The search for oil in Indian Territory began in 1882 with the drilling of wells in the Choctaw Nation on Boggy River near Atoka and in the Cherokee Nation on the Illinois River at Alum Bluff. Wildcat drillers increased each year in Indian Territory after the beginning of drilling in 1882. Their efforts yielded producing wells near Bartlesville and south into the Creek Nation near Tulsa. The Red Fork field near Tulsa opened in 1901 and was followed by rich finds at Coody's Bluff and Cleveland in 1904. The following year the famous Glenn Pool near Tulsa assured a rich oil future for Oklahoma. On the eve of statehood, Indian Territory wells were producing more than forty million barrels of oil annually.

Another industry that contributed to Indian Territory's economic surge after the Civil War was lumbering. Pine and mixed hardwood forests of the territory had supplied the settlers with wood for building homes and furniture and as fuel. Steam-powered lumber mills were installed in Indian Territory's eastern forests in 1868 and ushered in the modern era of lumbering for the state. Railroad development in the territory provided a rich market for lumbermen in the form of rail ties and bridge timbers. The railroads also hauled Indian Territory lumber and shingles to markets across the Southwest.

The Long Bell Lumber Company and the Fort Smith Lumber Company began cutting the dense forests of the Choctaw Nation in the early 1890s, and the Dierks Company began operations in 1898. The hardwood forests, consisting of oak, maple, pecan, and walnut, furnished lumber for several furniture factories on the Arkansas–Indian Territory border.

The tobacco industry was important in postwar Indian Territory. The Cherokee Treaty of 1866 with the federal government included a clause that allowed tribal citizens to manufacture and sell any product throughout the United States and be exempt from federal tax.

During 1868, Elias C. Boudinot and Stand Watie purchased a tobacco factory at Hannibal, Missouri, and moved it to the Cherokee Nation. They bought tobacco from local growers, manufactured chewing tobacco, snuff, and pipe tobacco, and sold their products tax free throughout the United States. Tobacco dealers complained that their business suffered from the competition of this tax-free tobacco produced by the Cherokee Nation. Congress responded to this and passed an act taking away the tax-exempt clause of the Cherokee Treaty.

Eventually the United States Supreme Court heard the case that grew out of the Cherokees' protest at congressional annulment of a treaty clause. In the *Cherokee Tobacco Case* decision, handed down in 1870, the Court ruled that the laws of Congress overruled the Cherokee Treaty of 1866. The ruling destroyed the thriving Cherokee Nation tobacco industry. More than that, however, it allowed Congress to make the Five Civilized Tribes of Oklahoma subject to its laws. This made it unnecessary in the future to use the treaty as a way to conduct relations with the tribes. In 1871, Congress passed a law providing that no new treaties would be made with the Indian tribes. Thereafter, all tribes were subject to the laws of Congress and the rulings of the president.

Indian Territory Population

ANOTHER REASON for the economic surge of Indian Territory after the Civil War was the rapid increase in population. At statehood Oklahoma had a population of nearly 1,500,000. At that time, Indian Territory, the eastern half of Oklahoma, had a total population of 750,000, with Indians and freedmen numbering about 100,000. The other 650,000 was made up of the foreign population.

To speed their economic recovery, the tribal governments had adopted permit laws allowing non-Indian mechanics and laborers and their families to settle in Indian Territory. The annual license or permit cost $2.50 for laborers and $5 for mechanics and farmers. This permit system was an impor-

tant source of money for the Five Civilized Tribes. Most of the farm labor force came from Arkansas, Alabama, and Mississippi. Workers for the mines came largely from Pennsylvania and foreign countries. Many business and professional people came to Indian Territory during these times. They included lawyers, bankers, coal and timber operators, and railroad promoters. By 1907 the Choctaw Nation alone had a reported population of 200,000, consisting of Indians, blacks, and whites.

Preparation for Statehood

NONCITIZENS in Indian Territory outnumbered Indians nearly seven to one, but they could not own land. The tribal schools were open only to Indian children. The only government provided for the increasing number of noncitizens came from federal judges and other government officials serving in Indian Territory. Increasingly the noncitizens demanded that the federal government change the system so they could own land, educate their children, and enjoy the general benefits of a government in which they would have a voice.

The federal government answered these demands by preparing Indian Territory for some form of statehood. A basic step was taken in 1871 when Congress adopted the act providing that no new treaties would be made with the Indian tribes and that all Indians were thereafter subject to the laws of Congress.

The federal government had been taking away the powers of the Five Civilized Tribes since the Civil War. The Federal District Court at Fort Smith, with the authority to rule on certain crimes committed in Indian Territory, was expanded in 1889 with the creation of a federal court at Muskogee. This court ruled in all cases of offenses against the laws of the United States that were not punishable by death or imprisonment at hard labor. The federal district courts also had authority over any civil dispute involving an Indian and a non-Indian.

For more serious criminal cases, formerly tried at Fort Smith, the southern parts of the Choctaw and the Chickasaw nations came under the Federal District Court at Paris, Texas. Cases from the other Indian nations were still tried in the Fort Smith federal court. In 1890, Congress created three federal courts for Indian Territory variously located at Muskogee, South McAlester, and Ardmore. The act setting up these courts applied the laws of Arkansas to Indian Territory in all cases except those in which all parties involved were Indian. The Indian courts continued to have jurisdiction over such cases.

Congress had passed the Dawes Allotment Act in 1887. This act provided for the end of tribal ownership in common of Indian lands and required each Indian to accept an allotment of individual land. The Five Civilized Tribes were exempted from this act, but the reservations of western Oklahoma were done away with under its terms.

Then, in 1893, Congress passed a law that applied the Dawes Allotment Act to the Five Civilized Tribes. This allowed the president to appoint a commission to negotiate with the leaders of these tribes to give each Indian citizen an allotment from the tribal lands. The commission, called the Dawes Commission, took its name from its first chairman, Henry L. Dawes of Massachusetts.

In 1895, Congress ordered the United States Geological Survey to prepare a survey plat of Indian Territory as a further step toward allotment and individual ownership.

The Dawes Commission traveled to Indian Territory and spent much time talking with leaders of the Five Civilized Tribes in an attempt to persuade them to submit to allotment voluntarily. The Indian citizens liked their old system of common ownership and were opposed to accepting allotments. To pressure the Indian leaders to agree to allotment, Congress regularly increased the powers of the Dawes Commission to the point that by 1895 this group could proceed with preparing tribal rolls and making land assignments to individual Indians without tribal approval.

The leaders of the Five Civilized Tribes gradually came to terms. The Choctaws and the Chickasaws were the first tribes to sign allotment agreements. In 1897 leaders from these two tribes signed an allotment pact with the Dawes Commission known as the Atoka Agreement. By 1902 leaders of all the Five Civilized Tribes had signed allotment agreements.

Allotments varied in size. Each Choctaw and Chickasaw received about 320 acres. Each Cherokee was assigned about 110 acres; Creeks received about 160 acres each and Seminoles got 120 acres each. The Cherokee, Creek, and Seminole freedmen and their descendants shared equally with the Indians in size of allotment. Choctaw and Chickasaw freedmen and their descendants each received an allotment of 40 acres. There were no surplus lands for sale to homesteaders in this part of Indian Territory, as had been the case for most of western Indian Territory.

There was mild opposition to accepting allotments among the Choctaws and Chickasaws, but among the Seminoles there was no outward opposition. Cherokee full bloods opposed allotments. Many from this group banded together under the name of an ancient Cherokee secret society, the Keetoowah, and refused to accept allotments. They declared they would continue to hold their lands in common. Federal marshals entered the Cherokee Nation to assist the Dawes Commission in making land assignments to this group. This was finally done peacefully.

The greatest resistance came from the Creeks. The old leadership viewpoint, which had flourished under Opothleyaholo, Sands, and Isparhechar, was kept alive by Chitto Harjo, called Crazy Snake. He led the Creeks' resistance to allotment. Chitto Harjo formed a separate government for his followers. They arrested and whipped Creeks who accepted allotments. They also refused to cooperate with the Dawes Commission or to accept allotments for themselves. Cavalry from Fort Reno rode through the Creek Nation and arrested Chitto Harjo's followers. They were tried in federal court at Muskogee and, faced with the threat of jail, most of them accepted allotments.

Another roadblock to statehood in some form for Indian Territory was the presence of five functioning Indian governments. A major step toward ending tribal government was accomplished in 1898 when Congress passed the Curtis Act. It provided for the survey and incorporation of towns, gave townsmen the right to vote, authorized the establishment of free public schools, and abolished tribal courts. All persons in Indian Territory, Indian and non-In-

Isparhechar, Creek traditionalist who opposed his nation becoming a part of Oklahoma.

dian, were thereafter subject to federal law and the laws of Arkansas. The allotment agreements with the tribes had provided for an end to tribal governments by 1906. This was confirmed by the Curtis Act.

The status of the citizens of the Five Civilized Tribes had been drastically changed. Each was now, through allotment, the owner of a piece of landed property. Each person transferred citizenship from his tribe to that of the United States. His tribal government was being phased out. His courts no longer functioned. All processes of his tribal government would end during 1906. Tribal leaders saw that statehood would come in some form in the American Union. Most of these leaders dreaded being attached to Oklahoma

Territory to form the proposed state of Oklahoma. In 1902 they began to meet and attempt to stop the plan to join the Twin Territories into a single state. They began to work for what was called "double statehood," a plan that would create two states, rather than one, from the Twin Territories.

Principal chiefs W. C. Rogers of the Cherokee Nation, Pleasant Porter of the Creek Nation, and Green McCurtain of the Choctaw Nation planned a meeting during 1905 for the purpose of discussing statehood for Indian Territory. Their efforts resulted in a convention that met at Muskogee on August 21, 1905. Its purpose was to prepare a constitution for an Indian state to be called Sequoyah.

The voters of Indian Territory selected 182 delegates to the convention. The delegates met and elected Pleasant Porter president of the convention, and they elected a vice-president from each of the five nations: W. C. Rogers, Cherokees; Green McCurtain, Choctaws; John F. Brown, Seminoles; Charles N. Haskell, Creeks; and William H. ("Alfalfa Bill") Murray, Chickasaws. Haskell, a non-Indian, was a businessman from Muskogee. Murray, an intermarried Chickasaw, was tribal attorney for the Chickasaw Nation. Alexander Posey, Creek poet and editor, was elected secretary of the convention.

The convention delegates drafted a constitution for the proposed state of Sequoyah. Its content followed the familiar pattern of the national and state constitutions by having separation of powers by dividing the functions of government into three branches—executive, legislative, and judicial, a system of checks and balances, and a bill of rights. A referendum or vote of the people of Indian Territory on the Sequoyah constitution resulted in its approval by a wide margin. Then tribal leaders carried the constitution and an all-Indian statehood proposal to Washington, D. C., and laid the plan before Congress.

Oklahoma Statehood

CONGRESS took no action on the plan because it finally had made its decision on the question of Oklahoma statehood. During 1906, Congress adopted a measure, the Hamilton Statehood Bill, which provided for the joining of the Twin Territories into a single state named Oklahoma.

The Hamilton Statehood Bill was signed into law on June 16, 1906, and became the Oklahoma Enabling Act (the law creating a state). This act, along with the Oklahoma Organic Act of 1890 and the Curtis Act of 1898, are the three most important federal laws in the development of Oklahoma as a state.

The Oklahoma Enabling Act of 1906 called for the people of Indian Territory and Oklahoma Territory to elect delegates to a constitutional convention. The seats of the convention were allocated on the following formula: Fifty-five delegates were to be elected from Indian Territory, fifty-five delegates were to be elected from the Oklahoma Territory, and two delegates were to be elected from the Osage Nation.

In writing this constitution, the delegates, were required to include the following things: (1) set up a republican form of government like the other states; (2) establish religious liberty; (3) prohibit polygamous marriages

120

Chitto Harjo (Crazy Snake), Creek traditionalist who opposed Indian lands being allotted to individuals.

Pleasant Porter, Creek chief, president of the Sequoyah Convention.

Green McCurtain, Choctaw chief, a Sequoyah Convention leader.

Allen Wright, Choctaw chief who was first to suggest the name "Oklahoma."

Oklahoma Constitutional Convention, Guthrie, Oklahoma Territory.

(marrying more than one person at a time); and (4) guarantee the right to vote regardless of race, color, or previous condition of servitude (slavery). In writing the constitution, the delegates also were required by Congress to provide for prohibition (no alcoholic liquor allowed) in the Indian Territory and the Osage Nation for twenty-one years. The new state capital would be located at Guthrie, and no change in this location would be considered until 1913.

During the summer of 1906, the Twin Territories were divided into 112 districts. The election of delegates was held on November 4, 1906. Democrats won 100 of the convention seats; Republicans won 12 seats. Thus the Democrats won the privilege of organizing the convention. Leaders of their party from the Twin Territories were the leaders of the convention.

Henry Asp, a Guthrie attorney, was the leader of the Republican minority. Charles N. Haskell was the leader of the Democratic majority. William H. Murray was elected president of the convention and Pete Hanraty, labor leader from Indian Territory, was elected vice-president. Haskell won the post of majority leader, and Henry Johnston of Perry was elected Democratic caucus (meeting) chairman.

The convention met at Guthrie on November 20, 1906, and was in session until July, 1907. The delegates wrote a constitution that reflected the reform thought of the times. The constitution called for the executive, legislative, and judicial branches of government; a system of checks and balances to prevent any one of the branches from becoming too powerful, including veto and impeachment powers; and a bill of rights. The document was very long, in fact,

122

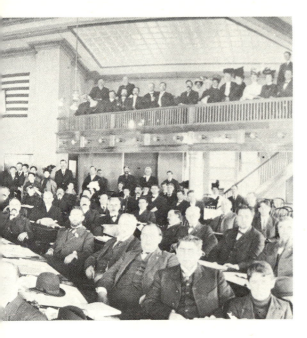

the longest state constitution in the nation. The delegates spelled out carefully in the text of the constitution their intent, believing this would reduce the necessity for interpretation by the judiciary.

The executive branch was to consist of twelve elected officials. For the times this was a reform in that it reduced the appointive power of the governor and made the officials responsible to the people. The judiciary, consisting of justices of the supreme court, justices of the district, county, and municipal courts, and justices of the peace, also were elective positions and thus responsible to the people.

Another reform for the times written into the constitution provided that the governor would be elected in off-years. Thus they would be unable to win election on the popularity of the presidential candidate. The governor's term was

set at four years, and he could not succeed himself. The intent of the delegates was that the legislature, the voice of the people, would be the most powerful agency of government.

The constitution created a bicameral body, with the house members to serve for two-year terms and the members of the senate to serve for four-year terms. Legislative power was shared with the people through adoption of the initiative and the referendum. This meant that 8 percent of the voters could initiate legislation by petition; 15 percent of the voters could initiate a constitutional amendment by petition; and 5 percent of the voters could obtain a referendum on an act of the legislature.

Social reforms written into the constitution included an eight-hour day on public works and in the mines and prohibition of child and convict labor. Primary elections were to be the method for nominating candidates for public office. Railroads, large businesses, utilities, and trusts were to be controlled by a corporation commission. The prohibition of alcohol as a reform measure, to be applied to the entire state, was submitted to the people in the form of an amendment separate from the constitution.

Territorial leaders arranged for an election to be held in the Twin Territories on September 17, 1907. The people were to vote on the constitution, the prohibition amendment, and the candidates for public office. The candidates winning election would not take office until the constitution was approved by Congress and Oklahoma was admitted to the Union.

Candidates for governor included Charles N. Haskell, the Democratic candidate; Frank Frantz (governor of

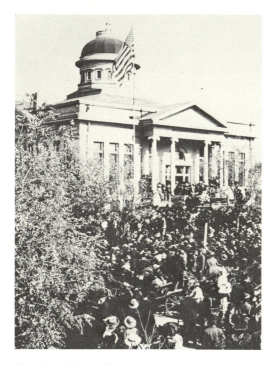

Statehood Day, November 16, 1907, Guthrie, Oklahoma.

Governor Charles N. Haskell.

Oklahoma Territory), the Republican candidate; and C. C. Ross, the Socialist party candidate. Haskell won the gubernatorial election with 137,599 votes to 110,292 votes for Frantz, and 10,000 votes for Ross. On the question of the constitution, Twin Territory voters ratified it by a vote of 180,333 to 73,059. The separate prohibition amendment carried by a vote of 130,361 to 112,258.

In this election Oklahomans also elected their first United States congressmen. The Oklahoma Enabling Act had given the new state five seats in the House of Representatives. Four Democrats, Scott Ferris (Lawton), James Davenport (Vinita), Charles D. Carter (Ardmore), and Elmer Fulton (Oklahoma City), and one Republican, Bird S. McGuire (Pawnee, former territorial dele-

gate) won election to Congress. At that time, United States senators were elected by state legislatures. Thus these two positions could not be filled until Oklahoma was admitted to the Union and the First Legislature could meet.

Oklahoma, on the threshold of admission to the Union, appeared to fulfill the theme set for it in a *Saturday Evening Post* (a popular weekly magazine) article describing the work of the Oklahoma Constitutional Convention: "It was not merely the birth of a new state, it was the birth of a new kind of state." On November 16, 1907, President Theodore Roosevelt signed the Oklahoma statehood proclamation, and the message was telegraphed to Guthrie. A large crowd had gathered for the occasion. Just before noon Charles N.

Haskell took the oath of office and was installed as Oklahoma's first governor. As a symbol of the joining of the Twin Territories into the new state of Oklahoma, a woman representing Indian Territory and a man from Oklahoma Territory were joined in a mock wedding.

Study Aids

Explain the significance of each term or phrase listed below:

1. *Cherokee Tobacco Case*
2. Dawes Allotment Act
3. Curtis Act
4. Sequoyah Convention
5. Glenn Pool
6. Dawes Commission

Identify each of these persons:

1. Pete Hanraty
2. Chitto Harjo
3. Henry Asp
4. Alexander Posey
5. Frank Frantz
6. Henry L. Dawes

On an outline map of Oklahoma locate the following places:

1. Krebs
2. Peoria
3. Cleveland
4. Ardmore
5. Lincolnville
6. Picher

Use the suggestions below for study guides:

1. Summarize the economic development of Indian Territory on the eve of statehood.
2. Discuss the work of the Dawes Commission.
3. Explain how the Curtis Act affected Indian Territory.
4. Give the terms of the Oklahoma Enabling Act.
5. Describe the work of the Oklahoma Constitutional Convention.

For Further Reading

Goble, Danney. *Progressive Oklahoma: The Making of a New Kind of State.* Norman, 1980.

Ellis, Albert H. *A History of the Constitutional Convention.* Muskogee, 1907.

Forbes, Gerald. *Guthrie: Oklahoma's First Capital.* Norman, 1938.

Franklin, Jimmie L. *The Blacks in Oklahoma.* Norman, 1980.

Hurst, Irvin. *The Forty-sixth Star: A History of Oklahoma's Constitutional Convention and Early Statehood.* Oklahoma City, 1957.

Maxwell, Amos D. *The Sequoyah Constitutional Convention.* Boston, 1953.

Journal of the Oklahoma Constitutional Convention. Muskogee, 1907.

Chapter 9. **OKLAHOMA STATEHOOD**

Character of the New State

WHEN Oklahoma was admitted to the Union in 1907, it had about 1½ million people. These Oklahomans came from different social, economic, religious, political, and ethnic backgrounds. Probably no state entered the Union with such variety. Joining the original Oklahomans —Indians and blacks—were white and black settlers from all sections of the country.

Most of the settlers in the Indian Territory section of the new state were from Missouri, Arkansas, Alabama, Mississippi, Louisiana, and Texas. In the western half of the state, the former Oklahoma Territory, great numbers of settlers had come from Kansas, Nebraska, and the states of the North and East. Many people from Texas also came into Oklahoma Territory. All these people brought with them the cultural traits —the attitudes, the language, dress and food habits, the economic practices, the

religion, and the politics—of their home regions.

The cultural traits they introduced into Oklahoma came to share a place with the local ways of Oklahoma's original settlers, the Indians and the blacks. The cultural mix of early Oklahoma was made even more colorful by the presence of foreign communities. German Mennonite settlements, Czech towns and farming communities, as well as Russian, Polish, Scottish, Welsh, Italian, and Greek settlements, particularly in the coal-mining areas of Indian Territory, further added to Oklahoma's ethnic-cultural diversity.

At statehood Oklahoma was a mixed ethnic and cultural community. This made it an interesting contrast to surrounding states. It did, however, to a large degree follow the regional and national pattern of the times in terms of where the people lived and worked. Mining, lumbering, and some limited manufacturing took place in the new

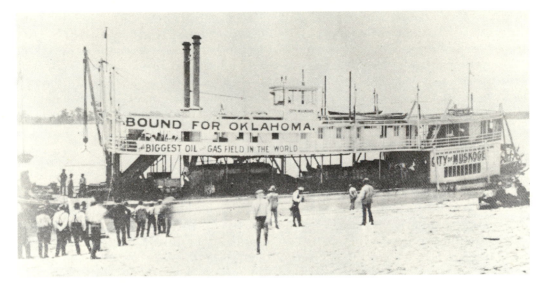

People from other states began to come to the new state of Oklahoma.

state. Oklahoma had several fast-growing cities, particularly Guthrie, Oklahoma City, Tulsa, and Muskogee. Most Oklahomans, however, lived in the country on farms. Oklahoma was about 75 percent rural and about 25 percent urban. Most Oklahomans supported themselves by farming and ranching.

The New Government

TAKING CARE of the needs of Oklahoma's varied communities was a difficult and challenging task. The new Oklahoma government, formed under the Constitution of 1906, had responsibility for guiding the new state. It had to provide leadership and direction, and it had to protect the rights and promote the varied interests of its people.

Officials who served in various positions in the government, most of them elected, were members of political parties. The main political parties in Oklahoma at the time of statehood were the Republican, the Democratic, and the Socialist. Most candidates running for public office in Oklahoma, whether local, state, or national, campaigned as Republicans, Democrats, or Socialists.

In the 1907 election, Democratic leaders of the constitutional convention were elected to high positions in the new state government. As stated earlier, Haskell, the convention majority floor leader, was elected governor. Several convention leaders won seats in Oklahoma's First Legislature. William H. Murray, the president of the constitutional convention, was elected to the house of representatives. The Democratic majority of the house elected Murray as speaker. Henry S. Johnston, also a convention leader, won a seat in the state senate, and members of that body selected him president pro tempore.

Democrats also won all elective state offices, including lieutenant governor and secretary of state. In most local elections of commissioners, sheriffs, and other elective county officials, Democrats were winners.

Winning control of the First Legislature was an important victory for the Democratic party. The First Legislature would be the most important one in Oklahoma history because it would write and pass the basic laws that would activate the state constitution and, in a sense, launch the new state. The Democratic party could then give the state laws the same direction and policies as the Democratic party's values.

For the long run, winning control of the First Legislature would allow the Democratic party to create the machinery in state government (staffed with members of its party) to build the party's strength, assure continual election of its members, and thus extend its power. One example was in the passing of laws providing for state and local elections, creating state and local election boards, and setting procedures for elections, including registration of voters.

The First Legislature largely achieved this goal, and through most of its political history Oklahoma has carried the image of a one-party state. The political scene has been dominated by the Democratic party. Every governor was a Democrat until 1962 when Henry Bellmon, a Republican, won election as Oklahoma's chief executive. In addition, most Oklahoma congressmen and United States senators, as well as most of the elected officials below the office of governor, have been candidates from the Democratic party.

In those American states where the one-party system has been strong, the key to control of state politics has been control of the legislature. In Oklahoma political history, the legislature from 1907 to the present, with one minor exception, has been controlled by the Democratic party. In 1920 the Oklahoma Republican party won control of the house of representatives, although Oklahoma Democrats continued control of the state senate.

The Work of the First Legislature

OKLAHOMA's First Legislature was in session for a long time, nearly six months. In that time it adopted those basic laws required to fulfill the constitutional charges and to organize the new state. The state government functioned at the state capital at Guthrie, the site of the capital of Oklahoma Territory. The new state government had no permanent capitol building. Governor Haskell and other officials in the executive branch had their offices in the Logan County Courthouse and in rented buildings about the town. The legislature met in the Guthrie Masonic Temple. The State Supreme Court and other agencies of state government also worked in rented buildings at Guthrie.

One of the first tasks of the First Legislature was to elect Oklahoma's two United States senators. Until 1913, the United States Constitution required that United States senators be selected by the state legislatures. The legislature, with a Democratic majority, selected two Democrats as Oklahoma's first United States senators—Robert L. Owen and Thomas P. Gore. Owen, a part-Cherokee from Muskogee, had enjoyed a proud career as an official for the federal Bureau of Indian Affairs in Indian Territory. Gore was from Lawton. Blind from an accident in his youth, Gore had become prominent in Oklahoma

128

Territory as an attorney and a leader of the Democratic party. He had a national reputation as a brilliant public speaker.

Among the basic actions of the First Legislature was the adoption of a series of laws creating the Oklahoma judicial system. The Oklahoma court system had a State Supreme Court, a Criminal Court of Appeals (later changed to be the Court of Criminal Appeals), and district, circuit, and superior courts, as well as municipal and justice of the peace courts. The Oklahoma code adopted by the First Legislature provided for staffing the courts, set their jurisdiction (their area of control), and established procedures for legal actions and appeals from lower court rulings.

On matters of local government, the First Legislature settled the question of Oklahoma counties. The number was eventually set at seventy-seven. They also made provision for the organization and administration of these units of local government. The legislature also provided for establishing towns and cities. Provisions were made for state and local elections, as well as the machinery of conducting elections, headed by the State Election Board and county and municipal election boards. The legislature passed laws settling the procedures for selecting state and local election board members, defined their duties, and established the qualifications of voters, particularly regarding residence requirements. The legislature also created the Oklahoma Board of Public Health and a state militia or National Guard.

The First Legislature passed laws setting up a system of free public schools. These laws made provisions for creating school districts, for the sale of bonds

Robert L. Owen, one of Oklahoma's first United States senators.

to build schools, for the construction of school buildings, and for the financing of the schools. The State Board of Education was created to work with the elected state superintendent of public instruction. The school code set requirements for the training and licensing of teachers. The legislature created the Oklahoma Textbook Commission and set up a system for uniform textbooks for the schools of the state. The new school code set certain course-of-study requirements for the public schools, including the teaching of agriculture to all students.

An attendance law was passed that required all children between the ages of eight and sixteen to go to school.

Oklahoma's first superintendent of public instruction was E. D. Cameron. He tried to improve instruction in Oklahoma schools by organizing a four-week teachers' institute in each county of the state. Teachers attended these institutes during the summers to improve their knowledge of the subjects taught. At statehood the terms of schools varied from three months in some districts to nine months in others.

Another basic step taken by the First Legislature was passage of a series of laws to produce money to pay the costs of government. This included a 2 percent gross revenue tax on pipelines, coal mines, and telegraph lines. A ½ percent gross production tax on oil, railroads, telephone companies, and electric utilities was also adopted. The new tax code included an inheritance tax to be collected on property as it passed to family members when the owner died.

Oklahoma was one of the first states to adopt an income tax, graduated in relation to income. The first tax rate on incomes ranged from ½ percent on yearly incomes of from $3,000 to $10,000, graded upward to 3½ percent on incomes more than $100,000. The tax code also provided for a tax on personal and real property. The revenue from these taxes was to go for the support of local government and the public schools.

Much of the basic legislation of the First Legislature to launch the new state of Oklahoma was of a progressive, reform kind. The spirit and drive behind this activity came from two sources. One was the personality of Governor Charles N. Haskell. A native of Ohio, this energetic adventurer won and lost several fortunes before coming to Indian Territory, where he developed banks and railroads. He was committed to the theme of the constitutional convention, which was "not just to create a new state, but to create a new kind of state."

The other source for the reform kind of legislation passed by Oklahoma's First Legislature was the times. It was the age of the muckrakers, a time of reform, of improvement, of progressive change. The delegates to the constitutional convention had been caught up in this spirit of the era, and its force continued as an influence upon the members of Oklahoma's First Legislature.

Basic to the economic health and prosperity of the state, the region, and the nation were the banks. In the early twentieth century banks were often unstable. Many times people lacked confidence in their local banks. Bank "runs," or withdrawal of deposits, by citizens because of the fear their money would be lost were common. A bank run could destroy a local bank, and if several banks were involved, this condition could set off an economic depression.

Governor Haskell believed that a strong, well-managed banking system was necessary for business confidence, for the expansion of credit, and for the economic development of the new state. To provide a strong banking system, the governor recommended that the legislature establish a system to protect bank deposits. Out of this came the bank guaranty law. This measure put a 1 percent tax on the daily balances of state banks. This money went into a state fund to protect deposits. The Oklahoma bank guaranty law had the desired effect. It served as an "ancestor" of the present Federal Deposit Insurance Corporation, which protects most bank deposits across the nation.

Other laws adopted by the First Legislature that made Oklahoma for years a pioneer in progressive legislation included a labor reform code. The laws in this group included a safety code for the mines, a child labor law, a factory inspection law, a health and sanitation code, and employer's liability for workers. In addition, laws were passed that set up ways to settle problems in labor disputes; that created public employment agencies; that prohibited unlabeled, convict-made goods; that prohibited any labor contracts restricting workers' rights to join labor unions; that allowed workers to bargain for their pay; and that declared Labor Day a state holiday.

The First Legislature also adopted a series of laws designed to protect the public from wrongdoing by public utilities, trusts, monopolies, and railroads. The Oklahoma Corporation Commission was assigned strong powers to set rates charged the public by these groups and to regulate these businesses. This group of laws also tried to control the influence of pressure groups and lobbyists by requiring them to register with the state, to declare their purpose, and to report regularly to the Corporation Commission.

The prohibition of intoxicating beverages, also regarded as a reform in 1907, came in for a good deal of attention by the First Legislature. Prohibition as a state policy created a problem for legislators and Governor Haskell. It continued to be a problem in state government until its repeal was adopted by Oklahoma voters in 1959. The prohibition law adopted by the First Legislature established an enforcement system. Since the author of the bill was State Senator Richard A. Billups, it was popularly known as the "Billups Booze Bill." The law forbade the manufacture,

Thomas P. Gore, one of Oklahoma's first United States senators.

transportation, sale, and possession of intoxicating beverages. A section of the Liquor Control Act established a system whereby each county was authorized to operate a public store where alcoholic liquors could be purchased with a doctor's prescription. This portion of the Oklahoma Liquor Control Act was repealed in 1908.

The state university, the state agricultural and mechanical college, the normal school, and other public institutions created by territorial legislatures were in the old Oklahoma Territory portion of the state. The First Legislature began a program, continued by other legislatures, to balance the location of higher education institutions by authorizing the building of additional ones over the state. During the First Legislature, a college for women was established at Chickasha, a school for the deaf at Sulphur, a school of mines at Wilburton, an orphanage at Pryor, and a mental hospital at Vinita.

Laws were adopted to put into effect the direct legislation features of the constitution. These pertained to the initiative and referendum provisions of the constitution by which qualified voters could initiate and adopt laws, as well as repeal laws adopted by the legislature.

If the First Legislature was progressive in most ways, it was prejudiced concerning race. This was shown by its adoption of a "Jim Crow" code for Oklahoma. Federal law and court decisions permitted the separation of the white and black races in those times. The Oklahoma segregation code required separation of the races in public places. Separate railway cars and waiting rooms, separate toilet facilities and drinking fountains, and separate schools for white and black children had to be provided. Marriage between white and black was forbidden.

Black leaders throughout Oklahoma protested the Jim Crow laws. By resolutions adopted in public meetings from Muskogee to Lawton, blacks spoke against the legislature and the unjust racial laws that body had adopted. Despite black protests, statutes separating the races in education, and in Oklahoma society generally, were enforced.

The Second Legislature

OKLAHOMANS participated in their first presidential election in 1908. In the state, the Democratic candidate, William J. Bryan, defeated the Republican candidate, William H. Taft. Taft, however, won nationally. In this election Oklahoma voters elected new United States congressmen and a new legislature. The Democratic party won a majority in both houses of the Second Legislature. One of the new house members was A. C. Hamlin, a black from Guthrie. He was elected on the Republican ticket.

Oklahoma's Second Legislature continued the work of the First Legislature in completing the organization of the new state government. It created the Oklahoma Board of Affairs, the purchasing agency for all government departments and institutions. It strengthened the bank guaranty law by increasing the levy on state banks to 5 percent of the daily deposits of each bank.

Additional institutions were established by the Second Legislature. These included normal schools (later called teachers' colleges, later called state colleges and today called state universities) at Ada, Durant, and Tahlequah, and the Panhandle Agriculture Institute at Goodwell. There was to be a mental hospital at Enid, a reformatory near Pauls Valley, and state prisons at McAlester and at Granite.

From early territorial days, Oklahoma criminals had been sent to the Kansas penitentiary at Lansing. There they were required to work in the coal mines to pay for their keep. Kate Barnard, a well-known reformer and womens' rights leader, had been elected to the office of state commissioner of the Department of Charities and Corrections. She visited the Oklahoma prisoners at Lansing and observed firsthand the bad conditions in which they lived. She returned to the state capital to demand that proper facilities be constructed in the state and that Oklahoma's prisoners be kept there.

The governor and the legislature responded with the necessary funds. The Oklahoma prisoners at Lansing were transported in heavily guarded railway cars to a site near McAlester where they were put to work building the walls and buildings that became the state prison.

The Democratic leaders in the Second Legislature added to the Oklahoma Jim Crow code by limiting black voting. Many states in the South at this time had amendments to their constitutions and laws called the "grandfather clauses." These clauses denied voting rights to most blacks. Oklahoma Democratic leaders were concerned at the increase in Republican voting strength in the 1908 election. Among other things, of the five Oklahoma seats in Congress, the Republicans had won three. This improvement in Republican strength was blamed on an increase in black voters.

A bill was prepared to be sent to Oklahoma voters. It provided that to be registered for voting one had to prove that he could read and write parts of the state constitution. Left out of this provision were the descendants of persons who were eligible to vote on January 1, 1866. This exemption explains the name "grandfather clause." The bill had the effect of excluding blacks from voting in two ways. First, election board officials could make the literacy test on the state constitution as difficult as they chose. Second, few if any of the blacks' ancestors had voted on January 1, 1866. The measure was approved by Oklahoma voters in 1910 by a 10,000-vote majority.

The Latter Part of Haskell's Term

THREE THINGS stand out during the last two years of Governor Haskell's term. These were the strict enforcement of the prohibition law, the effective control of railroads and trusts, and the moving of the state capital.

The bootlegging and manufacture of illegal whisky, called moonshine, flourished. Often a pact existed between the local police and the bootleggers, and no arrests were made. Governor Haskell, determined to enforce the prohibition law in all portions of the state, directed State Attorney General Charles J. West to "dry up" the state. West acted promptly. Grand juries and state lawyers brought charges that resulted in the removal of those county commissioners, sheriffs, and judges who were in league with moonshiners and bootleggers.

The Corporation Commission had the duty and the power to regulate trusts, monopolies, utilities, and railroads to protect the public from exploitation and to require effective service. Jack Love of Woodward was the first chairman of the Corporation Commission. He energetically enforced the laws and rules that applied to railroads, utilities, and other public enterprises within the state.

The railroads were very powerful during this period. State rates for passenger fares were two cents per mile. A fierce contest developed between the railroads, whose owners objected to this rate, and the Corporation Commission, which was determined to enforce it. The Commission won largely because of Love's dedication to the public interest. The victory over the railroads made Jack Love a popular hero in a day when there were few cars and the public depended on the railroads for transportation.

Of all his daring actions, Governor Haskell's most dramatic was in 1910. In a swift night-time move, he personally changed the state capital from Guthrie to Oklahoma City.

Oklahoma City civic and political leaders had worked for years to have this city named the capital. The Oklahoma Enabling Act of 1906 had required that the capital for the new state be at Guthrie at least until 1913. Guthrie had always been a Republican stronghold, and Democratic leaders throughout the state favored moving the capital to some other location. Governor Haskell supported this move for several reasons. One was his resentment at the Guthrie newspapers, which were strongly Republican in their editorial comment.

With Haskell's encouragement, a bill concerning the location of the capital was submitted to the voters on June 11, 1910, with no mention made as to when the move would occur if approved. The cities from which the voters had to choose were Guthrie, Oklahoma City, and Shawnee. In the election, Oklahoma City received a strong majority of votes.

On the night of the election when the voting results were tabulated, Haskell, who was away from the capital, sent his secretary to Guthrie for certain files of papers and the official state seal. These were carried to Oklahoma City. On the morning of June 12, shocked and surprised Oklahomans read in their newspapers a proclamation issued by Governor Haskell that Oklahoma City was the capital of the state. Haskell, with his secretary and the official state seal, established headquarters, and thus a temporary capital, in the Huckins Hotel in Oklahoma City.

Leaders at Guthrie sued in federal court seeking to force the governor to move the capital back to their city. They claimed that the removal action violated the Oklahoma Enabling Act requirement that the capital remain at Guthrie at least until 1913. Haskell's attorneys answered that Oklahoma was now a state and could not be bound by a law of Congress on what was a purely local matter. The United States Supreme Court upheld Haskell's action.

For several years the business of the state government was carried on in rented buildings and a school in Oklahoma City. At a special session of the legislature in November, 1910, Governor Haskell submitted plans for a new capitol This led to a gift of 650 acres of land and a $100,000 bond from Oklahoma City citizens. This provided the beginnings for the present state government headquarters completed in 1917.

Governor Haskell and the First and Second legislatures had launched Oklahoma's new state government. With the exception of the Jim Crow code, they left to future governors and legislatures a legacy of constructive leadership and positive action.

Study Aids

Explain the significance of each term or phrase listed below:

1. Urban
2. One-party system
3. Prohibition
4. Jim Crow code
5. Bank guaranty law
6. Grandfather clause

Identify each of these persons:

1. Robert L. Owen
2. Henry S. Johnston
3. E. D. Cameron
4. Thomas P. Gore
5. A. C. Hamlin
6. C. C. Ross

On an outline map of Oklahoma locate the following places:

1. Guymon
2. Miami
3. Woodward
4. Broken Bow
5. Alva
6. Haskell

Use the suggestions below for study guides:

1. Discuss the results of the election of September 17, 1907.
2. Show how prohibition was enforced in Oklahoma.
3. Describe the means by which Oklahoma blacks were segregated and stripped of their voting rights.
4. Outline the establishment of Oklahoma public institutions between 1907 and 1910.
5. Tell about the changing of the Oklahoma state capital.

For Further Reading

Blachly, Frederick F., and Miriam E. Oatman. *The Government of Oklahoma.* Oklahoma City, 1924.

Brooks, John S. *First Administration of Oklahoma.* Oklahoma City, 1908.

Bryant, Keith L. *Alfalfa Bill Murray.* Norman, 1968.

Fowler, Oscar P. *The Haskell Regime: The Intimate Life of Charles Nathaniel Haskell.* Oklahoma City, 1933.

Franklin, Jimmie Lewis. *Born Sober: Prohibition in Oklahoma, 1907-1959.* Norman, 1971.

———. *The Blacks in Oklahoma.* Norman, 1980.

Oklahoma Almanac. Oklahoma City, 1908.

Chapter 10. **THE OKLAHOMA POLITICAL SCENE TO 1930**

Legislative Versus Executive

GOVERNOR HASKELL had provided the new state of Oklahoma strong leadership. From 1910 to 1930, though, no governor was able to control the state legislature and give direction to state development as he had done. Beginning in 1910, the power in state government and politics shifted to the legislature, and this body controlled state government by threatening officials in the executive branch of government with impeachment (removal from office).

Not until William H. ("Alfalfa Bill") Murray won the governor's office in 1930 was the executive branch able to regain power. In the period from 1910 to 1930 the legislative and executive branches, rather than working together to do what was best for the state, fought for control of state government. The contest became so bitter at times that chaos ruled until, finally, the legisla- ture won by impeaching and removing from office those governors who tried to be strong leaders. In the process, the people were the losers because things that were needed for the good of the state were not accomplished.

In 1910, Oklahoma's second election for governor was held. Lee Cruce, an Ardmore banker, won the Democratic nomination. Joseph McNeal, a banker from Guthrie, won the Republican nomination. J. T. Crumbie was the Socialist party nominee. Cruce won in the general election in November, 1910. Democrats also won a majority of seats in the state legislature and three of the five Oklahoma seats in the United States Congress.

The Cruce Administration

GOVERNOR CRUCE was from Kentucky. Trained as an attorney, he practiced law and engaged in banking at Ardmore in Indian Territory days. His previous political experience included an unsuccessful attempt at the Democratic nomination for governor in 1907, and a term as regent at the University of Oklahoma. Governor Cruce was a pioneer in the movement to abolish capital punishment—the execution of condemned criminals. Thus during his term of office he pardoned or changed to life imprisonment the terms of those persons condemned to death.

Among the important things that happened during Governor Cruce's term was progress on the state capitol building. Having resolved that the state capital would be Oklahoma City, Cruce appointed the three-member State Capitol Commission. The legislature appropriated $750,000 for construction, plans were drawn, and a contract let for construction to begin during the summer of 1914.

Governor Cruce was committed to saving money. Oklahoma's First Legislature had allowed $4 million for state operations. Cruce's first legislature, Oklahoma's Third Legislature, allowed nearly $9 million for state operations. He tried to reduce this by combining state agencies and their jobs and abolishing certain state colleges and other public institutions across the state.

Legislative leaders were angered by the governor's tampering with local interests. They were also unhappy at his several vetoes (refusing to sign a law), including a bill providing for redrawing congressional boundaries. The number of seats Oklahoma was allowed in Congress had been increased to eight as a result of an increase in the state's population. The legislature was dominated by Democrats. They had adopted a plan that redrew the state into eight

Governor Lee Cruce.

congressional districts in such manner that Republican voting strength was minimized. Cruce regarded this gerrymandering (redrawing boundaries to help a particular group) as unfair to Republican voters, and he vetoed the bill. As a result, Oklahoma's three new seats in the Congress were filled by election on a statewide basis in 1912. Before he left office in 1913, Cruce signed a new bill establishing eight congressional districts. This plan remained unchanged until 1951.

The number of automobiles was increasing in Oklahoma, and the driving public demanded improved roads. On Cruce's recommendation, in 1911 the legislature established the Oklahoma Department of Highways. Sidney Suggs from Ardmore was named director. Income for the new state agency to finance public roads came from an annual one-dollar license fee charged for each automobile.

This period was a time of attempted moral reform through the adoption of "blue laws." These were laws written by cities to enforce Sunday closing of businesses, and to prevent prize fighting, gambling, bootlegging, and horse racing. On several occasions, Governor Cruce supported local reformers by calling out the militia to stop horse races and prize fights. On April 14, 1914, he declared martial law in Tulsa to stop a scheduled horse race.

In 1912, Oklahomans went to the polls to participate in their second presidential election. They gave the Democratic candidate, Woodrow Wilson, a majority of their votes over the Republican candidate, William H. Taft, and the Progressive (Bull Moose) candidate, Theodore Roosevelt. Eugene Debs, the Socialist candidate for the presidency, received 46,262 votes in Oklahoma. Robert L. Owen, incumbent United States senator and Democratic candidate for reelection, retained his seat in the Senate in a contest with J. T. Dickerson, the Republican candidate, and John G. Wills, the Socialist candidate.

The mostly Democratic Fourth Legislature, elected in 1912, met in anger at the governor for his attempt to abolish public institutions in their districts as a part of his economy program. They also were angry with Cruce for his opposition to their congressional redistricting plan. Thus this legislature took revenge on the governor and the executive branch of government by investigating executive departments and impeaching officeholders. The governor himself escaped impeachment by a single vote in the investigating committee. The state auditor, state insurance commissioner, and state printer were impeached. The auditor and the insurance commissioner resigned. The senate convicted the state printer on a charge of approving illegal claims against state funds, and he was removed from office.

Much of Governor Cruce's program for state development was stopped by the hostile legislature. He did, however, open up several areas of state development. Creation of the State Department of Highways has been noted. He also saw the need for long-range planning to promote industrial development in Oklahoma in order to vary the economy of the young state. Through his efforts, state and federal government surveys were made of Oklahoma coal, oil, and other mineral resources, and water-power locations.

Oklahoma's third gubernatorial election occurred in 1914. In the Democratic primary, Robert L. Williams, chief justice of the Oklahoma Supreme Court, was opposed by several candidates. Among them was Al Jennings, a colorful outlaw who had served a prison term for train robbery. Williams won the Democratic nomination. In the November general election he defeated Republican candidate John Fields and Socialist candidate Fred Holt. The strength of the Socialist party in Oklahoma at this time was shown by Holt's receiving 52,703 votes. Williams's vote was 100,597 and Fields's was 95,905.

In the first popular election for United States senator, Democratic incumbent Thomas P. Gore defeated Republican John Burford and Socialist Pat Nagle. In the congressional elections, Democrats won seven of Oklahoma's eight seats. The legislature continued with a Democratic majority in both houses.

The Williams Administration

GOVERNOR WILLIAMS was born in Alabama. He had come to Oklahoma during Indian Territory days. He practiced law at Durant and was a delegate to the constitutional convention. He had been elected to the Supreme Court in 1907 where he served as chief justice. Oklahoma's third governor was a strong-willed person and a good administrator. Perhaps he would have restored the power and prestige of the governor's office had it not been that much of his time was absorbed in pulling together the state's resources and manpower for World War I.

Today, Oklahoma legislatures operate under the budget-balancing amendment, which requires the state to live within its income. This means that the legislature can spend no more money than is available in expected revenue. Until this amendment was adopted in 1941, the legislature regularly authorized spending by state agencies in excess of revenue available. This resulted in the state going into debt each year. Governor Williams tried to reduce the state debt by passing laws to increase taxes, which in turn would increase state income. The governor also reduced state spending by consolidating state agencies and abolishing certain state institutions, including several of the district agricultural colleges.

The legislature continued its investigation and impeachment campaign against the executive branch of state government. A corporation commissioner was impeached, convicted, and removed from office on a charge of ac-

Governor Robert L. Williams.

cepting loans from companies that appeared before him. An insurance commissioner, impeached on a charge of improper relations with insurance companies, was acquitted.

During the Williams administration the state highway system was expanded. This was made possible by allowing more money for the new Department of Highways, and by the state beginning a sharing program with the federal government in the financing of highways. In a sense, the federal highway system in Oklahoma began during the Williams administration.

Social and economic legislation adopted by the Fifth Legislature included a minimum hour law for women in industry and welfare laws to support widows and orphans. This included a payment of ten dollars per month to be administered by the county commissioners.

The attempt by the Oklahoma Democratic party to restrict blacks from voting by means of the grandfather clause came under attack during the Williams administration. State election officials in several counties had been charged by federal grand juries for violating federal election laws by enforcing the grandfather clause. A number of officials were convicted and sentenced to prison. Later they were pardoned, but the decisions were appealed to the United States Supreme Court. That body in 1915 handed down the *Guinn* v. *United States* decision, which declared the Oklahoma grandfather clause null and void because it violated the Fifteenth Amendment to the Federal Constitution. After the *Guinn* case, Oklahoma Election Board officials attempted to keep blacks from voting by setting very brief registration periods for voters not already eligible. This included most blacks.

A highlight of the Williams administration was moving the scattered state agencies in Oklahoma City into the new capitol building, which was completed in 1917.

World War I began in Europe in 1914, but it did not directly involve Oklahomans until three years later. An important event before America entered the war was the presidential election of 1916. Democratic President Woodrow Wilson, opposed by Republican candidate Charles E. Hughes and Socialist candidate Eugene Debs, won in Oklahoma and the nation. Democrats won six of the congressional seats and heavy majorities in both houses of the state legislature.

Even before the United States entered World War I in 1917, Oklahoma fighting men were on active duty. The state militia had been a part of the force serving under General John Pershing to crush the Pancho Villa outbreaks on the Mexican border. Governor Williams pledged the state's resources to assist President Wilson in fighting the war when this nation entered the fray in 1917. The governor assisted in calling up troops through local draft boards; he also encouraged maximum farm production, promoted the saving of food and fuel for troops in Europe, and led Liberty Bond drives to help finance the war. More than 91,000 Oklahomans, including 5,000 blacks, saw active duty. Of these, 1,064 were killed in action, 502 were reported missing in action, 4,154 were wounded, and 710 died from illness.

The illness was usually Spanish influenza, which swept over Europe and the United States. It was rated as the worst outbreak ever to strike Oklahoma. The situation was worsened because more than a third of the state's doctors and even more nurses were with the military. More than 125,000 cases of influenza were reported in the state. Oklahoma Health Commission officials closed churches, schools, movie houses, and other public places, and forbade gatherings of more than twelve people, even for funerals. In some Oklahoma cities all businesses were closed except food stores, bakeries, and laundries. An estimated seven thousand deaths resulted in the state from the influenza epidemic.

The Socialists opposed the war and urged young men to resist being drafted. In eastern Oklahoma during 1915 and 1916 many tenant farmers were orga-

140

nized into a Socialist group called the Working Class Union. During August, 1917, members of this union in Pottawatomie, Seminole, and Hughes counties roamed the countryside burning bridges, barns, and other buildings, and firing upon officers sent to stop them.

Their activities are called the Green Corn Rebellion. Citizen posses broke up the wandering bands of Working Class Union members and arrested several hundred of the resisters. More than four hundred were held in the state penitentiary at McAlester. The prisoners were tried in federal courts for sedition, conspiracy, and resisting the draft. Many were sentenced to prison.

The announcement of the armistice on November 11, 1918, concluding the war in Europe, was greeted with great joy across Oklahoma. Oklahoma troops returned from Europe in 1919 and were met with great enthusiasm in victory parades in Oklahoma City, Tulsa, Enid, and Ardmore.

During the last months of the war in Europe, the 1918 election campaign to select Oklahoma's fourth governor was held. In the primaries, James B. A. Robertson won the Democratic nomination for governor over William H. Murray. In the general election Robertson met and defeated Horace G. McKeever, the Republican candidate, and Patrick S. Nagle, the Socialist candidate. Democratic incumbent United States Senator Robert L. Owen won reelection, defeating Republican candidate W. B. Johnson. Democrats won seven of the eight congressional seats and majorities in both houses of the state legislature. In this election a state constitutional amendment providing for women's suffrage (the right to vote) was adopted.

The Robertson Administration

OKLAHOMA's fourth governor, James B. A. Robertson, was born in Iowa, reared in Kansas, trained as an attorney, and had settled at Chandler during territorial days. He taught school, practiced law, and served as county attorney and as a member of the Oklahoma Supreme Court Commission. Robertson was Oklahoma's first governor from the old Oklahoma Territory part of the state.

One of Governor Robertson's primary interests was expanding the state highway system. He tried but failed to get voter approval for a $50 million bond issue to construct a system of paved roads across the state. Failing on this, he did get enough money for the Department of Highways to construct 1,300 miles of highways. This was more than the miles of highway built by the three previous governors combined.

The generally low standards of Oklahoma schools was a matter of concern for Governor Robertson. A particular problem was the great number of school districts unable to maintain school for more than three to six months each year. His interest led to the appointment of a special commission of state and national educators headed by William T. Bawden of the United States Bureau of Education. This commission was assigned the task of making a study of Oklahoma schools and recommending reforms.

The Bawden Commission Study urged improvement in preparation and certification of teachers, the upgrading of curricula, the beginning of consolidation of rural schools, a subsidized textbook program, and state aid to poorly financed school districts. Lo-

Governor James B. Robertson.

cal and legislative opposition held up many of these recommended changes in the Oklahoma school system until later times. During the second half of the Robertson administration, however, the legislature did appropriate $100,000 in state aid for poor school districts.

The legislature continued its pressure on the executive branch and held a number of impeachment hearings. Governor Robertson himself missed impeachment by only one vote in the house. Lieutenant Governor Martin E. Trapp was impeached on charges that he conducted improper transactions in his private business. During his trial in the state senate the charges were dismissed.

At Robertson's encouragement, the legislature approved the Eighteenth Amendment (national prohibition) and

the Nineteenth Amendment (national women's suffrage).

The second half of Robertson's administration was a time of problems. There occurred a series of crippling strikes, a race riot, and an economic recession. The Oklahoma economy depended primarily on agriculture and oil production. High wartime prices had encouraged farmers to expand and go in debt. Then the postwar decline in grain and beef prices caused extensive foreclosures on farms and bank failures. The state bank guaranty system collapsed because of the strain on its reserves by member-bank withdrawals.

Beginning in 1919, strikes became widespread, and nine thousand miners struck in eastern Oklahoma alone. Robertson sent two regiments of National Guard troops to Henryetta, Coalgate, and McAlester. Martial law was declared in the trouble zone. Labor unrest and strikes spread to the railroads, the building trades, and manufacturing plants.

The theme of disorder and trouble continued in race relations. In Tulsa a black youth was arrested in the spring of 1921 on a charge of molesting a white girl. A mob of whites gathered at the jail, apparently to lynch the accused youth. Violence flared when another mob of blacks sought to protect the prisoner. The conflict spread to the black section of Tulsa where fire gutted two miles of homes and businesses. Seventy blacks and nine whites died in the rioting. Order was restored only by calling out the National Guard and imposing martial law.

Adding to the unrest of this period was the rise of the Ku Klux Klan. By 1921 its membership in Oklahoma was said to number 100,000. The Klan was the champion of white supremacy. Its members claimed to be the "defenders" of traditional white Anglo-Saxon, native-born Protestant values. It was anti-Catholic, anti-Semitic, and anti-Negro. It was opposed to immigration and to involvement of the United States in the League of Nations. It was against labor unions and for business. The Klan, with its symbols, initiations, and secret operations appealed to citizens much like a lodge or club does. The Klan enforced its own code of moral law by warnings, whippings, mutilation, and burning crosses.

The election of 1920 was a turnabout for the one-party Democratic system of Oklahoma. Voters in Oklahoma and the nation were disillusioned with American participation in world affairs. They were opposed to the Wilson plan for the League of Nations. Many people suffered from the postwar economic recession. Republicans campaigned against the League of Nations and against any American participation in it. They promised if elected to return the nation to normalcy and prosperity.

Republican presidential candidate Warren G. Harding carried Oklahoma against Democratic candidate James M. Cox. The incumbent United States Senator Thomas P. Gore lost to Republican John W. Harreld. This was the first time that the Oklahoma Republican party elected a United States senator. Republicans won five of the eight Oklahoma congressional seats and several state offices, including seats on the State Supreme Court. For the first time in history, Oklahoma Republicans won a majority of seats in the state house of representatives.

Little constructive action occurred in Oklahoma state government for the sec-

ond half of the Robertson administration largely because of the split in the legislature. The house was dominated by the Republicans and the senate was dominated by the Democrats. One of the busiest officials in state government during this period was Oklahoma Attorney General George F. Short. He had the duty to supervise the liquidation of each bank that had collapsed during the crash of 1920.

As previously stated, the Ku Klux Klan became active during this period. It was countered by a radical liberal organization called the Farmer–Labor Reconstruction League. This was an organization of farmers and members of labor unions organized during 1921 for the purpose of gaining a greater voice in politics for farmers and working men. Its platform included a broad state aid program to help the poor, a demand that the state enter private industry and operate many of the basic businesses (particularly banking and transportation systems), and the elimination of private profits.

Both the Ku Klux Klan and the Farmer–Labor Reconstruction League were active in the election of 1922. The league leaders proposed that their organization use the Democratic party as the means to achieve their goals. They agreed to endorse those Democratic candidates who would agree, if elected, to put into effect the program desired by the league.

The winner of the Democratic primary for governor during the summer of 1922 was John C. (Jack) Walton, mayor of Oklahoma City. John Fields was the Republican candidate. Walton defeated Fields in the general election. The Democratic nominee for lieutenant governor, Martin E. Trapp, was re-

Governor Jack Walton.

elected. Democrats won majorities in both houses of the state legislature and won seven of Oklahoma's eight congressional seats.

The Walton Administration

GOVERNOR WALTON, a native of Indiana, was an engineer experienced in the building and management of city structures. He had served as commissioner of public safety and as mayor of Oklahoma City.

Most of Governor Walton's advisers were leaders of the Farmer–Labor Reconstruction League. They were impatient for the legislature to adopt their radical economic and social program. Few members of the legislature were obligated to the league, having won election in their districts through their own personal influence and efforts. Thus they largely ignored Governor Walton, his league advisers, and their pressure to adopt the league program. The legislature did adopt certain mild reforms, including an expanded farm cooperative program, revision of the workmen's compensation law to provide improved benefits, a free textbook law, and aid for weak schools to the amount of nearly $1 million.

Farmer–Labor Reconstruction League pressure to move farther and faster on its program irritated legislative leaders. Governor Walton angered the legislature by his appointments to political office. They were particularly concerned about his tampering with the regents for the A and M College at Stillwater and the University of Oklahoma at Norman. He also put pressure on the presidents of these two major institutions to resign so that he might appoint in their places his friends from within the Farmer–Labor Reconstruction League. Walton forced the resignation of the presidents at both of these institutions.

Increased Ku Klux Klan activity across Oklahoma during 1923 added to the turmoil. Beatings, mutilation, and other violence upon citizens by klansmen occurred daily. Okmulgee County was particularly well known for nightly raids by hooded klansmen. In June, 1923, Walton placed the county under martial law. Reports of Klan beatings in Tulsa caused the governor to place Tulsa County under martial law. He also suspended the right of habeas corpus, which protects citizens from illegal imprisonment, in Tulsa County. This was clearly forbidden by the national and state constitutions. When an Oklahoma City grand jury prepared to in-

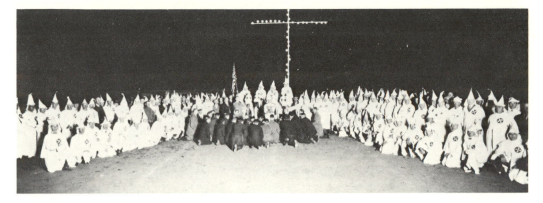

Ku Klux Klan rally at Bartlesville.

vestigate the governor's office, Walton placed the entire state under martial law.

The governor's actions caused several leading state newspapers to demand his impeachment. When the legislature tried to meet in special session for this purpose without the constitutionally required call by the governor, the members were dispersed by National Guard troops stationed about the capitol. Legislative leaders then circulated an initiative petition to permit the legislature to meet on the call of its leaders. The petition was approved by the required number of registered voters, and the proposition was placed on the ballot for a referendum election on October 2, 1923. The voters approved the proposal and legislative leaders called the house into session on October 17. The house brought twenty-two charges against the governor and voted for impeachment.

On October 23, Walton was suspended from office and Lieutenant Governor Trapp became acting governor. The senate convened to hear the impeachment charges and voted to sustain eleven of them. They included il-

legal collection of campaign funds, padding the public payroll, suspension of habeas corpus, excessive use of the pardon power, and general incompetency. On November 19, 1923, Governor Walton was convicted and removed from office. Acting Governor Trapp became Governor Trapp.

The Trapp Administration

MARTIN E. TRAPP came to Oklahoma from Kansas in 1889 and settled at Guthrie. After working with several newspapers, he entered a political career. He won election as lieutenant governor in 1914 and won reelection to that office both in 1918 and in 1922.

Governor Trapp first tried to restore confidence in the credit of the state by repealing several expenditures planned by former Governor Walton that totaled $10 million.

During 1924, Oklahoma voters went to the polls for the summer primaries to select candidates for public office. Then they went back to the polls in November to elect a new legislature, a United States senator, and their con-

Governor Martin E. Trapp.

gressmen, and to vote on presidential candidates. Robert L. Owen, United States senator from Oklahoma since statehood in 1907, decided not to seek another term. Interestingly, former Governor Walton, who had become somewhat of a popular hero because of his war against the Klan, won the Democratic nomination for United States senator. His Republican opponent was Okmulgee oilman William B. Pine. The Republican party won its second consecutive United States Senate seat when Pine rather easily defeated Walton. In the balloting for presidential electors, John W. Davis, the Democratic candidate, carried Oklahoma over the Republican presidential candidate, Calvin Coolidge. Oklahoma Democrats won six of the eight congressional seats

and substantial majorities in both houses of the legislature.

Governor Trapp maintained good relations with legislative leaders, and he was able to obtain passage of most of his program for state improvement. These included a three-cent increase per gallon in the gasoline tax, which enabled him to carry out an extensive highway construction program. So carefully did he manage state finances that he left office with a $2 million surplus in the state treasury.

Because of his interest in nature, Trapp provided leadership in establishing the Forestry Commission, the Conservation Commission, and the Fish and Game Commission. Opposed to the Klan, he gained adoption by the legislature of a law that reduced the power of the Klan by making it unlawful to wear the Klan mask and robes. The so-called "Invisible Empire" remained a force in Oklahoma social and political life for some time, but the beginning of the end of its influence began in Trapp's time.

The election for Governor Trapp's successor occurred in 1926. Henry S. Johnston of Perry won the Democratic nomination. His Republican opponent was Omer K. Benedict of Tulsa. Johnston won in the November election and was joined in the statehouse by Lieutenant Governor William J. Holloway, former president pro tempore of the state senate. With the continuing habit of the legislature to impeach officials of the executive branch, including the governor, the office of lieutenant governor was becoming increasingly important.

In the same election, Republican United States Senator John W. Harreld was up for reelection. His Democratic opponent was Congressman Elmer Thomas of Lawton. Thomas defeated Harreld and launched a career in the United States Senate that extended to 1950. Democrats won seven of the eight congressional seats and majorities in both houses of the legislature.

The Johnston Administration

JOHNSTON's relations with legislative leaders appeared good early in his administration. He passed several proposals including funds to establish a state crippled children's hospital and an increase in school aid to $1.5 million. This amount was the largest payment to local schools up to that time. Opposition to the governor among legislators began in the State Department of Highways over proposed changes by the governor in the makeup of the Highway Commission. The legislature attempted to impeach Governor Johnston. Charges were adopted by the house, but the senate refused to act on the indictment handed it by the house leaders.

The election of 1928 proved the undoing of Governor Johnston. The national Democratic party presidential nominee was Al Smith. Smith was a Roman Catholic and supported the repeal of prohibition. His Republican opponent was Herbert Hoover. Governor Johnston campaigned for Smith in Oklahoma, and this angered many groups, including the Women's Christian Temperance Union, Anti-Saloon League, and many of the Protestant clergy. In the November election, Hoover carried Oklahoma and the nation. Several Republicans won state offices, including three seats on the

Governor Henry S. Johnston.

State Supreme Court, a near-majority in the house of representatives, substantial gains in the senate, and three of Oklahoma's eight congressional seats.

Oklahoma Democrats blamed Johnston and his strong campaign for Al Smith for their local reverses. The day after the Twelfth legislature convened in regular session during January, 1929, a combination of anti-Johnston Democrats and Republicans joined to push for the governor's impeachment by the house. Thirteen charges were approved in the impeachment vote. The senate, sitting as a court, considered the charges, most of them trivial. That body voted on March 20 to remove Governor Johnston from office on the charges of general incompetency. Acting Governor Holloway became Governor Holloway.

The Holloway Administration

GOVERNOR HOLLOWAY, through his years of service as a state senate leader, had gained a reputation for sound administration. He was particularly concerned with educational reform.

Governor Holloway established a good working relationship with the legislature and gained increased aid to underfinanced schools. At his urging, the legislature adopted a new mining code that required employers to provide improved health and sanitation conditions for their workers. The legislature also approved the governor's recommendation that protection of state youth through improvement of the child labor code be expanded. The number of automobiles on Oklahoma highways was increasing. In the interest of safety, the legislature set the speed limit at forty-five miles per hour.

It was during Holloway's administration that the legislature adopted the primary runoff law. Thereafter, a candidate had to have a clear majority to receive the nomination.

Late in Governor Holloway's administration the Wall Street crash of 1929 occurred. There followed the Great Depression, which gripped Oklahoma for a decade. Future state leaders had to give the state economy their major attention.

Study Aids

Explain the significance of each term or phrase listed below:

1. Impeachment
2. Green Corn Rebellion
3. *Guinn* v. *United States*
4. Blue laws
5. Ku Klux Klan
6. Farmer–Labor Reconstruction League

Identify each of these persons:

1. William T. Bawden
2. Joseph McNeal
3. John W. Harreld
4. Sidney Suggs
5. William B. Pine
6. John Fields

On an outline map of Oklahoma locate the following places:

1. Enid
2. Sulphur
3. Chickasha
4. Wilburton
5. Shawnee
6. Broken Arrow

Use the suggestions below for study guides:

1. Discuss the highlights of the Cruce administration.
2. Summarize the construction of the capitol.
3. Trace the rise and decline of the Socialist movement in Oklahoma.
4. Trace the rise of the Ku Klux Klan in Oklahoma and show its impact on state politics.
5. Discuss the events leading to the Walton impeachment.

For Further Reading

Ameringer, Oscar. *If You Don't Weaken.* New York, 1940.

Bynum, Ernest T. *Personal Recollections of Ex-Governor Walton.* Oklahoma City, 1924.

Dale, Edward E., and James D. Morrison. *Pioneer Judge: The Life of Robert L. Williams.* Cedar Rapids, 1954.

McBee, William D. *The Oklahoma Revolution.* Oklahoma City, 1956.

Teall, Kaye M. *Black History in Oklahoma.* Oklahoma City, 1971.

Tucker, Howard A. *History of Governor Walton's War on the Ku Klux Klan.* Oklahoma City, 1923.

Scales, James R., and Danney Goble. *Oklahoma Politics: A History.* Norman, 1982.

Chapter 11. **OKLAHOMA IN DEPRESSION AND WAR**

A Period of Distress

TIMES WERE difficult in 1930. The nation was plunging into the worst economic decline in its history. The Great Depression would last for at least a decade. The stock-market crash on Wall Street and the spreading money panic was made worse in parts of the nation by destructive drouths, dust storms, and other problems. In Oklahoma and other states, farm prices were low, with few markets; banks were failing; mines and factories were closing; and the unemployment rate was the highest in history.

In those years there were no federal and state programs of relief and public help. Hungry, poverty-stricken citizens were issued emergency flour and other basic foods by the American Red Cross. In large cities like Tulsa and Oklahoma City, the unemployed formed long lines at church-sponsored soup kitchens. The times called for strong, energetic leaders. The election of 1930 produced for

Oklahoma a leader with such ability.

Just as Oklahoma Democrats were blamed by the voters for the depression of 1920, and were punished by being turned out of office, Oklahoma Republicans were blamed for the depression of 1930. Thus Democratic candidates profited from this voter reaction.

The election operated in 1930 for the first time in Oklahoma history under the runoff primary system. From the large number of Democratic candidates for governor, William H. ("Alfalfa Bill") Murray won the gubernatorial nomination for that party. His Republican opponent in the November election was Ira A. Hill, a state senator and an attorney from Cherokee. Murray won the governorship by a large margin.

The Democrats won substantial margins in both houses of the legislature and won seven of the eight congressional seats. Oklahomans also voted for United States senator in the 1930 election. The Republican incumbent, William B. Pine, sought reelection. Thomas P. Gore, former United States senator, won the Democratic party nomination. Gore defeated Pine in the November general election.

The Murray Administration

OKLAHOMA'S ninth governor, William H. Murray, was born in Texas. In his early life in that state he taught school, edited newspapers, and practiced law. He came to the Chickasaw Nation in 1895 and settled at Tishomingo to practice law. He married the niece of the Chickasaw Nation's governor, and served as adviser and counsel for the Chickasaw government until it was dissolved at statehood in 1907.

Murray was elected a vice-president of the Sequoyah Convention in 1905 and as president of the Oklahoma Constitutional Convention in 1906. His busy career had included service as speaker of the state house of representatives, several terms in the United States Congress, and a recent attempt to set up a colony of Oklahomans in Bolivia, South America.

No governor before or since faced the problems with which Murray had to deal. There was a $5 million deficit in state government finances. Banks were failing and closing all over the state. Many mortgages were being foreclosed, and people lost their homes and farms. Unemployment in Oklahoma was widespread.

The new governor turned first to the problem of hunger and poverty. From the Thirteenth Legislature he obtained money to provide free seed and emergency food rations for the needy. The governor also collected money from

Governor William "Alfalfa Bill" Murray.

businessmen and state employees, and gave much of his own salary to feed the hungry.

Since no federal program for relief had as yet developed, Governor Murray became a leader in the nation in finding solutions for the problems of bringing relief to the needy. Through his leadership the National Council for Relief was formed. It met at Memphis in June, 1931. The recommendations of this body served as a guide for the Congress as it developed a national program of emergency relief.

Another problem Murray faced was the threat of bankruptcy in state government. There was little hope of covering the $5 million deficit or of raising additional funds to meet the crisis

151

Governor Murray's soup line in Oklahoma City.

in the state's economy. This was because most taxpayers could not pay their local and state taxes.

At Murray's urging, the legislature created the Oklahoma Tax Commission. This agency tightened the system for collection of taxes, prevented tax evasion, and increased the amount of money coming to the state from existing laws. The Oklahoma Board of Equalization adjusted taxes on real property (land and homes), which gave relief for small property owners, and reduced the loss of property through tax sales. In the adjustment of tax rates, corporate property taxes were increased in the amount of $65 million.

In the face of many crises, Governor Murray frequently used National Guard troops and martial law to prevent resistance to what he thought was necessary for state recovery and progress. He used state troops and martial law to enforce his order closing all state banks. Murray took this step in order to check bank runs and bank failures. He used

National Guard troops and martial law to supervise elections, to stop oil field production, and to open highways and bridges to public traffic.

Murray used National Guard troops in Oklahoma's oil fields because heavy production from new producers in East Texas and Oklahoma wells in the Seminole and Oklahoma City fields had flooded the market. Producers ignored the attempts of the State Corporation Commission to regulate production, and prices fell to fifteen cents a barrel.

A main source of revenue was the gross production tax on oil. The industry and state finances faced disaster. On August 4, 1931, the governor placed 3,106 producing wells under martial law. Production stopped until a quota was assigned to each well. Oklahoma troops guarded the oil fields and watched over production until April 11, 1933.

Murray also met with the governors of Kansas and Texas, and all agreed to control future oil production in the Mid-Continent field. Murray's action caused a rise in oil prices. By the close of his administration, oil was selling for one dollar a barrel.

Governor Murray's most noted use of state troops and martial law grew out of the toll bridge issue. In the early days of Oklahoma highway development, there was very little public money for highways and most of that went for actual road construction. Expensive bridges over major streams often were built by private companies that charged tolls for use. These toll bridges generally were quite profitable. Thus when the state, in response to public demands, built free bridges across Red River and other major streams, the toll bridge companies objected.

During Murray's term, several public bridges were built across Red River close to privately owned bridges. The company operating a toll bridge at the Denison crossing on Red River challenged the right of the state to build and operate a free bridge that would destroy its business. The company brought suit in federal court at Houston. The presiding judge issued an injunction forbidding the opening and use of the new public bridge. Governor Murray declared that the courts were protecting toll bridge owners and were hurting the public welfare. He ordered the National Guard to close the toll bridge and to keep the free bridge open. State troops successfully opened the free bridge.

Murray required state officials to practice rigid economy. He greatly reduced the money for public institutions and required strict practices throughout state government. His concern that the state be debt free and his careful management of limited state money resulted in the restoration of full faith in state credit by the end of his administration.

Abandoned farm equipment during the dust bowl days.

The treasurer had previously paid state bills by issuing state warrants (a promise to pay). The state owed $13 million in unpaid warrants. The warrants could not be sold, and the operation of state government was threatened because it could not pay its employees or the businesses that supplied services and goods to state institutions. At Murray's urging, the legislature passed a law by which the state could issue treasury notes payable from one to four years. Those persons holding state warrants could exchange them for the new state treasury notes. A part of the gasoline tax was to be used to pay off the notes or bonds. The unpaid warrants were traded for the notes or bonds and warrants again could be sold.

The election of 1932 was one of the most dramatic in the history of Oklahoma and the nation. Governor Murray, with his direct approach and considerable success in meeting the problems of the depression, had become a national figure. This, perhaps, created

153

Many sharecropper families left for California to get away from the dust bowl days.

a desire on his part to seek the presidency. He was nominated at the Democratic Convention in Chicago, but Franklin D. Roosevelt of New York was selected as the presidential candidate for the Democratic party. In the November election, Roosevelt defeated Republican candidate Herbert Hoover in both Oklahoma and the nation.

Oklahoma Democrats won all seats in the Congress. By the 1930 census, Oklahoma's population had increased to 2,396,000, which gave the state a ninth congressman. The congressional districts were not reapportioned and this additional seat was filled by at-large voting each election until it was abolished in 1943. Democrats swept the state-

house and won heavy majorities in both houses of the state legislature.

Will Rogers, a Moore school teacher and a Democrat, capitalizing on the name of the famous entertainer, won this at-large congressional seat in each of five consecutive elections. Among the Oklahoma congressmen elected in this 1932 Democratic landslide was Ernest W. Marland, founder of the Marland Oil Company (later Conoco) of Ponca City. In two years he was to play an even larger role in Oklahoma politics.

The second half of the Murray administration saw the beginning of New Deal programs in Oklahoma. The New Deal was aimed at rebuilding the state economy. These programs included as-

CCC workers restoring the land in Oklahoma County, 1937.

sistance and direction in restoring factories, mines, farms, and transportation
systems, and in providing work for the
unemployed.

A vast program of public works, the
Public Works Administration (PWA),
the Work Project Administration (WPA),
and the Civilian Conservation Corps
(CCC), was begun by the federal government in Oklahoma and other states.
Oklahoma's problems had been made
more serious by a long drouth that blis-
tered crops, withered pastures, and reduced farmers and ranchers to ruin.
During 1933, nearly 93,000 Oklahomans
were on relief. They drew commodities
(food) and clothing from the new federal–state distribution system.

The federal programs required state
matching funds, particularly for social
programs, which included aid to the
aging and the handicapped. Governor
Murray called the Fourteenth Legislature into special session on May 24,
1933. At this session new tax laws were
adopted, including revision of the state
income tax law and the adoption of the
sales tax.

At this special session the legislation
also amended Oklahoma's "bone-dry"
prohibition law. Across the nation, the
Twenty-first Amendment to the Federal
Constitution had been adopted. This
had repealed the Eighteenth Amendment. Oklahoma was one of the few
states that remained dry. The legisla-

ture presented a proposition to the voters to legalize the sale and consumption of 3.2 beer (defined as nonintoxicating). This issue was approved at a special election held on July 1, 1933.

Governor Murray had not restored prosperity to Oklahoma. This would have been impossible because the depression was national in character. But his bold and determined leadership had turned back the threat of financial collapse. He had restored public solvency and credit.

In a sense, he also broke the legislature of its habit of impeaching governors who angered its members with an attempt to lead the state rather than to be led. Murray's tough leadership angered certain legislative leaders. They grumbled and threatened to give him the same treatment they had given Walton and Johnston. To these threats Murray responded, "If you've got any impeachment ideas in your heads, hop to it. It'll be like a bunch of jack rabbits tryin' to get a wildcat out of a hole."

William H. Murray's successor as chief executive of Oklahoma was selected in 1934. Congressman Ernest W. Marland won the Democratic nomination for governor. Oklahoma Republicans nominated William B. Pine, former United States senator, as their candidate. Marland campaigned on a platform to bring the New Deal to Oklahoma in the fullest sense in order to improve the state's economic situation. Marland won the governor's race in the November election. Democrats won all nine congressional seats and majorities in both houses of the state legislature. The Socialists reappeared on the Oklahoma political scene. Their candidate for governor, S. P. Green, received nearly 17,000 votes.

The Marland Administration

ERNEST W. MARLAND had come to Indian Territory from Pennsylvania to develop a vast oil empire. At one time his fortune was estimated at $85 million. His business headquarters was at Ponca City. One of his gifts to the state during his period of great wealth was the Pioneer Woman statue at Ponca City. Business connections with eastern bankers caused him to lose a fortune and by 1932 he had become an ardent New Dealer.

Marland's program for restoring prosperity in Oklahoma was called the "Little New Deal." By the time of his inauguration in 1935, an estimated 150,000 Oklahomans were out of work, and 700,000 were on relief. His program consisted of conservation, including the use of terraces, check dams, cover crops, and planting trees to halt erosion and restore soil production; the building of multipurpose dams on Oklahoma's rivers to provide electric power, flood control, manufacturing, and recreation; a program for old-age pensions, upgrading education, and reducing state indebtedness; and a planning board to develop state resources and attract new industry.

Oklahoma's Fifteenth Legislature was prone to economy in government rather than spending all that was necessary to put into effect the Marland New Deal. The speaker of the house, Leon Phillips, led the legislature in opposing Marland's program. New taxes were adopted by the legislature, but the money was more for the purpose of producing state solvency than for financing Marland's Little New Deal plans.

The 1 percent sales tax, adopted in Murray's administration, was increased to 2 percent. The revenue produced by the sales tax was used to match federal funds to provide old-age assistance and support for dependent children and the handicapped.

A special election in 1935 provided for a partial exemption of homesteads from taxation. The income lost by reducing taxes on real property, used largely for support of local schools, was made up in part by an increase in state aid to the schools in the amount of $8,200,000. The legislature forced state agencies and institutions to continue to operate on reduced funds. About the only state agency to receive increased funds was the Department of Highways. This made it possible to expand the Oklahoma highway network and to provide jobs for many unemployed persons in the state.

Oklahomans returned to the polls in 1936 to elect a president, and a United States senator, congressmen, and a new state legislature. United States Senator Gore was up for reelection. Oklahoma Democrats passed him over and decided between Governor Marland and Congressman Josh Lee. Lee defeated the governor in the primary and won the Democratic nomination for United States senator. In November, Lee defeated the Republican candidate, Herbert Hyde, an attorney from Oklahoma City. President Roosevelt, also up for reelection as the Democratic presidential candidate, carried Oklahoma and the nation, defeating the Republican candidate, Alf Landon. Democrats won the nine Oklahoma congressional seats and control of both houses of the state legislature.

Governor Marland, turned back in his bid for a seat in the United States Senate, returned to the business of his

Governor Ernest W. Marland.

attempt to lead the state in the direction of his Little New Deal. The Sixteenth Legislature adopted a series of laws providing for combined state and federal action in social security, welfare, and public works. Before the close of the Marland administration, nearly ninety thousand Oklahomans were employed on thirteen hundred WPA projects, which ranged from building sidewalks to courthouses.

Marland's achievements included providing leadership in the development of the Oklahoma Highway Patrol, the establishment of the Oklahoma Planning and Resources Board, and the Interstate Oil Compact. Murray had led the way on the compact by his agreement with the governors of Texas and Kansas, which brought some improve-

United States Senator Josh Lee.

sought reelection. In the primary he ran against Governor Marland. Thomas defeated Marland to win his party's nomination, then in November triumphed over the Republican candidate, Harry O. Glasser. The Democrats again won all nine of Oklahoma's seats in Congress (among them "Mike" Monroney from the Fifth District) and wide margins in the state legislature.

The Phillips Administration

GOVERNOR PHILLIPS's program was primarily concerned with saving money and making the state solvent. A low tax yield and increased state welfare and relief payments had caused a state debt of nearly $26 million. Phillips's first step in bringing that under control was to get legislative approval to issue $35 million worth of state bonds. This bond issue funded the state debt and provided the legislature a small surplus with which to work.

Phillips also urged passage of a series of tax increases on automobiles, tobacco, and other items. The legislature approved the tax increases, which included an increase in the gasoline tax from 4 cents per gallon to 5½ cents. To prevent future deficits, Phillips proposed that a budget-balancing amendment be adopted. It prohibited the state from spending more money than it received from its tax income. The amendment was adopted. Additional economy steps included a reduction in spending for public institutions and education amounting to 20 percent.

The conflict in viewpoint and program between national Democrats and Oklahoma Democrats over the New Deal flared in the election of 1940. Many lo-

ment in crude oil prices in the Mid-Continent field. Marland followed Murray with the plan to organize a group of oil-producing states that would help in conserving petroleum and in stabilizing production and prices for oil. The Interstate Oil Compact group elected Marland to serve as its first president.

Marland's successor was elected in 1938. Nine candidates ran for governor on the Democratic ticket, including two former governors—Walton and Murray. The Democratic nominee was Leon Phillips, former speaker of the state house of representatives and an advocate of economy in government. He was a leader in the growing group of Democrats who opposed President Roosevelt and the New Deal. The Republicans nominated Ross Rizley, a prominent Republican leader from Guymon. Phillips won the governorship in the November election.

United States Senator Elmer Thomas

cal Democrats objected to the New Deal because it brought federal control of many local matters. Governor Phillips was the chief spokesman for the anti–New Deal Democrats in Oklahoma.

Many local Democrats were very concerned when President Roosevelt announced that he would seek a third term. He defeated Wendell Wilkie, the Republican presidential candidate, but his margin of victory in Oklahoma was much lower than in previous elections. Oklahoma Republicans won their first seat in Congress since 1930. Ross Rizley defeated Phil Ferguson in the Eighth Congressional District.

A special target for Governor Phillips in opposing the New Deal was his attempt to stop the building of dams on Oklahoma waterways. The purpose of these dams, which created huge lakes, was to fulfill New Deal goals of water conservation, flood control, recreation, and electric power. Believing that the loss of farm land through flooding the lake bed would be a serious loss to the state, Phillips attempted to halt construction of Denison Dam on the Red River. He called out the National Guard to prevent completion of the Grand River Dam project, but was stopped by a court injunction.

It was during the Phillips administration that the state legislature proposed a constitutional amendment that removed most political limitations upon women. The amendment, making women eligible for all offices in the state, including governor, was defeated in 1940, but was resubmitted and approved in 1942.

Most of the energies of the governor and other leaders of the state during the second half of the Phillips administration were absorbed in mobilizing the

Governor Leon Phillips.

state for World War II. For the first time since 1929, the economic situation improved in the state as markets developed for farm and ranch products. The war effort placed a heavy demand on the petroleum resources of the state, and the oil industry boomed. The building of military training bases in Oklahoma and the development of war industries also produced full employment. The depression had ended in Oklahoma and the nation by 1942.

The election of 1942 in Oklahoma was more a battle between the New Dealers and the anti–New Dealers in the Democratic party than a contest between Democrats and Republicans. United States Senator Josh Lee was the leader of the New Dealers. Leon Phillips was the leader of the opposition. Lee was up for reelection. The Republican candidate for the United States Senate was Ed H. Moore of Tulsa. Outgoing Governor Phillips switched parties and actively campaigned for the Republican candidate for the Senate. In the November election Moore defeated Lee to become the third Republican United States senator in Oklahoma history.

In 1942, Oklahomans also elected a new governor. Robert S. Kerr was the Democratic nominee. The Republican nominee for governor was William J. Otjen. In a close race, Kerr defeated Otjen to become Oklahoma's twelfth governor.

The 1940 census showed Oklahoma's population as 2,336,434. This decline from the 1930 figure reduced Oklahoma's number of seats in the United States Congress to eight. The Democrats won seven of the seats. They also won majorities in both houses of the state legislature.

The Kerr Administration

ROBERT S. KERR was Oklahoma's first native-born governor. His birthplace was a log cabin in the Chickasaw Nation. Trained as an attorney and active as a civic and lay religious leader, Kerr had been successful as the developer of an Oklahoma-based oil company.

The Kerr administration was almost entirely within the World War II era. The state's activities were overshadowed and largely controlled by World War II. Thus his administration was for the most part uneventful. Both Kerr and the legislative leaders gave particular attention to the state debt. The result was that before the close of his administration the bonds to cover the state debt

issued in Phillips's administration were retired and the state treasury had a surplus of money.

The Kerr program included a proposal to provide free textbooks for the public schools. This was approved in 1946 on a referendum vote. Kerr accomplished reform in Oklahoma prisons by gaining adoption of a measure creating the Oklahoma Pardon and Parole Board. This shifted from the governor to the new board the responsibility for considering and granting applications for change of sentences, pardons, and paroles.

Kerr attempted with some success to calm the bitter feeling among certain Democratic leaders in the state toward President Roosevelt and the New Deal. He said that a cooperative attitude toward the federal government was essential if Oklahoma was to receive its share of federally supported dams, roads, and other income- and job-producing projects. He changed the stream of state-federal relations by pledging to support the national administration.

Kerr's leadership in smoothing state-federal relations was shown in the election of 1944. As one of the few southern governors to remain loyal to President Roosevelt and the New Deal, Kerr was selected to give the keynote address for the Democratic convention at Chicago. This was the first time an Oklahoman had received this honor, and Kerr, famous as a speechmaker, did not disappoint the large audience. President Roosevelt sought and won a fourth-term nomination.

The Republican presidential nominee was Thomas E. Dewey, governor of New York. Roosevelt defeated Dewey in Oklahoma and the nation to win a historic fourth term. Elmer Thomas won reelection to the United States Senate over the Republican candidate, William J. Otjen. Democrats also won six of the eight Oklahoma congressional seats and majorities in both houses of the state legislature.

As indicated, most of the interest and energy of the state was directed toward the war effort. Business boomed because of increased employment in war industries and military projects. Because of its mild climate that permitted ground and air training most of the year, Oklahoma was the center of intensive military building. Twenty-eight army camps, the best-known being the artillery center at Fort Sill, provided training for hundreds of thousands of troops for action in Europe and the Pacific. Thirteen naval bases were constructed, notably the Technical Training Center at Norman, which trained fifteen thousand navy men. In addition, several army air corps bases were established, including Will Rogers Field near Oklahoma City and Cimarron Field near Yukon.

The vast Tinker Field at Midwest City became the largest air depot in the world. The facilities at Tinker Field kept the army air corps' B-17s, B-24s, and B-29s in flying condition. Heavy bombers were adapted at Tinker Field for the atomic bomb strikes on Hiroshima and Nagasaki that ended the war with Japan in August of 1945. In addition, aviation training facilities at Miami and Ponca City were used for training British and Canadian pilots.

More than 193,000 Oklahomans enlisted in the armed forces. An additional 300,000 men were drafted. Oklahoma's battle casualties amounted to 6,500 killed and 11,000 wounded. On the home front, Oklahomans in the cities produced weapons of war or performed vital services.

Governor, later United States Senator, Robert S. Kerr.

Miners, oil-field workers, farmers, and ranchers supplied vast quantities of metals, fuel, grains, and meat for the military needs of the United States.

Looking to victory and peace, Governor Kerr carried on an active campaign to expand and diversify the Oklahoma economy by attracting new industries to the state. He also sought to develop and strengthen the functions of the Oklahoma Planning and Resources Board. He contributed greatly to the improved image and reputation of Oklahoma throughout the nation. He was in great demand nationwide as a public speaker, and he utilized these public appearances to acquaint his audiences with the resources and opportunities in Oklahoma. Probably no other leader took as much pride in

Governor Roy J. Turner.

The Turner Administration

IN PRIVATE business, Roy J. Turner had developed extensive oil and ranching properties. He also had gained international fame as a breeder of registered Herefords.

The new governor's program for Oklahoma urged economy in government, a reformed Highway Commission, the expanded use of state resources, soil conservation, and the development of Oklahoma's recreational facilities. He also advocated a tax reduction to attract industry to Oklahoma and a long-range highway development program.

In response to the challenge of Governor Turner's program, the state legislature adopted an act reducing the state income tax by one-third. Other laws offered additional attractions and advantages to businesses and industries. State lodges and other recreational facilities were built with funds from self-liquidating bonds. Governor Turner and other state leaders continued former Governor Kerr's national campaign to attract new industry to the state.

The 1948 presidential election occurred in the middle of the Turner administration. President Harry S. Truman was the Democratic candidate. Thomas E. Dewey won the Republican nomination. Ending discrimination and extending all civil rights to America's black population had become a political issue. The Democratic party and President Truman included the extension of civil rights in the party platform.

Many southern Democrats opposed this civil rights portion of the platform and withdrew to form the Dixiecrat party. In Oklahoma the leader of the Dixiecrat movement was William H.

being a citizen of Oklahoma or did as much to better the understanding of his home state.

Kerr's successor as chief executive of Oklahoma was elected in 1946. Roy J. Turner won the Democratic nomination for governor. Olney Flynn, former Tulsa mayor and son of the territorial delegate to Congress, was selected by the Republicans as their choice for the governorship. Turner defeated Flynn in the November general election to become Oklahoma's thirteenth governor. In that same election Democrats won control of a majority of seats in both houses of the state legislature and six of the eight Oklahoma congressional seats.

162

Murray. A radical group calling itself the Progressive party, with Henry Wallace as its presidential candidate, also ran in the 1948 campaign. Despite this splintering of the Democratic party, Truman defeated Dewey for the presidency both in Oklahoma and the nation. Oklahoma Democrats won all eight of the state's congressional seats and majorities in both houses of the state legislature.

The United States Senate term of Ed Moore had ended, and he was not a candidate for reelection. The Republicans nominated Ross Rizley for this seat in the Senate. However, former Governor Kerr won the Democratic nomination for this Senate seat. In the November election Kerr won this race to begin a long and distinguished career in the United States Senate. Many former governors of Oklahoma had sought a seat in the United States Senate, but Kerr was the first to accomplish this aim.

Several important developments occurred in the second half of the Turner administration. The enrollment on Oklahoma college campuses increased dramatically in the period after World War II. Most buildings were old and in need of repair. Buildings on the grounds of state hospitals and other public institutions needed work. Turner and legislative leaders worked out a plan for a bond issue in the amount of $36 million, which was used to finance the much-needed construction and repair of public buildings.

Legislation was also adopted that provided for construction of the Tulsa–Oklahoma City turnpike, which, when completed, was called the Turner Turnpike. The act created the Turnpike Authority and authorized the sale of bonds to investors to finance construc-

Ada Lois Sipuel Fisher, whose application for admission to the University of Oklahoma Law School began the drive for desegregation of Oklahoma higher education.

tion of a four-lane road 88 miles long. When finished it linked the state's two major cities. Construction began in December, 1949, and the toll road was opened to traffic on May 17, 1953.

Racial desegregation began late in the Turner administration. Oklahoma political leaders had kept the segregation laws passed by the First Legislature. A challenge against segregation on the graduate and professional school level occurred in 1946 when Ada Lois Sipuel, a Chickasha black who was a Langston University honor graduate, applied for admission to the University of Oklahoma School of Law. Since state statutes required university officials to deny her admission under penalty of fine and prison sentence, she was refused.

163

THE HISTORY OF OKLAHOMA

Miss Sipuel's attorney brought suit in the Cleveland County District Court to force university officials to admit her. The request was refused and the State Supreme Court upheld the lower court. In January, 1948, the United States Supreme Court ruled that the state must immediately provide the same instruction for blacks as that given to white students. Since the state segregation law was not thrown out by this decision, the Langston University School of Law for Negroes was set up in the state capitol building.

Unhappy with this arrangement, the National Association for the Advancement of Colored People renewed the attack. To achieve its goal, the organization sought out blacks who were willing to seek admission to other Oklahoma professional schools. George W. McLaurin, a former Langston faculty member, after some legal actions in state and federal courts, won admission to the University of Oklahoma graduate program. His success began the complete desegregation of higher education in Oklahoma.

As the Turner administration was drawing to a close during the summer of 1950, the United States as a member of the United Nations became involved in the Korean War. Under the Selective Service System, Oklahoma supplied men to the armed forces. Marine units from Oklahoma City and Tulsa, called at the beginning of the fighting, fought in early combat as part of the First Marine Division. This war, as all recent wars, stimulated industry and kept prices and wages relatively high. Many Oklahoma military installations, which either had been closed down or their activities reduced since the close of World War II, were reactivated or expanded to meet the new demands growing out of the Korean struggle.

The 1950s, the decade following Turner's administration, were times of intense political action in Oklahoma. Many of the issues that would confront state leaders and voters were anticipated in the Turner administration. These included attempts to establish a state merit system, to draft a new state constitution, and to repeal prohibition.

Study Aids

Explain the significance of each term or phrase listed below:

1. Budget-balancing amendment
2. Interstate Oil Compact
3. Dixiecrat
4. Mid-Continent field
5. "Bone dry"
6. Little New Deal

Identify each of these persons:

1. E. H. Moore
2. Ada Lois Sipuel
3. Josh Lee
4. William J. Otjen
5. S. F. Green
6. Olney Flynn

On an outline map of Oklahoma locate the following places:

1. Checotah
2. Noble
3. Gore
4. Cheyenne
5. Goodwell
6. Atoka

Use the suggestions below for study guides:

1. Explain the principal problems facing Governor William H. Murray.
2. Outline the steps taken by the Oklahoma state government to meet the depression crisis.
3. Describe the Marland program and account for its failure.
4. Compare the Phillips and the Kerr administrations, noting distinctive differences.
5. Trace the beginnings of racial desegregation in Oklahoma.

For Further Reading

Brookings Institution. *Report on a Survey of the Organization and Administration of Oklahoma.* Oklahoma City, 1935.

Bryant, Keith. *Alfalfa Bill Murray.* Norman, 1968.

Hines, Gordon. *Alfalfa Bill.* Oklahoma City, 1932.

Mathews, John J. *Life and Death of an Oil Man: The Career of E. W. Marland.* Norman, 1951.

Murray, William H. *Memoirs of Governor Murray.* 3 vols. Boston, 1945.

Scales, James R., and Danney Goble. *Oklahoma Politics: A History.* Norman, 1982.

Chapter 12. **OKLAHOMA POLITICS SINCE 1950**

Postwar Oklahoma

AFTER WORLD WAR II, Oklahoma was behind the other states in economic, educational, and social programs, and in public facilities. The 1950s was a time of catching up. The state's leaders were aware of the need for progress and for the most part they succeeded in accomplishing much-needed change and improvement.

Oklahoma's fourteenth governor was elected in 1950. In the primaries, Johnston Murray and William O. Coe fought a close race for the Democratic nomination. Murray was the son of former Governor William H. Murray, and Coe was an attorney from Oklahoma City. A recount was required and Murray received the Democratic nomination by only a 962-vote margin over Coe. Murray's Republican opponent in the November general election was Jo O. Ferguson, a Pawnee newspaperman. Murray defeated Ferguson by a margin of

16,103 votes. Democrats won six of the congressional seats, the Republicans two. Democrats also won control of both houses of the state legislature.

In this year, the Oklahoma voters elected a United States senator. Elmer Thomas, long-time United States senator, was defeated in the Democratic primary by Congressman Mike Monroney. The Republican candidate for the Senate seat was William Alexander, pastor of the First Christian Church of Oklahoma City. Monroney defeated Alexander to begin a long and distinguished career in the United States Senate.

Johnston Murray Administration

GOVERNOR MURRAY was an attorney and had held several positions in the Democratic party, including chairman of the Eighth Congressional District. He had served as chairman of the State Election Board and was a presidential elector in

The Oklahoma State Capitol, built during Governor Williams's term.

1940 and 1948. At his inauguration his father gave him the oath of office.

Early in Governor Murray's term, the legislature submitted to the people three issues for a vote. These provided for increasing the sales tax from 2 percent to 3 percent to permit increased payment to old-age pensioners; lowering the voting age to eighteen years; and giving bonuses to veterans of World War I, World War II, and the Korean conflict. All three issues were voted down.

Fearing Communists were active in state government, the state legislature adopted the loyalty oath law. This required all officials and employees of state government to take an oath of allegiance to the United States and the state of Oklahoma. Several teachers at Oklahoma colleges refused to sign the oath and they were dismissed. A United States Supreme Court decision in 1953 declared the law unconstitutional. A new loyalty oath, written in 1953, removed the objections of the Supreme Court.

Governor Murray and legislative leaders stressed economy in government, no new taxes, and a continuation of the program to recruit industry for the state. Economy in state spending included less money for public assistance. At the beginning of Governor Murray's administration, about 9 percent of the state's population received some form of welfare payment. State officials tightened the welfare program requirements. The result was that by the close of the Murray administration the number of Oklahomans on welfare was reduced to about 7 percent of the state's population.

Pioneers in the women's liberation movement had been active in Oklahoma for some time. One of their objectives was to remove the remaining political and legal limitations on women. During Murray's administration, the voters decided to permit women to serve on juries.

The 1950 census revealed Oklahoma's population to be 2,223,351, a decline of 113,083 from the 1940 census.

Governor Johnston Murray.

This was the second consecutive decade showing a loss in state population. A result of this loss was that the state's eight congressional seats were to be reduced to six. This required the state legislature to reapportion the state's congressional districts (redraw the districts' boundaries).

In 1952, Oklahomans went to the polls to elect a new president. The Democratic party nominated Adlai Stevenson, governor of Illinois. The Republican party chose Dwight D. Eisenhower, a World War II hero. Eisenhower defeated Stevenson in Oklahoma and the nation. Oklahoma Democrats, however, won five of the six congressional seats and majorities in both houses of the state legislature.

Murray and the Twenty-fourth Legislature (elected in 1952) succeeded in consolidating many rural schools to improve instruction. Reform was also brought about in the state's mental health facilities by increased funding from the legislature. Improved facilities and better treatment were the result.

An expansion of functions for the State Turnpike Authority made possible the construction of the Will Rogers Turnpike. This was a toll highway nearly ninety miles long between Tulsa and Joplin, Missouri. Another plan advanced by Governor Murray, though it did not gain acceptance, pointed the way for future development. His plan was to build four hundred miles of canals connecting lakes in the well-watered Ozark foothills of eastern Oklahoma with cities on the dry plains. An Oklahoma water authority, organized like a toll road company, would finance the canals by issuing $125 million in bonds to be paid from the water sold.

At the close of his administration, Governor Murray pointed out what Oklahoma needed in order to progress. Included were legislative reapportionment; the elimination of homestead exemption; a state merit system to reduce patronage and the "spoils system" and to provide continuity of service for state employees; making public buying more economical through central purchasing; reducing the number of Oklahoma counties; and reducing the power of county commissioners.

Governor Johnston Murray's successor as Oklahoma's chief executive came out of the election of 1954. Raymond Gary of Madill, a veteran legislative leader, won the Democratic nomination for governor. His Republican opponent in the November election was Reuben K. Sparks, a Woodward rancher and an attorney. Gary won the governorship by a substantial margin.

Democrats also won five of Oklahoma's six seats in the Congress and majorities in both houses of the state legislature. Oklahomans also voted for a United States senator in the 1954 election. Incumbent Senator Robert S. Kerr was up for reelection. His Republican opponent for the Senate was Fred Mock, an attorney from Oklahoma City. Kerr defeated Mock and was returned to the United States Senate.

The Gary Administration

OKLAHOMA's fifteenth governor, Raymond Gary, had been a schoolteacher, a county superintendent of schools in southern Oklahoma, a businessman, and an independent oil operator. He had won election to the state senate in 1940, and continued in that office until he became governor in the 1954 election.

Governor Gary's first legislature, the Twenty-fifth, created the Oklahoma Department of Commerce and Industry. Its function was to attract new industry to the state. The legislature also authorized additional toll roads, one of which was to run from Oklahoma City to Lawton and Wichita Falls, Texas. When finished, this toll road was designated the H. E. Bailey Turnpike.

Gary's first legislature also passed laws giving more money to higher education, public schools, the welfare program (notably old-age assistance), and mental hospitals. Strong legislative support of the state's mental health program made possible great reforms in the care and rehabilitation of the men-

Governor Raymond Gary.

tally ill. Before this support was possible, Oklahoma ranked near the bottom among the states in provision for care of the mentally ill. In the 1950s Oklahoma became a leader in mental health care.

Much of the time and energy of Governor Gary and the legislature was taken up in desegregating the public schools. Oklahoma's colleges and universities had been desegregated by the *Sipuel* and *McLaurin* decisions. The state's public schools continued to operate on a system that called for separate schools for white and black students.

On May 17, 1954, the United States Supreme Court handed down the historic *Brown* v. *Board of Education* deci-

169

sion. The decision declared that segregated schools were not equal and could not be made equal. Black students in segregated school systems were said to be denied basic rights guaranteed by the equal protection clause of the United States Constitution.

Governor Gary and other state leaders took steps to comply with the decision. Laws and amendments to the state constitution were adopted to abolish separate schools. This included correcting the formula for the financing of public schools that had kept black schools poor.

Governor Gary also took the lead in abolishing other forms of segregation. At the state capitol, separate washrooms, drinking fountains, and other reminders of "Jim Crow" days were removed. The Oklahoma National Guard was integrated, and the governor refused to attend any conference or meeting in the state held in a hotel or resort that practiced discrimination.

The drive to improve the status of blacks in the Oklahoma society was helped by the move toward equal education. This carried into other areas. More and more blacks registered to vote. They elected black representatives to governing bodies, including the Oklahoma City City Council and the state legislature. Thus they obtained a voice in the law-making process. Black leaders worked for equality in employment opportunity and in housing. They demanded repeal of all laws that were discriminatory. During the 1950s and the 1960s, these goals were achieved by local legislation as well as extension of federal laws and court rules.

Midterm in the Gary administration saw another presidential election. Dwight D. Eisenhower was again the

Republican candidate. For the second time the Democrats nominated Adlai Stevenson. President Eisenhower's nationwide victory in 1956 marked the fourth time that Oklahomans had supported a Republican presidential candidate. It was the first time that they had done so in two consecutive elections.

Democratic United States Senator Mike Monroney ran for reelection. His Republican opponent was Douglas McKeever of Enid. Monroney triumphed, as did five Democrats seeking the congressional seats. The Republicans won Oklahoma's sixth seat in Congress. Democrats won control of both houses of the legislature.

Oklahomans observed fifty years of statehood during the Gary administration. A state agency, the Oklahoma Semicentennial Commission, directed the show. Besides all communities in the state being represented, cities and states across the nation participated, as did nineteen foreign nations. The event was well advertised in local, state, and national newspapers. Held at the Oklahoma City Fairgrounds for three weeks in the summer of 1957, the celebration drew huge crowds, with visitors attending the celebration numbering 1½ million.

Governor Gary worked to improve the state and federal highways in Oklahoma and to build new ones. When he came into office, he announced that his goal was to provide the leadership and the means to construct 2,500 miles of new roads. At the close of his term in 1959, nearly 3,500 miles of new highways had been finished.

This increase in road building was made possible by the Federal-Aid Highway Act, passed by Congress in 1956.

170

It provided for the interstate highway system. The three branches of the Oklahoma portion of the system centered on Oklahoma City. The north-south route was designated as Interstate Highway 35. The east-west route was Interstate Highway 40. A northeast-southwest route, called Interstate Highway 44, included the Will Rogers Turnpike, the Turner Turnpike, and the H. E. Bailey Turnpike.

The Gary administration was a time of great activity by the State Department of Commerce and Industry to bring new industry into the state. The governor gave much personal attention to balancing the economy so that the state did not have to rely too heavily on agriculture, ranching, and oil production.

A key to achieving a balance in industry and agriculture was to increase water resources. At Gary's request the legislature passed a series of laws that allowed cities and towns to combine their resources through the organization of water conservancy districts, and to enter into long-range contracts to build and operate water facilities. This was to be done largely through the building of dams on creeks and rivers to create large lakes that would provide water to cities and towns and that could be used for recreation.

Raymond Gary's successor was elected in 1958. J. Howard Edmondson of Tulsa won the Democratic nomination. Because the office of lieutenant governor became an important position in the next administration, the candidate seeking that office should be noted also. George Nigh won the Democratic nomination for that office. The Republican candidate for governor was Phil Ferguson. Edmondson defeated Ferguson in November to become Oklahoma's sixteenth governor, and Nigh was elected as lieutenant governor. Democrats won five of the congressional seats and substantial majorities in both houses of the legislature.

The Edmondson Administration

J. HOWARD EDMONDSON was inaugurated in January, 1959, at the age of thirty-three. He was the youngest governor in state history, and the youngest in the nation at that time. Edmondson had established a statewide reputation as a capable county attorney for Tulsa County.

Edmondson's program had focused on reform in state government and the repeal of prohibition. At once he began working with legislative leaders to achieve repeal of prohibition. The new governor's first step was to require state officials to enforce the prohibition law as it had never been done before. Raids on bootleggers and illegal bars and private clubs happened daily.

State leaders asked Oklahomans to vote on a proposal to repeal the prohibition amendment to the state constitution. The bill provided for an Alcoholic Beverage Control Board that would issue licenses to privately owned package stores as liquor outlets. The election on this question was held on April 7, 1959. The question carried by a vote of 386,845 to 314,830. The Twenty-seventh Legislature put the amendment into effect by the Liquor Control Act. Legal liquor sales began on September 1, 1959.

The repeal of prohibition was in a sense a social revolution for Oklahoma. Governor Edmondson urged the legislature to adopt additional measures to

171

Governor J. Howard Edmondson.

tions. State Question 391 provided for the creation of the Oklahoma Industrial Finance Authority. This agency would be authorized to issue bonds to the amount of $10 million for loans to local agencies for industrial development. This proposition was also approved.

In 1960, midway through the Edmondson administration, Oklahoma voters went to the polls to elect a new president. The national Republican party nominated Richard M. Nixon. The Democratic party nominated John F. Kennedy. Nixon triumphed in Oklahoma, the third consecutive time a Republican presidential candidate had carried the state. Kennedy won the election, however.

In the same election, Robert S. Kerr ran for reelection to the United States Senate. His Republican opponent was B. Hayden Crawford, a Tulsa attorney. Kerr won the Senate race. Democrats also won five of the six congressional seats and maintained control of the state legislature.

The Edmondson reform program included a plan to make the Highway Commission a constitutional board and thus reduce the effect of patronage on its operation. He also wanted to redraw legislative boundaries in such manner as to provide greater voice for the growing urban centers of the state. His last plan was to reduce the power of county commissioners by allowing the State Highway Commission to control the funds for local highways and other improvements usually controlled by county commissioners. Edmondson failed to gain legislative support for these proposals. He therefore took the issues to the people by gaining a statewide vote on them by initiative peti-

bring about drastic change in other areas of state government. One of these was a withholding system to assure more efficient collection of the state income tax. Another was to set up a merit system for state employees that required a person's employment by the state to be based on qualifications and competency rather than on political affiliation. Both measures were passed by the legislature.

Edmondson's program included the expansion of buildings and facilities at public institutions, continued highway development, and the establishment of a state agency to promote and help finance industrial plants. The legislature submitted two of these matters to the voters for a referendum vote.

In the summer of 1960, Oklahoma voters approved State Question 393, which provided for a $35 million bond issue for construction at state institu-

President John F. Kennedy at Big Cedar, Oklahoma.

tion. All three proposals were turned down by the voters.

A reaction against Governor Edmondson's program developed in the second half of his administration. The Twenty-eighth Legislature reduced the effect of the merit system by exempting employees working for elective officials. Highway building did continue to grow, with more than two thousand miles of roads constructed, including expansion of the interstate system.

The election of 1962, which determined a new chief executive for Oklahoma, produced a political revolution. Midwest City builder William P. (Bill) Atkinson won the Democratic nomination and ran on a platform stressing the need for more money. He proposed that this additional revenue should come from an increase in the state sales tax. Henry Bellmon, a Noble County

wheat farmer and Republican leader, won his party's nomination for governor. His platform stressed rigid economy and denied the need for tax increase.

Bellmon won the November election and became Oklahoma's first Republican governor. Democrats dominated the other elective positions, including majorities in both houses of the legislature. Mike Monroney ran for reelection to the United States Senate. His Republican opponent was B. Hayden Crawford. Monroney won the United States Senate race, and Democrats also won five of the six congressional seats.

Bellmon's inauguration as governor would occur on January 14, 1963. On New Year's Day, 1963, Senator Robert S. Kerr died. According to the state succession law then in effect, the governor had the power to fill a vacancy

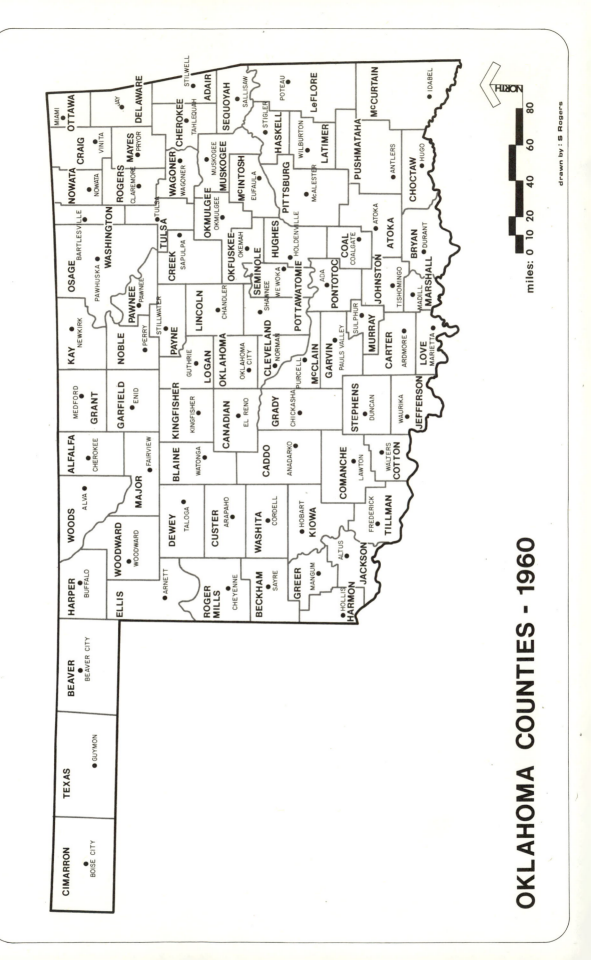

OKLAHOMA COUNTIES - 1960

miles: 0 10 20 40 60 80

drawn by : S Rogers

NORTH

in public office. The appointee would then hold office until the next general election.

Nine days before his term as governor ended, Governor Edmondson resigned and Lieutenant Governor George Nigh became the governor of Oklahoma. Governor Nigh then appointed Edmondson to the United States Senate as a replacement for the late Senator Kerr.

The Bellmon Administration

GOVERNOR NIGH was succeeded by Governor Bellmon on January 14, 1963. Even though the opposition party dominated the legislature, Governor Bellmon was able to work effectively with the body in achieving his goals for Oklahoma. The first half of his administration saw the sale of bonds for a new eastern turnpike to cost an estimated $31 million. The state oil depletion allowance was increased to 27.5 percent, and the merit system was strengthened by establishing an employees' retirement system.

Redrawing legislative district lines was one of the most serious problems facing the legislature. In 1962 a federal court ruled that the Oklahoma legislature improperly represented the people. It did not give enough voice to Oklahoma citizens living in the cities, which had absorbed much of the population of the once heavily populated rural areas.

In March, 1963, the legislature passed a reapportionment law, but a panel of three federal judges in Oklahoma City ruled that the new law did not satisfy the requirements of fair representation. The judges themselves then reappor-

Governor Henry Bellmon.

tioned the state to equalize representation in the house and senate. Primary elections for legislators under the plan were held September 29, 1964.

A presidential election year occurred in 1964, and it proved to be one of the most exciting periods in state political history. The election was colored by the right-to-work issue. The federal Taft-Hartley Labor Act allowed states to pass laws commonly called right-to-work laws. These made it illegal to force a person to join a union. Twenty states, including Kansas, Texas, and Arkansas already had right-to-work laws. Several business leaders in the state claimed such a law was necessary for Oklahoma to create a favorable business climate. Oklahoma labor unions opposed it.

The Oklahoma right-to-work proposition, a proposed constitutional amendment brought to the voters an initiative petition, appeared on the ballot as State Question 409. If adopted, it would restrict union activity by forbidding compulsory union membership as a condition for employment. In the May 5, 1964, election the proposition was defeated.

In the general election in November, 1964, President Lyndon B. Johnson, the Democratic candidate, was challenged by Senator Barry Goldwater, the Republican candidate. Johnson defeated Goldwater in Oklahoma and the nation by a landslide margin.

In this election Oklahomans also chose a new United States senator. State Senator Fred Harris won the Democratic nomination for this office. His Republican opponent was former University of Oklahoma football coach Bud Wilkinson. Harris defeated Wilkinson to win the final two years of Senator Robert S. Kerr's term. Democrats won five of the six congressional seats and a majority in both houses of the state legislature.

Serious problems, especially financing the public schools, faced Governor Bellmon and the legislature after the 1964 election. Great pressure to increase taxes to provide more money for public schools led Governor Bellmon, who opposed a tax increase, to propose a plan called "Giant Stride." The plan was a proposed $500 million bond issue to refinance the state bond-financed turnpikes, to build five new toll roads, and to provide $100 million for highways. This plan, Bellmon believed, would release enough money from the general fund to assure teachers an $800 pay increase over a two-year period.

The Oklahoma Education Association demanded a $1,000 increase for Oklahoma teachers and asked the National Education Association (NEA) to investigate the Oklahoma educational system. The NEA investigating committee studied Oklahoma education. Its report criticized the "subminimal conditions" in Oklahoma education, pointing out that the state ranked fortieth among the fifty states in per child spending for education. The state ranked thirty-seventh in the nation in salaries for its teachers. Based on its investigation, the NEA placed Oklahoma on a national blacklist and imposed professional sanctions.

The legislature tried to raise more money to improve education in Oklahoma. A sales-tax proposition was voted down by the people. Then the lawmakers passed a one-cent increase in the cigarette tax, and, with a higher estimate of general fund revenue, wrote an educational program providing for an average annual salary increase for teachers of $500 and allotted $5.2 million for textbooks for public school students.

Among the reforms adopted by the Thirtieth Legislature was the district attorney law. This replaced the county attorney system. This law divided the state into twenty-seven districts and provided each with a district attorney. These officials, elected for the first time in 1966 to four-year terms, took office in January, 1967.

The Thirtieth Legislature exercised its impeachment powers by removing an Oklahoma Supreme Court justice. The impeachment came from charges of corruption in the State Supreme Court. These evolved from a conviction in federal court of former Vice-Chief Justice Nelson Corn on charges of income tax evasion. Justice Earl

Welch was convicted in federal court on a similar charge.

While in prison, former Justice Corn gave federal and state investigators a statement saying his fellow State Supreme Court justices had accepted bribes. Justice Welch resigned from the court a few days before impeachment proceedings began. However, Corn's statement also involved Justice N. B. Johnson. The house investigated and voted charges of accepting bribes. After a week-long trial in the state senate, Justice Johnson was convicted and removed from the Oklahoma Supreme Court.

Governor Bellmon's successor was elected in 1966. The Republican party chose as its candidate state Senator Dewey Bartlett of Tulsa. The Democratic party candidate was Preston Moore, former national commander of the American Legion and an attorney from Oklahoma City. Bartlett defeated Moore to become not only the second Republican chief executive of the state but the first consecutive Republican to be elected to that office.

United States Senator Fred Harris, elected in 1964 to serve the last two years of Senator Robert S. Kerr's term, sought a full six-year term in 1966. He was challenged by the Republican candidate Pat J. Patterson of Oklahoma City. Harris defeated Patterson in the November election.

The Republicans, besides electing their second consecutive governor, for the first time in state history won the office of attorney general with the election of G. T. Blankenship. Democrats maintained control of both houses of the legislature and won four congressional seats. The Republicans won two congressional seats.

Governor Dewey Bartlett.

The Bartlett Administration

GOVERNOR DEWEY BARTLETT had campaigned and won on a platform similar to that of former Governor Henry Bellmon—a no-tax-increase promise. He pledged to manage the state government with existing revenue.

A change in legislative meetings from biennial (every other year) sessions to annual sessions took place in 1967. The legislature passed a redistricting bill that was based on the population shift from rural to urban areas and provided each congressional district with a better balance of population. The legislature also passed the Unclaimed Property Act. This law permits the State Tax Commission to take over accounts in banks, utilities, and oil companies that have not been used by their owners for fourteen years and spend the money as state revenue.

The State Supreme Court bribery scandal prompted a demand for judicial reform. The legislature passed a

177

court reform plan and sent it to the people in a special election on July 11, 1967. The measure provided for the nonpartisan election of members of the Oklahoma judiciary. The measure also abolished the justice of the peace system in Oklahoma. Voters approved the judicial reform plans.

Governor Bartlett vetoed (turned down) a number of legislative bills. Included among them were a salary increase for several state officials and a statewide kindergarten system. During 1967 the state senate investigated charges of conflict of interest among state officials. The study was begun when it was revealed that public utility lobbyists had provided cash and other gifts for public officials, including the state corporation commissioners.

Oklahomans went to the polls to vote for a new president in 1968. The Republican party nominated Richard M. Nixon., a former vice-president. The Democratic party nominated incumbent Vice-President Hubert Humphrey. A new political grouping, the American party, campaigned in Oklahoma. This party's presidential candidate was George Wallace, governor of Alabama. Nixon carried Oklahoma and the nation to win the presidency.

Mike Monroney sought reelection at this time as the Democratic candidate for the United States Senate. His Republican opponent was former Governor Henry Bellmon. Bellmon defeated Monroney. Bellmon's victory marked the fourth time an Oklahoma Republican won a United States Senate seat and the second time a former governor of Oklahoma won this high office. The Oklahoma voters in 1968 also repealed the state tax on intangible (personal) property.

Inflation, a national economic problem, affected state government. Public employees, including schoolteachers, faced reduced real income as small salary increases failed to keep pace with rapidly rising living costs. Increased costs of supplies and equipment required by state agencies, and contract charges for public construction, particularly highways, placed additional stress on the state's financial resources. Governor Bartlett's commitment to no new taxes placed limitations on increasing public funds to meet rising costs. This problem surfaced in the legislature several times during the second half of the Bartlett administration.

The legislative session of 1968 was particularly stormy. Public schoolteachers demanded higher salaries and improved conditions for Oklahoma schools. Their statewide organization, the Oklahoma Education Association, presented teacher demands to Governor Bartlett and the legislature. These included a state-supported kindergarten system, increased funds for educating handicapped children, improved library facilities, and smaller classes.

Early in the session, the legislature adopted several plans to meet the teacher demands. Bartlett always vetoed these plans because they included tax increases. In May, 1968, through the Oklahoma Education Association, the teachers voted professional sanctions against Oklahoma schools (they urged teachers not to come to Oklahoma). Finally, in cooperation with Governor Bartlett, legislative leaders adopted a school improvement program that included a salary increase of $1,300 for each teacher, spread over three years.

During the 1968 session, the legislature adopted a series of laws putting into effect the judicial reform propositions. It also adopted a speaker-control bill which kept controversial speakers from appearing in Oklahoma, particularly on college campuses.

Campus disorders were common across the nation. The possibility that student unrest might spread to Oklahoma caused the governor and the legislature great concern. The speaker-ban law was expected to keep agitators off the Oklahoma campuses. In 1969 the law came under attack in the state and federal courts. A year later Attorney General G. T. Blankenship declared the law violated the right of free speech.

To stop civil disorders in the state, especially on college campuses, Governor Bartlett in 1968 had created the Office of Inter-Agency Co-ordination. Its purpose was to collect information on persons suspected of radical activities and to make this information available to state and local law enforcement agencies. The Inter-Agency was attacked from several sources as an invasion of privacy. The agency and its operation became a campaign issue in the 1970 gubernatorial campaign.

The legislature tried during 1969 and 1970 to bring some reform to the state tax structure. The proposals for equalizing taxes ranged all the way from ending the tax-exempt status of Oklahoma insurance companies to requiring more fair and realistic assessments on real estate.

Another reform idea was to rewrite the state constitution and bring it up to date. State leaders varied in their view on how to accomplish this. One group favored calling a constitutional convention to draft a new constitution. Another group favored reforming the constitution by amendments, with the state legislature directing the process. The question of calling a constitutional convention was submitted to Oklahomans for a referendum vote. A second proposal would authorize state officials to carry out a $70 million industrial bond issue. The issues were voted down.

As the Oklahoma political parties prepared for the 1970 gubernatorial race, Governor Bartlett came in for considerable attack by Democratic party leaders for what they called lack of progressive leadership for the state. A recent constitutional change approved by the voters made it possible for the governor to succeed himself. Thus it was expected that Governor Bartlett would seek reelection.

The election of 1970 was a very close contest in the governor's race. Governor Dewey Bartlett, the Republican candidate, sought a second term as Oklahoma's chief executive. From a very intense Democratic primary, David Hall, a Tulsa attorney, emerged as the party's candidate. Initial returns in the November election showed that Hall was the winner, but only by a margin of 2,190 votes. Governor Bartlett requested a recount of the ballots, but the recount sustained Hall's margin of victory.

In this election of 1970, Republicans won two of Oklahoma's six congressional seats; Democratic candidates won four. One of the Democrats returned to Congress was Carl Albert of McAlester, destined by his victory to receive high national office. Democrats also won all the state's elective offices and a majority of seats in both houses of the legislature.

When the United States Congress

Congressman Carl Albert, Speaker of the United States House of Representatives.

opened in January, 1971, Congressman Carl Albert was sworn in as Speaker of the House. This is the highest national office ever held by an Oklahoman. For several years Albert had served as majority floor leader of the United States House of Representatives while John McCormack of Massachusetts was speaker.

The Hall Administration

FOLLOWING his inauguration, Governor Hall turned his attention to the problems facing Oklahoma. His first official act was to fulfill a campaign promise to abolish the controversial Office of Inter-Agency Co-ordination.

The new governor said the first prob-lem in state government was money. Continued rising costs because of the national inflation and increasing revenue needs of state operations were complicated by state income not match-ing agency needs. The most pressing crisis was in public education. Okla-homa ranked forty-fifth among the fifty states in the amount of money spent on each student, with only Idaho, Ten-nessee, Arkansas, Mississippi, and Ala-bama ranked lower than Oklahoma.

Governor Hall proposed a system of tax increases to raise $82,700,000 in new state money. The legislature responded by approving increases in the oil and gas tax, the state income tax, and the liquor tax. All these together would in-crease state income by $43 million. Pub-lic schools, higher education, and high-ways received most of this new money.

The legislature approved the pub-lic kindergarten law, which had been sought by Oklahoma teachers for many years. The legislature also passed a re-apportionment law to provide more ef-fective representation in state govern-ment for the growing towns and cities of the state.

Besides providing leadership in re-ducing the crisis in state government finance, Governor Hall carried out an intensive industry recruitment pro-gram that extended into 1972. The ded-ication of the vast Arkansas River navigation project in 1971 ranked as an outstanding highlight of the early portion of the Hall administration.

Oklahoma politics for the rest of the decade of the 1970s were substan-tially altered by voter response in state and national elections and by reforms adopted by the state legislature. In 1972, Oklahomans went to the polls to vote for their presidential choice—Republican

Richard Nixon and Democrat George McGovern. Nixon carried Oklahoma and the nation to win reelection. Incumbent United States Senator Fred Harris chose not to seek reelection. Former Republican Governor Bartlett and Democratic Congressman Ed Edmondson contested for this position; Bartlett won. The year before Oklahoma voters had approved a proposition reducing the age for voters to eighteen, allowing persons in the 18-to-21 age group to vote in this presidential election.

During 1974, Oklahomans selected a new chief executive. David Boren, a Democratic state representative from Seminole won the governorship in a contest with Republican candidate Jim Imhoff, state senator from Tulsa. United States Senator Bellmon ran for reelection. He was challenged by Ed Edmondson, but was able to retain his Senate seat in a disputed election. The dispute was finally settled by a United States Senate committee. Other important elections in the state during this decade included the 1976 presidential race. Former Georgia Governor Jimmy Carter ran against Republican President Gerald Ford, successor to President Nixon, who had resigned. Ford won the Oklahoma electoral vote, but Carter triumphed nationally.

Two years later Oklahomans returned to the polls to elect another governor. Democratic candidate George Nigh, governor for a few days at the close of the Edmondson administration and a frequent lieutenant governor, was contested by Republican Ron Shotts. Nigh won. When Senator Bartlett chose not to seek reelection, Republican Robert Kamm, former president of Oklahoma State University, and Democratic Gov-

Governor David Hall.

ernor Boren sought the position. Boren won to become the first Democratic senator from Oklahoma in six years. In 1980, at the end of his second term, Senator Bellmon chose not to seek reelection. His Senate seat was sought by Democrat Andrew Coats, the Oklahoma County district attorney, and by Republican businessman Don Nickles. The latter triumphed. Also in the 1980 election, President Jimmy Carter was defeated for reelection by Republican Ronald Reagan in Oklahoma and the nation.

Throughout the decade of the 1970s the Democratic-dominated Oklahoma legislature had three primary concerns. They had to attempt to keep pace with rapidly rising costs of state government primarily due to inflation. The execu-

Governor, later United States Senator, David Boren.

of State John Rogers. Rogers was impeached by the house on charges of corruption concerning investment of state retirement funds, but he resigned before his trial began in the senate. Hall later was indicted in federal court on charges of extortion and conspiracy to commit bribery; he was convicted and sentenced to a three-year term in a federal prison.

Reforms adopted by the legislature during the decade of the 1970s included lowering the voting age to eighteen. In addition, the legislature submitted a proposal for referendum vote to shorten the ballot. The measure authorized the governor to appoint the secretary of state, the labor commissioner, and the chief mine inspector. The proposition was approved. The legislature also adopted a series of so-called "sunset laws," which require an annual review of state agencies to decide if they should continue to operate. The 1980 census revealed that Oklahoma's population had increased from 2,559,253 (in the 1970 census) to 3,025,266, the first time in state history for the Sooner population to reach and exceed three million.

The decade of the 1980s began with several significant happenings. During 1982, Oklahoma voters considered a number of questions and candidates. A gubernatorial election year, incumbent George Nigh was contested by Republican State Auditor Tom Daxon. Nigh triumphed to become the first chief executive in state history to succeed himself. Voters approved State Question 553, which permits parimutuel betting, an issue strongly supported by the Oklahoma Horsemen's Association.

Among other developments of significance that ushered in the 1980s were grim revelations centering on

tive branch required investigation, and state government needed to be reformed. An increasing need for money to meet the spiraling costs of state government is reflected in appropriations for the decade of the 1970s: 1972, $325 million; 1975, $700 million; well over $1 billion in 1980; and slightly more than $2 billion (including federal funds) in 1983. Much of this increase in funding went to highway construction and maintenance, and for the support of public schools, colleges, universities, and other state institutions.

During the decade of the 1970s the legislature spent much time investigating the executive branch. Legislators considered impeachment proceedings against several state officials, including Governor Hall and Secretary the county commissioners' scandal. Federal investigators discovered that county commissioners had been involved in unlawful transactions called kickbacks (taking money) with suppliers of heavy equipment and road and building materials. By early 1982, at least two hundred county commissioners, former commissioners, and suppliers had been arrested, tried, convicted, and fined or sentenced to terms in federal prison, or were awaiting trial, or were being investigated.

Careless or faulty treatment given youth in the care of the Department of Human Services surfaced in 1982. Newspaper and television investigative reporters published reports of this improper treatment. As a result of this, longtime Director Lloyd Rader retired. Former governor and former United States Senator Henry Bellmon was appointed director to remove those causes of criticism and to improve management of the Department of Human Services.

Throughout the 1970s, the Oklahoma economy prospered from business and industrial expansion and there was nearly full employment. The primary support for the state's economy was the widespread oil and natural gas explorations, and the production, processing, and marketing of the oil industry. The boom seemed to peak in 1982, and as the oil industry's prosperity declined so did private and state wealth. Unemployment increased substantially. All of this was a reflection of a general decline in the nation's economy.

One of the most sensational indicators of the growing recession was the failure of Penn Square Bank in Oklahoma City, which had been a heavy money lender for many drilling and production com-

Governor George Nigh.

panies. The Penn Square Bank failure set off shock waves and money losses were felt in banking circles all across the nation because Penn Square Bank had borrowed heavily from larger banks in other states.

More signs of the decline in Oklahoma's economy during 1982 were startling increases in business bankruptcies, reduced production by industrial plants, or in some cases even closings, and mounting layoffs of workers. Oklahoma state government had had several years of increasing revenue. State agencies and the services they provide were brought up short in 1982 by a drastic decline in revenue. Late in that year Governor Nigh told all agencies to cut spending, and the legislature prepared to apply a more cautious approach to funding state government.

Women in Oklahoma Politics: Former Mayor of Oklahoma City Patience Latting; State Representative Hannah Atkins; State Representative Cleta Deatherage.

184

Study Aids

Explain the significance of each term or phrase listed below:

1. Merit system
2. Legislative reapportionment
3. "Giant Stride"
4. Arkansas River Project
5. Right-to-work
6. Withholding system

Identify each of these persons:

1. B. Hayden Crawford
2. William O. Coe
3. William P. Atkinson
4. Douglas McKeever
5. Reuben K. Sparks
6. William Alexander

On an outline map of Oklahoma locate the following places:

1. Maramec
2. Frederick
3. Eagletown
4. Orienta
5. Thomas
6. Madill

Use the suggestions below for study guides:

1. Describe the Edmondson reform program.
2. Show how repeal of prohibition came about and explain the Alcoholic Beverage Control Board program.
3. Discuss the 1962 revolution in Oklahoma politics.
4. Describe Governor Bartlett's approach to state problems.
5. Characterize the first part of the Hall administration.

For Further Reading

Debo, Angie. *Footloose and Fancy Free.* Norman, 1949.

Franklin, Jimmie Lewis. *The Blacks in Oklahoma.* Norman, 1980.

McReynolds, Edwin C. *Oklahoma: A History of the Sooner State.* Norman, 1954.

Morgan, Anne Hodges. *Robert S. Kerr: The Senate Years.* Norman, 1977.

Directory of the State of Oklahoma. Oklahoma City, 1961.

Directory of the State of Oklahoma. Oklahoma City, 1981.

Scales, James R., and Danney Goble. *Oklahoma Politics: A History.* Norman, 1982.

Chapter 13. **HOW OKLAHOMANS EARN A LIVING**

The Farming Industry

TODAY, Oklahomans earn their living in many ways. Some work in factories and plants, some work in the mines, and others work in the oil fields and refineries. Many Oklahomans are tradesmen, construction workers, transportation workers, and professionals, such as teachers, doctors, and lawyers. A surprising number of citizens are employed in public works, particularly at federal military bases. A decreasing number of people are working in farming and stock raising. Today, most people in the state live in towns and cities. Not long ago, however, most Oklahomans lived in rural areas and were farmers and stock raisers.

Oklahoma agriculture is very old, perhaps going back four thousand years. Prehistoric Oklahoma farmers grew beans, squash, corn, melons, and tobacco. At the time of the entry of Europeans into Oklahoma in 1540, several

Indian tribes then living in Oklahoma were farmers.

With the arrival of the Five Civilized Tribes from east of the Mississippi River, beginning around 1820, the agricultural development continued. The Indian settlers established farms, ranches, and plantations. They began planting cotton in Oklahoma. These Indian pioneers exported grains and cotton to markets on the lower Mississippi River and the Gulf Coast. They sold their livestock and other products in the settlements on the Missouri-Arkansas border.

Intensive agriculture in Oklahoma began with the arrival of the homesteaders in 1889 and continued throughout the territorial period. In central and western Oklahoma, settlers found a deep layer of rich topsoil covered with grass. They turned under the native grass cover with sod plows and began producing cotton, corn, and other cash crops.

Early Oklahoma farmers did not know how to prevent erosion. Contour plowing was not practiced. Crop rows were plowed up and down the slopes, and pasture and meadow lands were burned over. Then, when heavy rains and strong winds occurred, thousands of acres of soil, no longer held by vegetation, were eroded. An estimated 80 percent of Oklahoma's soil has suffered some erosion.

Cotton was the most important cash crop from territorial days to the 1930s. In recent times it has become a surplus crop in the nation's economy. Federal controls restrict its production in order to stabilize prices. Production on Oklahoma farms runs from about 350,000 to 400,000 bales per year. As late as the 1940s more than forty thousand persons were required each fall to hand-pick the cotton crop. This compares with fewer than five hundred today because of the increased use of mechanical pickers.

Wheat has replaced cotton as the state's leading cash crop. Wheat production in Oklahoma varies from 100 million to 200 million bushels a year. In 1979, Oklahoma farms produced 217 million bushels of wheat. Like cotton, wheat has been a surplus crop and production has been controlled by federal acreage allotments and government price supports. Wheat is Oklahoma's most important foreign export. About 40 percent of the annual harvest is sent abroad.

Dairy farming, poultry raising, and broomcorn and peanut production are also important segments of the state's agricultural industry. Orchards produce fruits for export. Eastern Oklahoma is the scene of considerable bush fruit and strawberry culture.

The Livestock Industry

OKLAHOMA was a part of the once vast range-cattle industry. Stock raising con-

Modern harvesting of cotton. It was once harvested by hand.

tinues as an important part of the agricultural industry. Included are sheep, hogs, cattle, and horses, but cattle are the most important. Because of the mechanization of agriculture, less intensive cultivation, and the application of conservation practices, more of Oklahoma's farmland in recent years has been returned to grass and livestock-support crops. Alfalfa, sorghums, bermuda, and other hay and feed crops are grown widely in the state to support the livestock industry.

Related to the increased production of livestock feed is the business of feedlot operation in Oklahoma. Each year Oklahoma ranch and farm herds produce more than 2 million calves. About half of this calf production is shipped to Iowa and other corn-belt states for sale to feedlot operators. In recent years an increasing number of calves have been

187

Modern wheat harvesting is often done by harvest crews that travel from state to state.

taken to feedlots in Oklahoma. During the 1970s, more than a half million animals were processed annually in the state's expanding feedlot facilities.

An important phase of stock raising is marketing. The livestock trade has long been a leading industry in Oklahoma. Livestock markets are found in every part of the state. One of the principal livestock outlets in the Southwest is the Oklahoma City Stockyards. It is rated as a leading cattle center of the nation.

New Farm and Ranch Practices

OKLAHOMA farmers and ranchers have been active in applying conservation practices to their fields and pastures. Years of intensive farming with row-crop agriculture, the one-crop system, and overgrazing reduced the productivity of farms and ranches. Experts es-

timate that wind and water erosion has carried away one-third of the state's top-soil.

After the extended drought that caused widespread dust storms during the 1930s, Oklahoma farmers and ranchers began to adopt conservation methods. The uses of contour plowing, gully control, regrassing and reforestation, planting cover crops and trees to create shelter belts, and strip farming helped to reduce erosion, to restore the soil, and to improve the productivity of Oklahoma soils.

Irrigation is another modern development in Oklahoma agriculture. Rainfall varies considerably across the western half of the state. By 1940, farmers in that part of the state had applied irrigation to 5,000 acres to supplement the natural rainfall.

Large-scale irrigation came to Oklahoma in 1947 with the opening of the W. C. Austin project near Altus. With-

Central Oklahoma dairy herd.

in three years, 50,000 acres were under irrigation. By 1965 this had increased to more than 350,000 acres. Jackson County, served by the Austin project, had 60,000 acres under irrigation. In 1970, Texas County in the Panhandle had more than 250,000 irrigated acres, served by six hundred wells. By 1980 more than a million acres of Oklahoma farmland was under irrigation.

Scientific research is an important part of the Oklahoma economy. Farming and stock raising have benefited from some of this research. Oklahoma State University, with its agricultural experiment station headquarters at Stillwater and regional stations distributed over the state, carries on extensive studies on improvement of farming and stock raising. Scientists in the state laboratories work closely with specialists in the United States Department of Agriculture. Research by Oklahoma State University scientists in fertilizer alone

has added more than $50 million to the state wheat crop value.

Farming and stock raising are less a way of life than in former times and are more of a business. Fewer people live in the rural areas on farms and ranches because it takes fewer people to run the farms and ranches. With the application of mechanization and new technology to farming and ranching, one person can produce enough food to sustain from twenty-five to thirty people.

Yet agriculture is one of Oklahoma's most important businesses. It amounted to more than a billion dollars in value in 1980, rivaling the income from petroleum and other leading industries. Oklahoma's labor force consists of about one million workers. More of these are engaged in agriculture-related activities than any other business or industry. An estimated 200,000 persons, 20 percent of the state labor force, are engaged in

Cattle being fattened for market at a western Oklahoma feedlot operation.

meat and dairy processing, canning and freezing food products, grain milling and processing, and other agriculture-based industries.

Oklahoma Mineral Resources

NATURE richly endowed Oklahoma with minerals. The mining of Oklahoma mineral resources is an old business. The first quarries in northeastern Oklahoma were opened by prehistoric craftsmen. They used the hard stone material, called chert, to make lance and arrow points, stone knives, scrapers, and axe heads. Salt springs and flats, found in most parts of the state, and surface-exposed pieces of lead or galena were used by Indians and frontiersmen to supply their needs for salt and ammunition.

Salt springs near present Salina and on the Illinois River were mined commercially soon after 1800. Salt water was boiled in huge kettles over wood-burning fires to evaporate the water from the salt. Salt produced in frontier Oklahoma was sold locally for food seasoning and preserving meat, and was exported to Gulf markets. Salt is still produced in Oklahoma from salt springs or salt-water wells and sold largely for livestock. The state has an estimated reserve of one billion tons of rock salt.

Coal is an important Oklahoma mineral. Early visitors to Oklahoma, including Bernard de La Harpe in 1719 and Thomas Nuttall in 1819, observed the presence of rich coal seams in east-

Modern irrigation methods bring water to Oklahoma Panhandle farms.

ern Oklahoma. Before the Civil War, limited amounts of coal were mined to supply blacksmith forges.

In 1871, J. J. McAlester developed the first commercial coal mines in Oklahoma near present McAlester. He organized the Osage Coal and Mining Company. The principal markets for Oklahoma coal in those times were the railroads. The engines required huge amounts of coal to fire the locomotive boilers. The MKT Railway Company was the first line to use Oklahoma coal.

In Indian Territory times, coal deposits were opened in the Choctaw Nation, the Creek Nation, and the Cherokee Nation. Miners were imported from Pennsylvania and from foreign counties, including Greece, Italy, Russia, Poland, France, and Great Britain. The coal

seams were tapped by deep-shaft mining and by strip-mining methods. By 1903, Indian Territory coal mines were yielding 3 million tons annually. Peak production in Oklahoma coal mines occurred in 1920 when nearly 5 million tons of coal were taken.

A gradual decline in coal mining took place because of the development of other power sources, notably fuel oil, gasoline, and natural gas. With the movement of heavy industry into the Southwest after World War II, coal production in Oklahoma picked up. In 1949, more than a hundred coal workings produced 3,430,152 tons of coal and employed 2,500 miners.

As with agriculture, the mechanization of local mines has reduced the labor force. In 1962 coal mining employed

Lead and zinc mining, northeastern Oklahoma.

six hundred men. Much of the Oklahoma coal during the 1960s was exported to East Texas steel mills. By 1972 the market for Oklahoma coal had grown, with much of it being sold to Canada, Mexico, and Japan. During the 1970s, Oklahoma coal production steadily increased as public utilities and other industrial users of fossil fuels reduced their dependence on oil and turned more to coal.

Among Oklahoma's mineral riches, lead and zinc have been of great importance. These two minerals, found together, are often joined in the earth as a mixture of flinty chert. Commercial mining of lead and zinc began in 1890 at Peoria in Ottawa County. It was a part of the Tri-State District operations from southwestern Missouri and southeastern Kansas extending into Oklahoma. Rich lead and zinc discoveries at Peoria made the Oklahoma portion of the Tri-State field the richest in the district.

In 1913 a heavily mineralized zone was found at Picher. The production from the new mines, added to those of the Missouri and Kansas portions of the Tri-State District, made it the heaviest producer of lead and zinc ores in the world. Between 1900 and 1950 more than a billion dollars worth of mineral ores was taken from Tri-State mines.

Heavy mining, however, has depleted the rich mineral lodes of the Tri-State. Only marginal deposits remain, and to operate at a profit mine owners must have some sort of government assistance. During 1960, twenty-four mining companies produced 193,295 tons of lead and zinc. Three mines at Cardin yielded most of the tonnage. Operations declined during the 1960s and had ceased by 1970.

The Petroleum Industry

OKLAHOMA's industrial image in the nation and the world is oil. Certainly the petroleum industry has been one of

Oklahoma's main sources of wealth, employment, and money for state government. Beginning in 1882 with crude equipment, local production was hardly worth recording, amounting to about thirty barrels annually. The chief uses of petroleum at that time were as medicine, as kerosene or coal oil to illuminate homes and businesses, and as grease for lubricants. Production gradually increased to a few hundred barrels each year.

Authorities rate the Bartlesville field, opened in 1897 by the Cudahy Oil Company with the drilling of Number One Nellie Johnstone, as the first important oil discovery in present Oklahoma. The Red Fork field, near Tulsa, was opened in 1901, and its wells produced the first commercially significant volume of oil. Drillers searched Indian Territory and Oklahoma Territory for favorable oil signs as the demand for petroleum products increased. New fields were opened at Coody's Bluff and Cleveland in 1904, and in 1905 the famous Glenn Pool near Tulsa was opened. This gave rise to Tulsa being called "The Oil Capital of the World." On the eve of statehood, Oklahoma oil wells were producing more than 40 million barrels a year.

Improved equipment and increased demand brought additional exploration, and by 1920, Oklahoma had become the nation's leading oil producer with more than a billion barrels a year. One of the richest petroleum fields in the world was discovered in the heart of Oklahoma City in 1928. Of the 1,658 wells sunk in the Oklahoma City field, all but 113 produced oil and gas. Since its opening, the Oklahoma City district alone has yielded nearly a billion barrels of crude oil.

Osage County, famous not only for

Kerr-McGee Corporation's first oil well rig.

193

Sunray refining facility, Tulsa.

large production of petroleum, but also for the rich Osage Indian oil headrights, was opened in 1904 with the discovery of oil at Avant. Osage County wells have produced close to a billion barrels of oil. By 1957, the Cushing field, discovered in 1912, had yielded half a billion barrels from 1,830 wells. Glenn Pool, with 1,804 wells, produced at its peak more than a quarter-billion barrels of oil. Both the Wheeler Pool in Carter County and a heavily producing field near Okmulgee were brought in during 1907. These were followed after 1912 by the Hewitt, the Garber, and the Healdton openings.

The vast Healdton field helped Oklahoma achieve national oil leadership in 1920 by boosting the total production for the state that year to a record of one billion barrels of crude oil. It is said that the wells at Healdton fur-

nished 50 percent of all oil for the Allied Powers in World War I. At the end of 1957 its 2,046 wells had produced a quarter-billion barrels.

The Tonkawa and the Three Sands fields opened in 1921. At the time of discovery they were the westernmost of Oklahoma's oil-producing district. Nearly every year throughout the decade saw a new field opened. Among the major discoveries were the Sholem Alechem of southern Oklahoma in 1923, and the Saint Louis field in Pottawatomie County in 1925. Heavily flowing wells there yielded 200 million barrels of crude oil by 1957.

The Seminole field, opened during 1926, made a record output during the 1930s. The Little River field was discovered during 1927, followed by the Earlsboro in 1930. Fitts field in Pontotoc County opened in 1933. In more recent times, the Golden Trend, a vast district spread through Garvin, Grady, and McClain counties, was tapped first in 1946. Followed by discoveries at Ringwood and Hennessey, the Golden Trend accounts for many of the new completions recorded since the close of World War II.

Oil discoveries have marched across the state so that virtually every county now records some production of oil and its common underground associate, natural gas. While oil and natural gas often occur together, drillers frequently open wells containing only natural gas. In early oil-field history, operators wasted most of the natural gas to get at the more valuable crude oil.

New uses for natural gas gradually developed, at first principally as an illuminant; many homes and cities at the turn of the century were lighted by natural gas. Today natural gas is used for home heating and cooking, and to fire the boilers of industry, even those producing electric power. Most of the large gas wells are in western Oklahoma and the Panhandle; but recently in eastern Oklahoma drillers discovered a new natural gas district, Arkoma Basin, situated in Le Flore, Latimer, Haskell, and Pittsburg counties.

The oil industry is important to the state for many reasons. In all of its production stages, it provides employment for more than a hundred thousand Oklahomans. Processing oil is an important industry for the state. Fourteen refineries operate with a capacity to handle nearly half a million barrels of crude oil daily.

Transportation of petroleum products is another important phase of the industry. Motor tank trucks, railroad tank cars, and 12,000 miles of pipeline move the daily crude production to market.

The oil industry also is important for the growth of towns and cities in Oklahoma. Generally oil has been found in remote areas. Boomtowns sprang up overnight next to each new oil field. The houses in the boomtowns were often no more than one-room shacks. The boomtowns' streets were dusty when dry and deep in mud when wet.

These oil boomtowns attracted hardworking roughnecks, drillers, and other workmen. They also attracted the reckless and the lawless, the gambler and the gunman. Law and order problems were common to all such communities. If the field was rich and had a long life, the boomtowns changed into orderly communities with permanent homes and business buildings. Many leading Oklahoma towns got their start as boomtowns after an oil discovery.

Other Mineral Industries

OTHER mineral industries that add to the variety and importance of the Oklahoma economy are tripoli mining, gypsum production, quarrying for building stone and cement, sand conversion into glass, and clay uses.

Tripoli, a fine abrasive material used for delicate grinding and polishing and filtering, is mined in Ottawa County of northeastern Oklahoma. Gypsum is found in many parts of the state. It is mined and processed into a soil conditioner and wallboard, called sheetrock, used in home and business construction.

Building stone and gravel are quarried and processed for construction, including highways and public buildings. Crushed limestone is used for fertilizer

Modern lumbering in southeastern Oklahoma's pine forests.

eration by business leaders of the Five Civilized Tribes soon after their arrival from the East. Before the Civil War, a few steam-powered sawmills were in operation in Oklahoma's eastern forests. In 1889 eleven commercial sawmills, all powered by steam, operated in Indian Territory forests.

In the modern lumber industry, the principal timber that is milled is softwood—shortleaf and loblolly pine—although hardwoods are also commercially important. Of these hardwoods the most widely used are white and red oak, ash, hickory, black and sweet gum, sycamore, cypress, maple, black cherry, and walnut. Red cedar is also a widely used commercial wood. Eastern Oklahoma mills turn out construction lumber, bridge timbers, fence posts, telephone poles, pulpwood, fiberboard, charcoal, and furniture woods.

The Manufacturing Industry

FARMING, stock raising, mining, oil production, and lumbering are basic industries. Through the years Oklahoma leaders have worked hard to diversify the Oklahoma economy and add to the basic industries a variety of job-producing manufacturing industries. In 1900, Oklahoma had five hundred manufacturing plants with 2,600 workers. The annual production was valued at $2.7 million. By 1929 the number of workers in industry had grown to 30,000 with a production value of $150 million.

Through active industrial recruitment after World War II, manufacturing employed 78,000 workers in 1952, with an annual production value of $493 million. By 1965 more than 100,000 persons held industrial jobs, and the

and in railroad construction. Red granite, quarried in southwestern Oklahoma, is esteemed for use in monuments and public buildings. Oklahoma-produced cement is an important product for state use and export in the construction business.

A combination of high-quality sand and plentiful natural gas gave rise to a thriving glass manufacturing business for Oklahoma. Glass plants in eight cities employ nearly five thousand persons and produce glass products valued at nearly $20 million a year. In several Sooner plants, Oklahoma clays have been converted to construction bricks, tile, and ceramics.

The Lumbering Industry

AN OLD INDUSTRY in Oklahoma that is growing in importance is lumbering. Water-powered sawmills were put in op-

Executive aircraft are manufactured in Bethany, Oklahoma.

value of manufacturing was more than one billion dollars.

Some of Oklahoma's older job-producing manufacturing industries have been meat packing, brewing, and refining petroleum products. Some refining and smelting of metals, particularly zinc, also occurred in Oklahoma. Glass manufacturing has already been noted. Processing food items produced on Oklahoma farms and ranches is a growing industry.

All of the old established industries —meat processing and packing, poultry and egg preparation, and grain milling—have grown. Milling wheat and corn into flour and meal are important industries in the grain-producing portions of the state. Stock raising has changed from the open-range type of operation to controlled breeding and production, including the feedlot. Because of this, grain milling and process-

ing have been expanded to include preparation of special grain and silage rations required to "finish out" (fatten) livestock for market.

New Oklahoma industries produce finished consumer goods ranging from airplanes to clothing, gloves, footwear, carpets, and appliances. Executive-type jet planes are manufactured at Bethany and Norman. Plants at Tulsa and Oklahoma City produce parts for space systems and ground-support equipment. Industrial laboratories at Ponca City, Bartlesville, Tulsa, and Oklahoma City conduct research in missile fuels, metallurgy, and plastics. Plants across the state assemble automobiles and manufacture automobile tires, boats, oil-field equipment, sporting goods, and chemicals. New industries include a uranium conversion plant in eastern Oklahoma.

The industry recruitment program carried on by governors, other state

197

The tourism industry in Oklahoma brings thousands of visitors to Sequoyah State Park (*above*), Beavers Bend State Park (*opposite page, above*), and Tenkiller Lake and State Park (*opposite, below*).

leaders and officials, and local chamber of commerce groups have increased the industrial employment pool in Oklahoma from 100,000 jobs in 1965 to more than 200,000 jobs in 1980.

The Service Industries

OKLAHOMA's service industries are many, but three that create the most widespread employment opportunities in the state are tourism, government, and transportation.

An expanding industry in Oklahoma is tourism. This industry nets about $1.2 billion each year and attracts about 30 million visitors to Oklahoma annually. The natural beauty of the Sooner State, its variety of landforms, its plant life, its scenic wonders, and its general raw beauty are appealing to outsiders. Thus

these resources rank among the state's most valuable.

In addition to the state's natural beauty are the many waterways, including clear streams in eastern Oklahoma and giant lakes scattered across the state. State parks at Lake Tenkiller, Lake Eufaula, Lake Texoma, Lake Thunderbird, and the Chickasaw Recreation Area, formerly Platt National Park at Sulphur, are prime attractions. A system of state lodges including Western Hills, Roman Nose, Lake Murray, and Quartz Mountain, add to tourist attractions.

In the Oklahoma economy, one of the biggest employers is government. In 1980 more than 200,000 persons were engaged in working for local, state, and federal governments. Fifty thousand of these are employees of the federal government, working at Tinker Air Force Base and the Federal Aviation Agency

Tinker Air Force Base, Oklahoma City, is a source of employment for thousands of Oklahomans.

at Oklahoma City, Fort Sill at Lawton, Altus Air Force Base at Altus, and other military installations.

Another factor in the expansion of the Oklahoma economy is transportation. An extensive grid of railroad lines furnishes transport facilities for Oklahoma's expanding production from farms, ranches, mines, and factories. Improved highway systems, notably the interstate system, provide truck-transport operators easy access to cities and towns and supplement the railway freight service.

Oklahoma's transportation resources were enlarged in 1971 with the completion of the Arkansas River navigation system, with the terminal port at Catoosa near Tulsa. Oklahoma businessmen can now ship their varied products at rates competitive with rail and truck freight rates.

The Oklahoma Labor Force

THE EXPANSION of the Oklahoma economy is caused by several factors. One is the state labor force. Oklahoma has been attractive to industries seeking new locations because of its high-quality labor supply. The state labor force varies from migratory workers—harvesting vegetables, fruit, cotton, and broomcorn—to highly trained electronic technicians, construction workers, industrial chemists, and space engineers.

Unionism began in Oklahoma in 1882

when the Knights of Labor established assemblies in the coal camps of the Choctaw Nation. Gradually the United Mine Workers (UMW) took over the organization of laborers in the coal fields of Indian Territory. Unions for the building trades were active in Oklahoma Territory, and in 1903 these organizations fused into the Twin Territories Federation of Labor. At statehood this organization became the Oklahoma Federation of Labor, an affiliate of the American Federation of Labor (AFL). The railroad brotherhoods contained the largest membership, both before and after statehood, when railroads were the principal carriers of men and goods and were heavy employers of workers.

During World War I, unskilled workers and tenant farmers were drawn into both the Industrial Workers of the World and the Working Class Union. These groups were radical, and each had a brief life. The Committee on Industrial Organization (CIO), a part of the American Federation of Labor, entered the state in the 1930s as a part of the national movement to organize the unskilled and industrial workers. Various units of the CIO seceded and maintained an independent existence until a few years ago when the national AFL and CIO merged. Today the official name for the spokesman of organized labor in the Sooner State is the Oklahoma Federation of Labor, AFL-CIO.

Other Economic Factors

AMONG other contributing factors to the Oklahoma economy are the state's capital resources (money) and research activities. Expanding its capital resources is basic to Oklahoma's growing economy. In early times eastern capital largely financed businesses in the state. This had the effect of maintaining only the basic industries without being able to diversify into the multiple job-producing kind of manufacturing. Recently, however, several individuals and companies in Oklahoma have developed capital resources sufficient to finance many local industries. Grants and loans from state and federal agencies also have expanded the state's capital resources.

Supporting all industries in the Oklahoma economic spectrum and pointing the way to new industries is scientific research. Much scientific research is done on the campuses of the University of Oklahoma at Norman and the Oklahoma State University at Stillwater. Some of the vital services provided by these institutions include: research, consulting, guidance, and direction for new businesses; developing new techniques and new products; and training leaders for Oklahoma's business future.

Study Aids

Explain the significance of each term or phrase listed below:

1. W. C. Austin project
2. Tri-State District
3. Erosion
4. Three Sands
5. Contour plowing
6. Arkoma basin

On an outline map of Oklahoma locate the following places:

1. Covington
2. Hardesty
3. Muldrow
4. Walters
5. Erick
6. Clinton

Use the suggestions below as study guides:

1. Explain the causes of soil erosion in Oklahoma.
2. Describe the methods used to check soil erosion.
3. List the Oklahoma mining industries.
4. Explain the importance of the oil industry and its related industries to the Oklahoma economy.
5. Describe the modern Oklahoma economy.

For Further Reading

Bell, Max W. *This Fascinating Oil Business.* Indianapolis, 1940.

De Graff, Herrell. *Beef: Production and Distribution.* Norman, 1960.

Dikeman, Neil J., and Marjorie E. Earley. *Statistical Abstract of Oklahoma, 1982.* Norman, 1982.

Glasscock, C. B. *Then Came Oil.* Indianapolis, 1938.

Kerr, Robert S. *Land, Wood and Water.* New York, 1960.

Knowles, Ruth Sheldon. *The Greatest Gamblers: The Epic of American Oil Exploration.* Norman, 1980.

Rister, Carl C. *Oil! Titan of the Southwest.* Norman, 1949.

Chapter 14. EDUCATION IN OKLAHOMA

Early Education in Oklahoma

THE ESTABLISHMENT of good schools so that its children could be taught is a continuing theme in Oklahoma history. Thus education has been discussed in several previous chapters in connection with the Indian tribes and with territorial and state government. Because education is so important to the future of Oklahoma, it seems proper to draw together in a separate chapter a summary of educational history and add to it those essentials to round out the story of education in Oklahoma.

The Five Civilized Tribes had established schools for Indian children before moving from the East to Indian Territory. Soon after their arrival in the West over the Trail of Tears, the leaders of these five tribes began establishing schools in the wilderness. Missionary teachers from the Baptist, Methodist, and Presbyterian churches assisted them. Soon each of the Indian nations had a system of schools for educating tribal youth. In each nation there was a superintendent of public instruction who supervised the curriculum, looked after the credentials of teachers, and generally managed the tribal education system.

Schools ranged from neighborhood elementary schools to Indian nation secondary schools. These were generally called academies or seminaries. Each tribal government set aside part of the tribal funds for the support of its schools. Tribal scholarships also financed the education of qualified tribal youth in eastern colleges and universities. Before the Civil War several Indian students from the Five Civilized Tribes studied at Yale, Dartmouth, and other institutions of higher learning in the East.

Tribal schools suffered during the Civil War. Most of them were closed because of a lack of teachers and funds. Several schools in the Choctaw and

Chickasaw nations were converted into military training camps for Indian troops for service in the Confederate army. Schools were also used as military hospitals. From the ruin of the Civil War and Reconstruction, the Five Civilized Tribes reopened their schools, and by 1870 each had its national educational system working again.

During this period segregated schools were established by the Five Civilized Tribes in that Indian children and the children of former slaves were required by tribal law to attend separate schools. Thus Oklahoma's segregated school system, in operation until the 1950s, did not begin with statehood in 1907. It was well established long before that time.

On Indian Territory's western side, the land taken from the Five Civilized Tribes after the Civil War was used to settle tribes from other parts of the United States. Each reservation had at least one school. Most had several. The purpose of these schools was to help Indian children learn American ways more quickly. Missionaries did some teaching in these schools. The Quakers (Society of Friends) were the most active of the religious bodies working among the tribes of western Indian Territory.

Education in Oklahoma Territory

AFTER WESTERN Indian Territory was opened to homesteaders, settlers quickly set up schools for their children. It was some time before local taxes were levied to raise money to support public schools.

In the early frontier period, the children of the settlers attended one-room subscription schools. The family of each student paid a portion of the total cost of maintaining the school. The men donated their labor for hauling materials and building the schoolhouses. Some of the pioneer schoolhouses were of the sod-house type. Others were constructed of logs placed horizontally to form a wall, or of cedar posts placed vertically into the ground to form a picket wall. Dirt floors were common. Drinking water was carried from a spring or well.

The only textbooks were those books the parents had brought from their original homes. The pupils studied reading, home economics, writing, arithmetic, geography, and oratory (public speaking). School seldom was in session for more than three months each year. Teachers received about twenty-five dollars each month.

The first territorial legislature did much basic work to establish the Oklahoma educational system. It adopted a law, patterned after the Kansas school law, which divided each township into four school districts. A rural school was to be established in each district. Towns of 2,500 population or more could establish their own independent school districts.

Oklahoma Territory's first public school fund came as federal aid in the amount of $50,000 provided for in the Organic Act of 1890. This sum was to replace local revenue lost by the tax-exempt status of land. Indian allotments could not be taxed, and the homesteads of settlers were exempt from local taxes for a period of up to five years.

Gradually the public school situation improved in Oklahoma Territory. By 1895 there were more than 75,000 children of school age in the territory, and more than three thousand school districts had been organized by 1907, the year of statehood. As the towns and cities of Oklahoma Territory grew, it

Pioneer children in western Oklahoma Territory attended schools built from picket logs, with sod roofs.

became easier to set up schools in the larger towns than in the rural areas. More taxable property was found in the larger towns, and teachers were more easily hired. As the towns grew larger and richer, better school buildings were built and high schools began to appear throughout the territory.

Oklahoma Education, 1889 to 1907

OKLAHOMA had two school systems operating from 1889 to 1907—one for the children of Oklahoma Territory, the other for the children of Indian Territory. This dual educational system caused problems in 1907 when Oklahoma educational officials tried to establish one public school system for the entire state.

Until 1907 each of the Five Civilized Tribes in Indian Territory had schools for Indian and black children. After the Civil War the non-Indian population increased greatly, and the children of immigrants had few educational opportunities. Non-Indian children were able to attend only private schools.

In 1898, Congress tried to create a uniform educational system for whites, blacks, and Indians in Indian Territory by passing a law that gave the secretary of the interior the authority to assume management of tribal finances and schools. Under government management, only Indians and blacks attended the tribal boarding schools. White children could attend day schools upon payment of tuition.

Indian schools in eastern Indian Territory and western Indian Territory, some started by tribal governments, some by missionaries, and some by the federal government, educated the young people from a number of tribes. These schools included the Creek Academy, the Cherokee Male and Female seminaries, the Seminole Academy, the Choctaw Academy at

205

Tuskahoma, the Jones and Goodland academies, and Rock Academy for the Chickasaws. Some of the better-known Indian training schools in western Indian Territory were Fort Sill School, Riverside School, Concho School, and Chilocco School. Seneca Indian School at Wyandotte in northeastern Indian Territory provided an education for Indian children of that region.

Oklahoma Education After Statehood

PUBLIC EDUCATION received much attention by the First Legislature. This body adopted laws establishing the Textbook Commission, which began the systematic adoption of textbooks for all public schools in the state. This was to assure a uniform education for each of the grades in the state's public school system. The First Legislature also established a system of teacher certification and a compulsory attendance law requiring the enrollment in schools of all children between the ages of eight and sixteen.

The Oklahoma constitution provided that the state superintendent of public instruction be elected. E. D. Cameron was the first person to be elected to this office. His energetic leadership got the Oklahoma school system off to a good start. One of his major problems was to unite the system of education in the former Oklahoma Territory with the system of education in the former Indian Territory. His efforts resulted in an orderly joining of the two systems and the creation of a uniform school system throughout the state.

During that period, persons could be certified to teach with an eighth-grade education. Cameron was concerned that

these minimally educated teachers receive additional training. For this purpose he organized a four-week teachers' institute in each county. Teachers attended these institutes during the summer to improve their knowledge of subjects taught. The length of school terms ranged from three months in some districts to nine months in others.

As a part of the Jim Crow code, the First Legislature established a system of separate schools: one for the white and Indian students, and another for the black students. It was made unlawful for black students to attend the same school as the other students. It was also unlawful for white teachers to teach black students, or for black teachers to teach the other students.

Segregation was not a new practice. It had been in force in Indian Territory schools soon after the close of the Civil War. In Oklahoma Territory the first schools were not segregated. But as the number of black homesteaders increased, by 1893 the territorial legislature had begun to adopt laws separating the races in the schools of Oklahoma Territory. The practice of having white and black public schools continued until the 1950s.

In the administration of the Oklahoma public school system, the focus is on the Oklahoma Department of Education, headed by the superintendent of public instruction. This elected official and the department work together to plan the total state school program and to set policy for public education. A county superintendent supervises the dependent rural schools of the county. A district school board hires teachers and supervises spending. A superintendent of schools is in charge of each independent or city school district within

The Five Civilized Tribes built schools for their children, such as the Cherokee Male Seminary at Tahlequah (*above*) and the Choctaw Female Seminary at Tuskahoma (*below*).

the county. This superintendent, hired by a five-member board of education, supervises the schools of that city or district.

Highlights in School Development

FROM TIME to time, the quality and support of Oklahoma's educational system have been a matter of concern for state leaders. Their interest and action have resulted in improvement in the state's educational system.

Highlights in the improvement of public education in Oklahoma include the Bawden Survey of 1921. Governor J. B. A. Robertson was worried by the generally low levels of Oklahoma schools, particularly the great number of schools unable to hold classes for more than three to five months each year. The governor's interest led to the appointment of a special commission consisting of leading national and state educators. It was headed by William T. Bawden of the United States Bureau of Education. Robertson assigned this group the task of making a searching study of Oklahoma's schools.

From the Bawden Survey came such recommended reforms as improvement in the preparation and certification of teachers, upgrading curricula, the beginnings of consolidation of rural schools, a subsidized textbook program, and state aid to poorly financed districts. During the second half of the Robertson administration, an appropriation of $100,000 was made in response to the state aid recommendation. This appropriation began the system of school finance, which, in recent years, has become an important source of support for public schools.

Other highlights of educational development in Oklahoma include the growing consolidation of rural schools and the drastic reduction in the number of school districts in the state; the desegregation of public education that began in the 1950s; and the gradual shift in the financing of public schools from the local to the state level.

Historically, public schools were financed by taxes on property in each county and by the income obtained from leasing state school lands. Most of the land in eastern Oklahoma, however, was owned by the Five Civilized Tribes. In lieu of land for public schools in that part of the state, the federal government gave the state of Oklahoma $5 million as a trust fund for public schools.

In western Oklahoma the federal government gave the state of Oklahoma section 16 and section 36 of the land in each township to help support common schools. Some of this land was sold, but most has been leased to farmers and ranchers and the rent is used to support local public schools.

Since most school income has been provided by local district taxation, inequality of education arose because some districts were wealthier than others. The inequality in taxes collected has kept some school children from getting a quality education, but it has prompted the legislature to vote more and more money to aid poorly financed schools. State aid amounted to only $100,000 in 1921, but has been gradually increased until by 1955 the legislature was spending more than $30 million each year. Ten years later, school aid appropriations were in excess of $100 million for a two-year period.

Because the amount of state aid to

208

public schools was becoming larger each session, state educational leaders in 1955 proposed an amendment to the state constitution that would allow each school district the right to increase its tax by five mills. In a special election held on April 5, 1955, this amendment was adopted by a large margin.

Each year the margin of support to public schools in Oklahoma from federal aid increases. This aid is granted to districts and to the state system for special vocational programs, for school lunch programs, for educating pupils of certain ethnic groups (particularly Indian children) and the handicapped, and for "impacted" areas where there are many federal workers to compensate for revenue loss because of the tax-exempt status of military bases.

Other developments in public education include adoption of a statewide kindergarten system in 1971 and the expansion of technical and vocational education across the state. Other than vocational and technical training programs, which were a part of local high school systems, the only such training institution in the state for many years was Okmulgee Tech. Since 1969 the number of such schools has increased. Vocational and technical training schools have spread from Okmulgee to every region of the state. The increase in the number and importance of these training schools was needed because of the state's increased industrialization that caused the Oklahoma economy to become more varied and complex.

Oklahoma Higher Education

AN IMPORTANT extension of education in Oklahoma is the state's system of colleges and universities. Most institutions of higher learning in the state are supported by the public. A few colleges and universities, however, are privately supported. All Oklahoma colleges and universities, public or private, are under the direction of the Oklahoma State Regents for Higher Education.

The first territorial legislature established the Territorial University at Norman, the Territorial Agricultural and Mechanical College at Stillwater, and the Territorial Normal (teacher training school) at Edmond. In 1897, in response to the requirements of the segregation statutes of Oklahoma Territory, the legislature established the Colored Agricultural and Normal University at Langston. Langston was an all-black town founded east of Guthrie in 1890. As the territory grew, other towns demanded their share of public institutions. The result of this demand was the establishment of a second normal school at Alva in 1897, and a third normal school at Weatherford in 1901. The last school established before statehood was the University Preparatory School at Tonkawa in 1901.

At statehood in 1907 all state-supported institutions of higher learning were located in western Oklahoma. The extension of the public school system over Indian Territory increased the need for more and better-trained teachers. The Oklahoma College for Women was located at Chickasha in 1908. The following year the state legislature created three new normal schools, one each at Durant, Ada, and Tahlequah.

As a rural state with much agriculture, Oklahoma's greatest educational need was agricultural. The legislature responded to this need by establishing a number of agricultural colleges—one

The University of Oklahoma Bizzell Library.

each at Miami, Warner, Tishomingo, Lawton, and Goodwell.

In 1980 the Oklahoma state system of higher education included the University of Oklahoma at Norman, Central State University at Edmond, East Central State University at Ada, Langston University at Langston, Northeastern State University at Tahlequah, Northwestern State University at Alva, Oklahoma State University at Stillwater, University of Science and Arts of Oklahoma at Chickasha, Panhandle State University at Goodwell, Southwestern State University at Weatherford, Southeastern State University at Durant, Cameron University at Lawton, Northeastern Oklahoma Agricultural and Mechanical College at Miami, Murray State College at Tishomingo, Northern Oklahoma College at Tonkawa, Connors State College at Warner, Eastern Oklahoma State College at Wilburton, and Rogers State College at Claremore.

In addition to these institutions, local school districts and cities, with some state support, maintain junior colleges at Altus, El Reno, Muskogee, Poteau, Sayre, Seminole, Midwest City, Oklahoma City, and Tulsa.

Several private and denominational (church-owned) colleges and universities also function in Oklahoma. These include Hillside Free Will Baptist College at Moore; Oklahoma City University, Midwest Christian College, Oklahoma Christian College, and Southwestern College at Oklahoma City; Tulsa University and Oral Roberts University at Tulsa; Phillips University at Enid; Bethany Nazarene College at Bethany; Bacone College at Muskogee; Saint Gregory's College and Oklahoma Baptist University at Shawnee; and Bartlesville Wesleyan College at Bartlesville.

Study Aids

Explain the significance of each term or phrase listed below:

1. Federal aid
2. Dependent district
3. Bawden Commission
4. State school land
5. Impacted area
6. Subscription school

On an outline map of Oklahoma locate the following places:

1. Jay
2. Frederick
3. Anadarko
4. Hartshorne

5. Pawhuska
6. Thackerville

Use the suggestions below for a study guide:

1. Outline the kinds of schools in Indian Territory to 1889.
2. Describe education in Oklahoma Territory.
3. What were the findings of the Bawden Commission survey?
4. Discuss the forms of federal aid available to the schools of the state of Oklahoma.
5. Explain the great number of institutions of higher learning in Oklahoma.

For Further Reading

Constant, Alberta. *Oklahoma Run.* Oklahoma City, 1982.

Dale, Edward E., and Jesse I. Rader (eds.). *Readings in Oklahoma History.* Evanston, 1930.

Douglas, C. B. *The History of Tulsa.* 3 vols. Chicago, 1922.

Kerr, W. F., and Ina Gainer. *The Story of Oklahoma City.* 3 vols. Chicago, 1922.

Pugmire, Ross D. *Oklahoma Children and Their Schools.* Oklahoma City, 1950.

Teall, Kaye M. *Black History in Oklahoma.* Oklahoma City, 1971.

Smallwood, James (ed.). *And Gladly Teach: Reminiscences of Teachers from Frontier Dugout to Modern Module.* Norman, 1976.

Chapter 15. OKLAHOMA'S ARTISTIC HERITAGE

Primitive Creativity

THE WORDS of a well-known philosopher of olden times remind us that "man shall not live by bread alone." From earliest times Oklahomans have been creative and have expressed their artistic talents in many ways.

Prehistoric people sketched animal figures and other subjects on the walls of their cave and ledge dwellings. Paleo-Indian artists decorated conch shells, pottery, and animal skins with with native art forms. Sculptors struck figures from stone and clay. Native artisans also wove designs in their fabrics.

Native art was also expressed in tribal music, rhythms, and dance. From primitive flutes, drums, and rattles came musical expression. A variety of dances, communicating symbolically various attitudes, values, and goals, suggests that dancing was for purposes other than exercise or entertainment. Aboriginal religion had a delicate and intimate tie with nature which, in its observance by performance of specific rituals, also amounted to an art form.

The culture of the Five Civilized Tribes provided a bridge between the wilderness frontier and civilization. Besides introducing constitutional government, schools, and other familiar tokens of an advanced way of life in Oklahoma, they added to the Sooner legacy of creative expression.

The Cherokee Indian intellectual leader, Elias Boudinot, had written fiction and nonfiction before he came to Indian Territory. He began the *Cherokee Phoenix,* a tribal newspaper published at New Echota, Georgia, capital of the Cherokee Nation in the eastern United States. He continued his writing, study, and publication in the Oklahoma wilderness.

With Samuel Austin Worcester, the missionary-teacher serving the Cherokees, Boudinot established the town of Park Hill near Tahlequah. Park Hill was a center of learning. Worcester and Boudinot constructed a church and a school at Park Hill. They imported a printing press from the East and established Oklahoma's first publishing house, the Park Hill Press. Boudinot and Worcester translated many works, including the Scriptures, from English to Cherokee by using the Cherokee alphabet created by Sequoyah. They published papers and books on the Park Hill Press both in English and Cherokee.

During the era of the homesteader, Oklahoma was the scene of much creative and cultural activity, both in performance and in interest and support by citizens generally. Most frontier towns in Oklahoma Territory supported literary societies. Its members wrote poetry, short stories, and plays, and discussed the issues of the day. Traveling Chautauqua groups were popular and well received in early-day Oklahoma. These groups provided lectures by nationally known figures, and performed plays, musical performances, and other forms of entertainment.

Modern Creativity

BUILDING on these pioneer foundations of participation in fine arts activity as performers and supporters of artistic endeavors, modern Oklahomans display increasing interest in creative pursuits. More Oklahomans than ever before are joining writers' clubs and artist federations, supporting local theatrical productions, attending symphony orchestra presentations, and patronizing art galleries and museums. This is encouraging an expansion of the Sooner State's aesthetic resources.

Several Oklahoma towns support sym-

phony orchestras. The best-known are the Oklahoma City Symphony, the Tulsa Philharmonic, and the Lawton Symphony. The growth in number of private teachers of voice, piano, and instrumental music reflects the interest of Oklahomans in providing fine arts opportunities for their youth.

Music clinics are popular among educators and young musicians. One of the highlights of the music year for young Oklahomans is the world-famous Tri-State Music Festival held each spring at Enid. Here performers gather from all over the nation to show their talents.

The fine arts departments at the University of Oklahoma, Oklahoma State University, the state colleges, and the private institutions of higher learning offer instruction and courses in music, drama, and art. These courses provide training for the specialist as well as for the general student seeking courses of appreciation.

Several Oklahoma towns feature annual folk plays, operas, festivals, and pageants. One of the best-known pageants in past years is the Wichita Mountains Easter Pageant. In 1949 fine arts patrons at Tulsa formed the Tulsa Opera Company to produce light operettas. This group attracted regional and even national attention in its presentation of *Madame Butterfly*.

In the art of the dance, one national critic declared that Oklahoma has unquestioned leadership among the states. Five of the major names in ballet are from Oklahoma and are of Indian descent. Yvonne Chouteau at the age of fourteen was the youngest American ever accepted for the Ballet Russe de Monte Carlo. She was a member of this famous group for fourteen years as the acclaimed ballerina. Later she was co-

Young Indian dancer at the Anadarko Indian Exposition takes pride in keeping his tribal dances alive.

homa is the Indian dance. It provides a modern expression of tribal lore, religious sensitivity, and artistic movement. With sixty-seven tribes represented in Oklahoma, much of the dancing has an intimate tribal association and provides a means of fellowship with other tribes. Many of these tribes hold powwows during the summer and autumn months.

The color, rhythm, movement, and the vivid tableau of native dancing appeal to non-Indians too, with the result that the powwows often are attended by outsiders. Annual events like the Indian Exposition at Anadarko provide outlets for a more commercial application of the Indian dance.

From earliest frontier times Oklahomans have shown a keen interest in the theater. Guthrie, Kingfisher, and other homesteader towns supported dramatic productions. Even the rough mining camps of the Choctaw Nation supported crudely fashioned Shakespearean plays.

This theatrical tradition continued into present times, and nearly all junior and senior high school dramatic clubs present a round of comedy and tragedy each year. Fine arts departments at the various colleges and universities provide training for drama teachers and professional actors, and present a variety of productions for students and townspeople.

The little theater and community theater groups receive support in several towns. They present productions ranging from musicals to melodrama.

Art activity is an important sign of interest in the fine arts. Oklahomans have produced art, collected it, and supported galleries and museums which show it. In early times the Sooner

director of the Oklahoma City Civic Ballet, and presently she is artist in residence in the University of Oklahoma.

Other Oklahoma celebrities in the ballet world include Maria Tallchief, at one time the ranking ballerina in the United States; her sister Marjorie Tallchief, noted for her career with the Paris Ballet Company; Rozella Hightower of Ardmore; and Moselyne Larkin of Miami, former soloist and later ballerina of the Ballet Russe de Monte Carlo. Miss Larkin's career included a teaching assignment in Tulsa and being codirector of the Tulsa Civic Ballet.

Another form of the performing arts becoming increasingly popular in Okla-

This drama about the Trail of Tears was presented at the Tsa-La-Gi Theater, near Tahlequah.

Indian dancers at a powwow often allow outsiders to watch.

Indian encampment at an Anadarko Indian Exposition.

State's natural beauty and varied population attracted world-famous painters like George Catlin, John Mix Stanley, Frederic Remington, and Elbridge Ayer Burbank.

In modern times, certain Oklahomans have used their great wealth to support the arts. Ernest W. Marland's early financial successes and aesthetic tastes account in part for the beauty of Ponca City and made possible his greatest gift to the state, the *Pioneer Woman* statue by Bryant Baker. Thomas Gilcrease devoted his personal fortune to collecting art treasures, including the fabulous Remington and Russell galleries at Gilcrease Museum in Tulsa. Philbrook Art Museum, also at Tulsa, is in part the gift of oilman Waite Phillips. The Woolaroc Museum near Bartlesville is the gift of Frank Phillips.

Other Oklahoma art collections include the Oklahoma City Art Center, the University of Oklahoma Art Museum, and the Saint Gregory's Art Museum at Shawnee. Father Gregory Gerrer was a pioneer artist and collector who became art director at Saint Gregory's College at Shawnee in 1908. A painter

and art authority of international reputation, Father Gerrer brought together a gallery of some two hundred paintings.

The most notable development in the Oklahoma art world was the school of Indian artists developed by Dr. Oscar Jacobson at the University of Oklahoma. He encouraged the Indian students to use native themes and a simple form derived from the Indian's historical style in pictorial art. Jacobson's school produced more than thirty native artists from ten different tribes. Among his students were five young Kiowas, Stephen Mopope, Monroe Tsato-ke, James Auchiah, Jack Hokeah, and Spencer Asah, who came to the University of Oklahoma campus in 1928. These and other Indian painters brought fame to Jacobson's school through their achievements as painters and muralists.

Other prominent Indian artists have been Acee Blue Eagle, Woodrow Crumbo, Allen Houser, Black Bear Bosin, Archie Blackowl, Jerome Tiger, and Carl Sweezy. One of the most famous of modern Indian artists is Dick West, a Cheyenne.

Non-Indian painters include John Noble who, after making the run of 1893 into the Cherokee Outlet, studied art in Paris, Brussels, and London. *The Run* is one of his best-known works. Howell Lewis and Nellie Shepherd painted beautiful landscapes showing Oklahoma's hills and prairie before 1920. In modern times Charles Banks Wilson, Dick Goetz, and the late Augusta Metcalf rank as the state's most popular artists.

Wilson has been honored by the United States Department of State as well as by the International Institute of Arts and Letters in Geneva. His

Tulsa opera production.

The Philbrook Art Center in Tulsa.

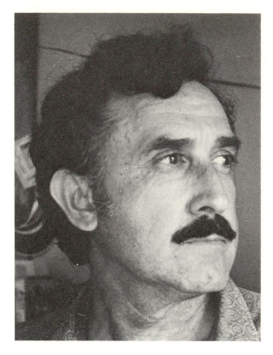

Oklahoma artist Charles Banks Wilson.

Oklahoma artist Augusta Metcalf.

works, mostly southwestern scenes and subjects, have been shown in more than two hundred exhibitions in this country and throughout the world. He is the recipient of Oklahoma's first state-commissioned art projects, which were to create portraits of prominent Oklahoma leaders and four historical murals for permanent installation in the state Capitol rotunda. Augusta Metcalf's appeal to the art-loving public was through her perceptive skill in interpreting life in western Oklahoma and her technique with color and attention to detail.

The art created by the faculties at the major state institutions of higher learning and of the private institutions are regularly exhibited in Oklahoma, the Southwest, and across the nation. Eugene Bavinger of the University of Oklahoma School of Art faculty is prominent in this regard. The late Sam Gibson won regional acclaim for his Oklahoma landscapes in watercolors. Frank Draper, a Norman artist, has received high praise from critics who have evaluated his work at state and regional exhibits. And the late George Miksch Sutton, University of Oklahoma ornithologist, attracted national attention through his research and bird paintings.

Architecture is an art form expressed in many notable buildings in Oklahoma. Most buildings and homes follow conventional themes, but some Oklahomans with great wealth, particularly from oil during the 1920s and 1930s, had their homes designed as Spanish villas, French chateaux, colonial mansions, and English baronial homes.

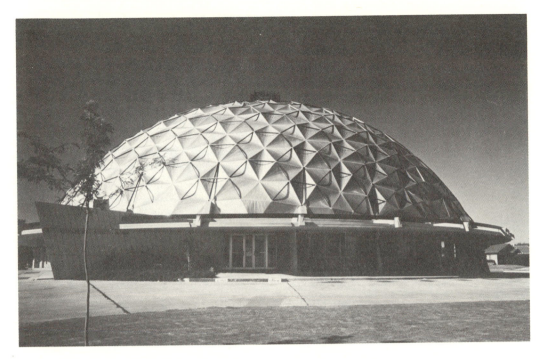

Oklahoma architecture, Oklahoma City bank building.

Architectural forms in Oklahoma's new industrial and institutional buildings show the influence of Frank Lloyd Wright. One of Wright's most popular designs is the Price Tower at Bartlesville. Church architecture in Oklahoma has shown a daring newness, a departure from the traditional gothic. The new state Capitol office buildings in Oklahoma City and the Center for Continuing Education complex on the campus of the University of Oklahoma are other examples of architectural change.

An important part of Oklahoma's cultural resources preserving and displaying the state's heritage is the wide variety of historical museums scattered about the state. One of the oldest museums is at the State Historical Society in Oklahoma City. One of the newest is at Lawton, the Museum of the Great Plains. Others are the Will Rogers Memorial at Claremore, the Panhandle Museum at Goodwell, the Pioneer Woman Museum at Ponca City, the Black Kettle Museum at Cheyenne, the Stovall Museum at the University of Oklahoma, the Gilcrease Museum at Tulsa, the Woolaroc Museum near Bartlesville, the Museum of the Five Civilized Tribes at Muskogee, and the Museum of the Western Prairie at Altus. A museum of national prestige that includes much of the life and traditions of Oklahoma is the National Cowboy Hall of Fame and Western Heritage Center at Oklahoma City. Seventeen western and southwestern states are participants in its displays.

Libraries are symbols of nonmaterial interest and signs of cultural advance. Most towns in the state have public

Oklahoma architecture, Price Tower, Bartlesville.

libraries. Knowledge resources contained in the Oklahoma State Library in Oklahoma City are available to all citizens. Smaller communities of the state can draw on the knowledge resources of larger libraries through traveling libraries serviced by bookmobiles.

As a part of its cultural resources, Oklahoma has a number of special research collections of international fame. These include the works in the Oklahoma Historical Society Library in Oklahoma City, the Gilcrease Museum Library in Tulsa, the Cherokee Collection at Northeastern State University at Tahlequah, and the Choctaw Collection at Southeastern State University at Durant.

The library at the University of Oklahoma has over two million volumes. Its special research collections in the history of science and business history, the Bizzell Bible Collection, and its collection on Indian, Oklahoma, and Western history rank with the best in the nation. The Oklahoma State University Library has received special recognition in such fields as science, technology, agricultural economics, and government documents.

In all the areas of artistic expression available to Oklahomans, the most popular seems to be writing. Writers' clubs, poetry societies, and folklore groups are active across the state. Oklahoma has a national reputation for producing able writers. Some of the better-known Oklahomans who have achieved fame in writing are John Rollin Ridge, Alexander Posey, George Milburn, John Okisson, Ralph Ellison, and Lynn Riggs. Riggs's *Green Grow the Lilacs* was used as a basis for the well-known Broadway show *Oklahoma*. Will Rogers, Okla-

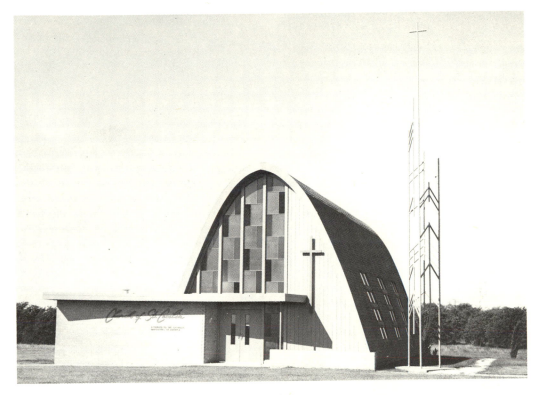

Oklahoma architecture, Church of Saint Cecilia, Ardmore.

homa's foremost humorist who won international acclaim as an entertainer, also achieved widespread recognition for his writing, notably through his autobiography and his newspaper column. During the 1930s, Woody Guthrie established himself as a writer and composer of national note.

Oklahoma has received added recognition in the world of authors and publishers from the School of Professional Writing developed at the University of Oklahoma by the late Walter Campbell (Stanley Vestal). Students trained in this program write and publish in a wide area, including biography and fiction.

Oklahoma poets have received wide acclaim from the days of the Five Civ-ilized Tribes through the work of John Rollin Ridge, a Cherokee, and Alexander Posey, a Creek. Prominent twentieth-century poets have included Kenneth Kaufman, George Riley Hall, Melvin Tolson, Welborn Hope, Vera Holding, and Mamie Culver Fry.

Publication outlets are vital for writers, and from earliest times Oklahoma authors have had local publishing facilities available. The best-known of the frontier publishing houses in the Southwest was Park Hill Press, noted earlier in this chapter. The tradition for excellence in publishing established by the Park Hill Press is carried on today by the world-famous University of Oklahoma Press. Under the leadership of former Director Savoie Lottin-

Will Rogers Memorial, Claremore, built to honor Oklahoma's most famous entertainer.

Gilcrease Museum, Tulsa, one of many fine museums in Oklahoma.

ville, several popular series were established. These include "The Civilization of the American Indian Series," the "Western Frontier Library," and the series entitled "Centers of Civilization." The University of Oklahoma Press publishes more than fifty new books each year.

Several magazines have been published in Oklahoma. Each provides an outlet for local writers. Three territorial publications were *McMasters' Oklahoma Magazine, Twin-Territories Magazine,* and *Sturm's Oklahoma Magazine.* These magazines contained articles on the history and lore of the territory and on promoting the development of its resources. The best-known periodical since statehood was *Harlow's Weekly,* a news magazine rich in political writing and containing poetry and other works by Oklahoma writers.

The principal surviving periodicals are *Chronicles of Oklahoma,* the official publication of the Oklahoma Historical Society; *World Literature Today* (formerly *Books Abroad*), a literary quarterly published on the campus of the University of Oklahoma; the *Great Plains Journal,* published by the Museum of the Great Plains and containing articles on archaeology, anthropology, and history of the Great Plains; the *Gilcrease Magazine of American History and Art,* a quarterly published by Gilcrease Museum of Tulsa; and *Oklahoma Today,* a quarterly published by the State Planning and Resources Board that contains articles on Oklahoma history, poetry and art, and on the modern developments in industry.

During the 1960s there was increasing interest in Oklahoma's aesthetic heritage. This trend continued into the 1980s. One example was the creation

Lynn Riggs, playwright.

in 1967 of the Oklahoma Arts and Humanities Council. This organization has served the state with council members drawn from all walks of life, both lay and professional fine arts people. Its purpose is to find out what resources Oklahoma has, to generate public interest in these resources, and to encourage even wider participation by Oklahomans in art, literature, music, and the other artistic fields.

An Oklahoma Arts and Humanities Council study on the state of the arts in Oklahoma revealed an increasing degree of public interest and concern in the arts. Among other findings, the survey revealed that the greatest interest and activity was in the visual arts, mainly painting and drawing. Almost every town and city responding to the survey reported numbers of interested local residents working and displaying their work in art shows.

Oklahomans celebrated the Diamond Jubilee of Statehood in 1982. The Diamond Jubilee Commission and staff was coordinated through the Oklahoma Historical Society. They supported many local and statewide pageants, tableaus, musical and dramatic programs, and publications interpreting the Oklahoma heritage and honoring seventy-five years of Sooner Statehood. The Diamond Jubilee's dominating theme, besides public acknowledgment of the state's progress through seventy-five years, was a strong civic commitment to advance positively along the path to the Oklahoma Centennial in 2007.

Study Aids

Explain the significance of each term or phrase listed below:
  1. Park Hill Press
  2. Ballerina
  3. Paleo-Indian
  4. Arts and Humanities Council
  5. *Cherokee Phoenix*
  6. Indian Exposition

Identify each of these persons:

  1. Lynn Riggs
  2. George Riley Hall
  3. Oscar Jacobson
  4. Dick West
  5. Gregory Gerrer
  6. Augusta Metcalf

On an outline map of Oklahoma locate the following places:

  1. Lehigh
  2. Sapulpa
  3. Saline
  4. Sayre
  5. Picher
  6. Perry

Use the suggestions below for study guides:

  1. Summarize the Indian influence on Oklahoma fine arts.
  2. Discuss architectural development in Oklahoma.
  3. Describe Oklahoma's leadership in ballet.
  4. Show the results of the Jacobson School of Indian Art.
  5. Explain the function of the Oklahoma Arts and Humanities Council.

For Further Reading

Campbell, Walter. *The Book Lover's Southwest.* Norman, 1955.
Foreman, Carolyn. *Oklahoma Imprints.* Norman, 1936.
Goins, Charles R., and John W. Morris. *Oklahoma Homes: Past and Present.* Norman, 1980.

Hollon, W. Eugene. *The Southwest: Old and New.* New York, 1961.
Marable, Mary Hayes, and Elaine Boylan. *A Handbook of Oklahoma Writers.* Norman, 1939.
Peyton, Green. *America's Heartland: The Southwest.* Norman, 1948.

Chapter 16. OKLAHOMA IN A CHANGING WORLD

Heritage and History

GREAT SOCIAL, economic, and political changes are occurring today in Oklahoma and in the world. These changes largely are the result of developments in science and technology. Many people are disturbed by the changing world and find it difficult to understand and accept the changes. It is important, however, that citizens make rapid and effective adjustments to the drastic changes brought about by the developments in science and technology.

One can make effective adjustment to this rapidly changing world. At the same time one can help to adapt these changes to purposeful goals. One way is to develop *perspective.* Perspective comes from knowledge and appreciation of one's heritage and history. By using this perspective and knowledge, one is better able to understand what is going on and thus be strengthened to face the future with poise and purpose.

From perspective one also gains wisdom and energy to give some direction to the future. Oklahoma history is a rich storehouse from which to draw knowledge, to form an appreciation of heritage, and to gain perspective.

An important part of the Oklahoma heritage is pride. Oklahomans are a proud people, and their pride stems from the frontier values of self-reliance, adaptability, and resourcefulness. Nourished by these characteristics, they tamed the southwestern wilderness. More recently, these values helped them to recover from the dreadful drought-ridden 1930s. Oklahomans became national leaders in soil conservation and in restoring wasted grasslands. Oklahoma's determination to improve explains in part the state's economic growth and expansion of industry during the past thirty years.

Oklahomans can take pride in the character of their heritage. The Oklahoma story is a rich one, full of variety,

Jim Thorpe, famed Oklahoma athlete of Indian heritage.

Oklahoma's human differences—biological and cultural—also gives it a rich background and provides a source of strength for the future. Oklahoma's people came from all directions; they were both rich and poor and they brought a variety of political and religious traditions. Constitutional government, schools, newspapers, churches, and other fixtures of an advanced way of life did not suddenly begin in 1889 with the coming of the homesteaders, nor in 1907 with statehood. These institutions of civilization were well established in Oklahoma in the 1820s by the Five Civilized Tribes.

Southern institutions, including slaveholding brought here by the Five Civilized Tribes, were a part of Oklahoma culture. Oklahoma was a Confederate province during the Civil War. Later it faced a Reconstruction program like the former states of the Confederacy. This explains in part that to this day the southeastern section of the state is known as Little Dixie.

The settlement of the Plains tribes in western Oklahoma after the Civil War added to the state's cultural variety. In many ways these Indians were quite different from the Five Civilized Tribes who occupied eastern Oklahoma.

Aside from soldiers, missionaries, and traders, the first large-scale immigration of non-Indian settlers to Oklahoma after the Civil War occurred during the mining boom in the Choctaw Nation in the 1870s. Descendants of these Italian, Slav, Greek, Welsh, Polish, and Russian miners still reside in the old Choctaw Nation and increase the richness of Oklahoma's ethnic community. Add to these the scattered German Mennonite and Czech settlements, many still practicing their Old World

uniqueness, and drama that very few of the other forty-nine states can match. A part of this drama, this uniqueness, comes from the prehistoric part of the Oklahoma story—the fact that representatives of what may be America's first human family (Clovis man and Folsom man) flourished here. In addition, when the analysis of Spiro culture is completed, Oklahoma quite possibly will receive recognition as the locale for the golden age of American prehistory.

During the period from 1500, when the prehistoric age ended and the historic age began, to 1907, when Oklahoma achieved statehood, the theme of uniqueness continued. The development of Oklahoma into a state is different from any other state in the American Union.

Changes on Oklahoma's face: Tulsa in 1900 and Tulsa as it is now.

customs and colorful festivals, and one can sense the variety of Oklahoma's cultural elements.

At about the same time as the European immigration, cowboys and ranchers came into the territory, as did crews of railroad workers. When the rush of homeseekers began with the famous Land Run of 1889, settlers came from all directions, from many states, and from foreign countries. They brought with them customs, religions, and politics as different as the areas from which they came.

The blacks are an important part of the Oklahoma ethnic community. They now comprise about 10 percent of the state's population. Blacks were among the first settlers in Oklahoma. They came to Indian Territory over the Trail of Tears as slaves of the Five Civilized Tribes. In early times, with few exceptions, the blacks' role was lowly and suppressed. As slaves they could not be active in politics or society, but their contribution to early Oklahoma economic life was of great importance. Blacks did most of the work on the Indian Territory frontier. They cleared land for farms and plantations, labored in the fields, built the roads, and helped tame the wilderness.

Blacks were freed after the Civil War, and as early Indian Territory settlers they worked on the railroads, in the mines, and on farms and ranches. Blacks from the South and other parts of the country participated in the land runs that settled Oklahoma Territory. Early-day black homesteaders settled towns all across western Oklahoma. A principal black homesteader town established after the Run of 1889 was at Langston.

A special role was played by freed blacks at the Oklahoma military posts. After the Civil War the War Department established several all-black cavalry units that served at Indian Territory forts, particularly Fort Supply, Fort Reno, and Fort Sill. They were called the "buffalo soldiers." They helped tame the Plains tribes and bring peace to the frontier of the Southwest. The best-known black unit in Indian Territory was the Tenth Cavalry stationed at Fort Supply.

Through the years Oklahoma blacks, largely by their own efforts but assisted by United States Supreme Court decisions, federal laws, and local leadership, have sought new opportunities and made great strides in the professions, the arts, and in creative labor.

The strength of a state is found, too, in the spiritual interests of its people. In this regard, Oklahoma has great diversity, for just as its people are varied, so too are its religions. Most Protestant groups are represented. Southern Baptists and Methodists are the most numerous. Also included are the Disciples of Christ (Christian churches), the Congregationalists, the Presbyterians, the Pentecostal groups, the Church of Christ, the Evangelical United, and virtually every other sect of Protestantism. Greek Orthodox, Roman Catholic, and Jewish worshippers are among the believers.

A reflection of the European immigration to the old Choctaw Nation mining camps is found at Hartshorne, where one of the few Russian Orthodox churches in the entire Trans-Mississippi West is located. The Oklahoma religious scene is further enriched by the presence of traditional Indian religions. Such historic observances as the Sun Dance and the Ghost Dance have been vital spiri-

Oklahoma City today.

tual forces among tribes of western Oklahoma, and the popular Native American (Peyote) Church is a denomination recognized by state charter.

One of the most important steps taken in recent years to prepare Oklahomans to play vital roles in the changing world and to meet the demands of the Space Age occurred in 1954. In that year a committee of Oklahoma business, professional, and scientific leaders met and formed an organization to keep Oklahoma at the forefront of the new scientific and technological revolution.

Out of this meeting came the Frontiers of Science Foundation of Oklahoma, established on October 1, 1955, as a voluntary association of state business, educational, professional, and governmental leaders. The stated purpose of the Frontiers of Science Foundation is to develop and maintain ways to describe, interpret, and expand the new frontiers in science, industry, and education in the Sooner State. One of the founders declared, "Frontier-mindedness is attached to geographic frontiers. The new frontiers are of the mind—frontiers of intelligence and of the spirit." Many Oklahomans have adopted this credo to guide them in fashioning the state's direction and destiny toward the Centennial of Statehood in 2007.

INDEX

Osage County: 5, 22, 193
Osage Hills: 6
Osage Indian oil headrights: 194
Osage Nation: 120
Osage Reservation: 90, 106
Osage River: 21
Osage village: 21–22
Osceola: 33, 45, 58
Oskisson, John: 220
Otjen, William J.: 160–61
Oto and Missouri reservation: 106
Otoes: 92
Ottawa County: 11, 115
Ottawas: 93
Ouachita Mountains: 5, 6
Owen, Robert L.: 128, 146
Ozark Mountains: 5, 12

Pacific Ocean: 24
Pageants: 213
Panhandle: 5, 8, 77, 102, 189
Panhandle Agriculture Institute: 132
Panhandle Museum: 219
Panhandle State University: 210
Pardon and Parole Board: 160
Parimutuel betting: 182
Paris Ballet Company: 214
Paris, Texas: 118
Park Hill: 56, 212
Park Hill Press: 213, 221
Parker, Isaac: 78
Parker, Quanah: 94
Patterson, Pat J.: 177
Pauls Valley, Oklahoma: 132
Pawnees: 92
Payne, David L.: 97
"Payne's Oklahoma Colony": 98
Pea Ridge: 68
Pegg, Thomas: 70
Penn Square Bank: 183; failure of, 183
Peoria: 93, 115
Permit laws: 117
Perryman, Benjamin: 52
Perryman, J. M.: 81
Perryville: 54, 70
Pershing, John: 140
Petroleum industry: 116, 192
Philbrook Art Museum: 216

Phillips, Frank: 216
Phillips, Leon: 156, 158–59
Phillips University: 210
Phillips, Waite: 216
Phillips, William A.: 69
Picher Lead Company: 115
Picket wall: 204
"Piecemeal absorption": 112
Pike, Albert: 65
Pine, William B.: 146, 151, 156
Pike, Zebulon M.: 21
Pioneer Woman Museum: 219
Pioneer Woman statue: 156, 216
Pipeline: 195
Pirogues: 21
Pittsburg County: 5
Plains: 6
Plains Apaches: 15
Planning and Resources Board: 161
Plantation: 52, 54
Platte River: 23
Pleistocene Age: 10–11
Polish settlements: 126
Pomeroy, Samuel: 73
Ponca Agency: 93
Ponca City, Oklahoma: 156
Poncas: 92
Pontotoc County: 194
Population: 160, 168
Populist: 109, 110
Porter, Pleasant: 120
Posey, Alexander: 120, 220–21
Poteau: 210
Poteau River: 22, 26
Pottawatomi County: 51, 194
Pottawatomies: 91, 141
Pourtalès, Albert de: 41
Powell, J. W.: 14
Powell system of classifying Indian tribes by language: 14
Prairies: 6
Prehistoric age: 12
Presbyterians: 56, 58; missionaries, 57
Price, Sterling: 68
Price Tower: 219
Primary Runoff Law: 139
Primordial bison: 9
Prize fighting: 138
Progressive Party: 163
Prohibition: 123, 131, 171
Prohibition amendment: 123
Public education: 206
Public Land Strip: 102

Public school system: 54
Public works: 157
Public Works Administration (PWA): 155
Pushmataha: 26, 35

Race relations: 142
Race riot: 142
Rader, Lloyd: 183
Railroad Brotherhood: 201
Railroad building: 84
Railroads: 133
Railway Companies: 96
Rainfall: 7
Ramsey, James R.: 58
Ranches: 52, 54, 82
Ranching: 127
Range cattle industry: 84, 187
Reagan, Ronald: 181
Reapportionment: 168, 175
Recession: 142
Reconstruction: 79, 81, 88–89; plan, 73
Reconstruction treaties: 75, 77, 78, 91
Red Bird, Oklahoma: 79
Red Fork field: 116, 193
Red River: 3, 5, 19–24, 28–29, 41, 62, 71, 87, 153, 159
Red River expedition: 21
Red River Valley: 52
Referendum: 123
Refineries: 195
Reforestation: 188
Reformatory: 132
Relief: 151
Remington, Frederic: 216
Renfrow, William C.: 109
Rentiesville, Oklahoma: 79
Republic of Texas: 5
Republicans: 65, 109–10, 112, 122, 127, 133, 141, 150
Revolutionary War: 33
Ridge, John: 38, 50
Ridge, John Rollin: 220–21
Riggs, Lynn: 220
Right-to-work issue: 175
Ringwood: 195
Rio Grande: 18, 54
River steamers: 52
Riverside School: 206
Rizley, Ross: 158–59, 163
Robbers' Roost: 103
Robertson, James B. A.: 141,

The History of Oklahoma,
designed by Sandy See, was
composed by the University of Oklahoma Press
in eleven- and ten-point Baskerville
and nine- and eight-point Helvetica
and printed offset on sixty-pound Glatfelter
Smooth Antique with presswork by Cushing-Malloy, Inc.
and binding by John H. Dekker & Sons.